Enterprise Internet of Things Handbook

Build end-to-end IoT solutions using popular IoT platforms

Arvind Ravulavaru

BIRMINGHAM - MUMBAI

Enterprise Internet of Things Handbook

Commissioning Editor: Gebin George
Acquisition Editor: Prachi Bisht
Content Development Editor: Trusha Shriyan
Technical Editor: Vishal K. Mewada
Copy Editor: Safis Editing
Project Coordinator: Kinjal Bari
Proofreader: Safis Editing
Indexer: Priyanka Dhadke
Graphics: Jisha Chirayil
Production Coordinator: Shraddha Falebhai

First published: April 2018

Production reference: 1270418

Published by Packt Publishing Ltd.
Livery Place
35 Livery Street
Birmingham
B3 2PB, UK.

ISBN 978-1-78883-839-9

www.packtpub.com

`mapt.io`

Mapt is an online digital library that gives you full access to over 5,000 books and videos, as well as industry leading tools to help you plan your personal development and advance your career. For more information, please visit our website.

Why subscribe?

- Spend less time learning and more time coding with practical eBooks and Videos from over 4,000 industry professionals

- Improve your learning with Skill Plans built especially for you

- Get a free eBook or video every month

- Mapt is fully searchable

- Copy and paste, print, and bookmark content

PacktPub.com

Did you know that Packt offers eBook versions of every book published, with PDF and ePub files available? You can upgrade to the eBook version at `www.PacktPub.com` and as a print book customer, you are entitled to a discount on the eBook copy. Get in touch with us at `service@packtpub.com` for more details.

At `www.PacktPub.com`, you can also read a collection of free technical articles, sign up for a range of free newsletters, and receive exclusive discounts and offers on Packt books and eBooks.

Contributors

About the author

Arvind Ravulavaru is a platform architect at Ubiconn IoT Solutions, with more than 9 years, experience in software development and 2 years, in hardware and product development. For the past 5 years, he has been working extensively on JavaScript, both on the server- and client-side. And for the past couple of years in IoT, building a platform for rapidly developing IoT solutions, named The IoT Suitcase. Prior to that, Arvind worked on big data, cloud computing, and orchestration.

Thanks to my dear friend Amit Kumar Sharma for all the conversations we have had on technology, life, and the universe. I have learned a lot from your perspective.
A special thanks to Dexter for allowing me to use his pictures in this book. I also sincerely thank Prachi B., Trusha S., Vishal M, and the Packt team for their awesome support.

About the reviewer

Yatish Patil works with Saviant Consulting as a technical project manager. He has delivered enterprise IoT and analytics applications using Microsoft Azure, ASP.NET, MVC, C#, SQL Server, and NoSQL. He has worked in different domains, as IT, Utilities, manufacturing, and engineering.

He is a Microsoft Azure Certified professional and was among the industry speakers at India IoT Symposium, 2016. He has delivered a session on remote asset monitoring with Azure IoT Suite. Yatish is the Author of *Azure IoT Development Cookbook* and has reviewed *Microsoft Azure IaaS Essentials*.

Packt is searching for authors like you

If you're interested in becoming an author for Packt, please visit `authors.packtpub.com` and apply today. We have worked with thousands of developers and tech professionals, just like you, to help them share their insight with the global tech community. You can make a general application, apply for a specific hot topic that we are recruiting an author for, or submit your own idea.

Table of Contents

Preface

The Internet of Things is one of today's hottest topics. There is a lot of work that is being done in this space, and, according to Forbes, the global IoT market will grow from $157 in 2016 to $457 billion by 2020. It is an amazing market both in terms of technology advancement and money.

This handbook covers almost all of the essential knowledge that is needed for an architect or a developer to build an IoT solution. Right from understanding what IoT is and exploring various off-the-shelf IoT platforms, this book has it all. This book also covers machine learning IoT at a basic level, using Azure Machine Learning Studio.

Who this book is for

This book is targeted toward IoT architects and engineers and any stakeholders working with enterprise IoT solutions. This book also caters for decision makers and professionals from small- and medium-sized enterprises looking to build an IoT strategy for their venture.

What this book covers

Chapter 1, *Introduction to IoT*, introduces you to the concept of the Internet of Things or IoT and talks about how it all started. This chapter also elaborates on the IoT market and what it would be for an enterprise. Once we understand the market, we will be looking at various building blocks of IoT.

Chapter 2, *Applications of IoT*, covers various applications that are possible in the IoT space. This chapter showcases two major domains, healthcare and industrial IoT, and how enterprises can easily expand their horizons and penetrate the IoT market.

Chapter 3, *Getting Started with IoT Platforms*, talks about what off-the-shelf IoT platforms are and how they reduce the time and effort needed for anyone to quickly build enterprise-grade IoT solutions. This chapter introduces you to the five platforms that we are going to work with in this book. We will also be setting up Raspberry Pi 3, along with ThingSpeak platform to build an end-to-end solution that showcases the platform idea in its simplest form.

Chapter 4, *AWS IoT*, explains how to use the AWS IoT service to build an end-to-end solution with Raspberry Pi 3 as our main hardware. We will explore concepts such as Things, shadows, and rules services. To create a real-time dashboard, we will be working with Elasticsearch and Kibana.

Chapter 5, *Azure IoT*, explains how to use the Azure IoT service to build an end-to-end solution with Raspberry Pi 3 as our main hardware. We will explore concepts such as the IoT Hub and device twins. In order to create a real-time dashboard, we will be working with Power BI and stream analytics job.

Chapter 6, *Google Cloud IoT*, explains how to use Google Cloud IoT Core service to build an end-to-end solution with Raspberry Pi 3 as our hardware. We will explore concepts such as device registry, topics, and Pub/Sub subscriptions. To create a real-time dashboard, we will be working with BigQuery and Google Data Studio.

Chapter 7, *IBM Watson IoT*, explains how to use Watson IoT platform to build an end-to-end solution with Raspberry Pi 3 as our main hardware. We will explore concepts such as device registry, topics, and Pub/Sub subscriptions. In order to create a real-time dashboard we will be working with Watson IoT platform boards by creating schemas.

Chapter 8, *Kaa IoT*, explains how to use the most popular open source Kaa IoT middleware to build an end-to-end solution with Raspberry Pi 3 as our hardware. We will explore concepts such as applications, appenders, and Kaa schemas. In order to create a real-time dashboard, we will be working with REST appenders and the ThingsBoard platform.

Chapter 9, *IoT and Machine Learning*, demonstrates the true capability of IoT through the power of machine learning. In this chapter, we will understand machine learning at a high level and, using Azure Machine Learning Studio, we will build a simple web service that will predict the chance of rain based on the temperature, and humidity.

Chapter 10, *Platform Comparisons*, concludes this book by comparing the five IoT platforms we have worked on, based on various parameters. This chapter also talks about various IoT architectural solutions that can be built using these platforms.

To get the most out of this book

To work with the content of this book, you will need the following hardware:

- Raspberry Pi 3
- DHT11 temperature and humidity sensor
- Three jumper cables
- One breadboard

For the software, we need a Raspberry Pi 3 with Raspbian OS installed and Wi-Fi or Ethernet configured. We will be installing Node.js as we work through the book.

You will also need another machine that supports the installation of Node.js. We will be installing Node.js as we work through the book.

Download the example code files

You can download the example code files for this book from your account at `www.packtpub.com`. If you purchased this book elsewhere, you can visit `www.packtpub.com/support` and register to have the files emailed directly to you.

You can download the code files by following these steps:

1. Log in or register at `www.packtpub.com`.
2. Select the **SUPPORT** tab.
3. Click on **Code Downloads & Errata**.
4. Enter the name of the book in the **Search** box and follow the onscreen instructions.

Once the file is downloaded, please make sure that you unzip or extract the folder using the latest version of:

- WinRAR/7-Zip for Windows
- Zipeg/iZip/UnRarX for Mac
- 7-Zip/PeaZip for Linux

The code bundle for the book is also hosted on GitHub at `https://github.com/PacktPublishing/Enterprise-Internet-of-Things-Handbook`. In case there's an update to the code, it will be updated on the existing GitHub repository.

We also have other code bundles from our rich catalog of books and videos available at https://github.com/PacktPublishing/. Check them out!

Conventions used

There are a number of text conventions used throughout this book.

CodeInText: Indicates code words in text, database table names, folder names, filenames, file extensions, pathnames, dummy URLs, user input, and Twitter handles. Here is an example: "Now, we will construct the GET URL that we will use to send the data: https://api.thingspeak.com/update?api_key=R9XY4AXEG52DJHIT&field1=25&field2=30."

A block of code is set as follows:

```
[default]
var Protocol = require('azure-iot-device-mqtt').Mqtt;
var Client = require('azure-iot-device').Client;
var Message = require('azure-iot-device').Message;
var async = require('async');
```

When we wish to draw your attention to a particular part of a code block, the relevant lines or items are set in bold:

```
[default]
var Protocol = require('azure-iot-device-mqtt').Mqtt;
var Client = require('azure-iot-device').Client;
var Message = require('azure-iot-device').Message;
var async = require('async');
```

Any command-line input or output is written as follows:

```
$ curl -sL https://deb.nodesource.com/setup_7.x | sudo -E bash -
$ sudo apt install nodejs
```

Bold: Indicates a new term, an important word, or words that you see onscreen. For example, words in menus or dialog boxes appear in the text like this. Here is an example: "Update the previous URL with your **Write API Key**."

 Warnings or important notes appear like this.

 Tips and tricks appear like this.

Get in touch

Feedback from our readers is always welcome.

General feedback: Email `feedback@packtpub.com` and mention the book title in the subject of your message. If you have questions about any aspect of this book, please email us at `questions@packtpub.com`.

Errata: Although we have taken every care to ensure the accuracy of our content, mistakes do happen. If you have found a mistake in this book, we would be grateful if you would report this to us. Please visit `www.packtpub.com/submit-errata`, selecting your book, clicking on the Errata Submission Form link, and entering the details.

Piracy: If you come across any illegal copies of our works in any form on the Internet, we would be grateful if you would provide us with the location address or website name. Please contact us at `copyright@packtpub.com` with a link to the material.

If you are interested in becoming an author: If there is a topic that you have expertise in and you are interested in either writing or contributing to a book, please visit `authors.packtpub.com`.

Reviews

Please leave a review. Once you have read and used this book, why not leave a review on the site that you purchased it from? Potential readers can then see and use your unbiased opinion to make purchase decisions, we at Packt can understand what you think about our products, and our authors can see your feedback on their book. Thank you!

For more information about Packt, please visit `packtpub.com`.

Introduction to IoT 1

When was the last time you felt that someone or something was watching you? Maybe after watching a horror movie or when you were home alone? Worry not! This is going to happen to you every day and every moment in the near future. Welcome to the world of **Internet of Things (IoT)**, where everything around you is always watching and understanding you to make your life better.

In this book, *Enterprise Internet of Things Handbook*, we are going to look at these Things and understand what they are and how they contribute to making the next biggest revelation in technology.

In this chapter, we are going to get started with our journey by defining what IoT is then go through the history of IoT and understand how and why it is going to be a game changer for humans.

After this, we are going to get into the basics of the IoT technology stack. We are going to look at the end-to-end architecture of a typical IoT solution and deep dive into every section of it.

In this chapter, we will cover:

- Introduction to Internet of Things
- History of IoT
- IoT enterprise market
- IoT technology stack
- Understand the building blocks of the IoT Stack
- Understand cloud computing
- Understand fog computing
- IoT and security

Internet of Things

The Internet of Things is a state where the things on the face of the earth connect to the internet and start talking to each other. Things here can be electronic, electrical, mechanical, or electro-mechanical objects.

Imagine waking up in the morning to your favorite music playing in the background; once you walk into the bathroom, the lights come on automatically and the mirror greets you with the latest Instagram or Twitter feed while it analyzes your sleep pattern to see how well you have slept to show you a feed based on your mood.

You wash and move to the kitchen to find the coffee machine has already turned on a few minutes ago to serve you a cup of hot coffee. Your toaster has auto-inserted the last couple of slices of bread from its tray and checked with the refrigerator to see there is any more bread. The refrigerator checks its inventory and discovers that it is out of bread and adds the bread to your shopping cart and places an order with an online grocery store.

Meanwhile, your self-driven car is reading your calendar for meetings that you need to attend across town and plans the routes for an optimal and smooth journey. The moment you walk out of your home, the environment sensors detect the lack of humans, shut down everything that is consuming power, and move into a hibernate mode.

Now, this is Internet of Things, where all the things talk to each other and make your life an absolute pleasure.

What I have described is no longer a vision or a dream. It is how we may live one day in the very near future. There are already things such as smart fridges, smart washing machines, and smart water purifiers on the market today and people are buying them one at a time to get acquainted with the technology. Soon, we will have a system in place that will interface with all these devices; that is when we will realize the true power of IoT.

The example I have given centers around a smart home. It is very important to understand that IoT is not limited to smart homes. The same technology that we used to make our refrigerator order groceries online can be used to tell us when our car needs to be serviced next, the duration of traffic light signals at a particular hour of the day, or when a conveyer belt in a factory floor needs to be changed.

With IoT, you no longer need to worry about a diet plan; you can tell your refrigerator, your stove, and your weighing scales that you are on a diet and they will take care of that for you.

There are two sides to any coin. IoT can be very helpful and at the same time can be very annoying.

Imagine every move of yours is monitored and relayed to other services so everything is connected and in sync; this may be a bit of a challenge at times. Imagine your doctor calling you when you are going to eat a second serving of a cake... pretty annoying, right?

We rely heavily on connectivity and synchronization between devices and if things don't sync well, then the chaos will be in the order of n, where n is number of devices that this device needs to sync with.

On the lighter side of things, imagine a world where all your smart devices have an active online presence posting information about themselves and all you need to do is follow them on social media and you will know everything about them.

And if any two devices do not want to talk to each other, because they have an *ego* issue, we are doomed for sure.

The next key thing in the world of IoT is data privacy and security. Since all the devices talk to each other and share this information over the internet there is always an onlooker who is interested in that data. They may be monitoring your door sensor data that is being transmitted and then may act in your absence. Or they can tamper with the data by intercepting the packet and sending a spoofed packet on behalf of the door sensor itself.

Imagine a time and age where you need to buy a firewall for your toaster, because someone is tampering with the crispness of your toast.

We will talk more about security and data privacy in the coming chapters.

All this loosely summarizes the major part of what IoT is. We will deep dive into various areas as we go along.

In the next section, we are going to look at the history of IoT.

History

In the last section, we have seen what IoT is and we have looked at a few examples as well. In this section, we are going to take a look at the history of IoT.

Even before Kevin Ashton coined the term Internet of Things in 1999, this technology existed in other forms and shapes, pretty much doing the same thing.

 Read more about Kevin Ashton's thoughts on the term Internet of Thing at: `http://www.rfidjournal.com/articles/view?4986`.

To put things into perspective, the first TCP/IP communication was made in 1974 (`https://en.wikipedia.org/wiki/Internet_protocol_suite`), which stemmed from the success of ARPANET (`https://en.wikipedia.org/wiki/ARPANET`) in 1969.

Automated Teller Machines (ATMs) one of the first connected devices, were launched in 1969. It was a very exciting time in the banking domain, where people could get instant cash.

Take a look at this demo of an ATM from 1969 named *'Instant money': ATM comes to Australia (1969)*: `https://www.youtube.com/watch?v=yuClDSofyJs`.

Then there came the famous **Internet Coke Machine**, built by four students of Carnegie Mellon University in 1982. This machine used ARPANET to communicate and could be queried in real-time remotely using a finger interface. This machine lets you know about the stock of Coke in the machine along with the information about the Coke's coldness.

The next notable and documented incident that happened in the connected devices space was **The Internet Toaster** in 1989. John Romkey connected a toaster to the internet using a TCP/IP protocol and controlled it using a **Simple Networking Management Protocol Management Information Base (SNMP MIB)**. This internet toaster could be turned on remotely and the darkness of the toast was controlled by the duration of the toaster being powered on.

In 1991, Sir Timothy Berners Lee and CERN announced the **World Wide Web (WWW)** outside the CERN. Do note that until this time no one had seen a web page or HTML document in the outside world; it was all packets of data transmitted over wire.

With the invention of the WWW, people started working with the world of connected things with more ease.

The next event in history that brought in a new dimension to the connected things world was the **Trojan Room coffee pot** created by Quentin Stafford-Fraser and Paul Jardetzky in 1993. Using a video frame-grabber present inside the **Trojan Room**, they were able to take pictures of a coffee pot present inside the Trojan Room every few seconds and then send these to a server. The client application on the other side could show these images and if the coffee in the coffee pot was low, people could remotely get to know and then refill the coffee pot.

As you see from this series of incidents, the concept of connected devices is quite old. And the industrial sector is no stranger to it. Machines connected to each other over PLC can each be controlled, monitored, and managed from far away.

As you can see, the world of connected devices and the Internet of Things is evolving faster than ever. *The motivation is: laziness. I believe that in this time and age, laziness is the mother of invention!*

That concludes this walk down memory lane. In the next section, we are going to look at IoT and the market.

IoT and the market

In the last section, we went through the history of IoT. In this section, we will take a brief look at the IoT market and reports published by Gartner and Forbes.

IoT is identified as one of the key emerging technologies and is currently in the **Peak of Inflated Expectations** phase, as per Gartner (July 2017): `https://blogs.gartner.com/smarterwithgartner/files/2017/08/Emerging-Technology-Hype-Cycle-for-2017_Infographic_R6A.jpg` and `https://www.gartner.com/smarterwithgartner/top-trends-in-the-gartner-hype-cycle-for-emerging-technologies-2017/`.

Given the report, one can only imagine how this technology could evolve into a market, where a world of connected things leads to intelligent things.

Take a look at the *Gartner Top 10 Strategic Technology Trends 2018*: `https://www.youtube.com/watch?v=TPbKyD2bAR4`. David W. Cearley, VP and Gartner Fellow, Gartner research explains how intelligent devices are key items in emerging technology trends in 2018 and how they are going to impact overall growth in the next 5 years.

Here is an interesting article published on Forbes by Louis Columbus, titled *2017 Roundup Of Internet Of Things Forecasts*: `https://www.forbes.com/sites/louiscolumbus/2017/12/10/2017-roundup-of-internet-of-things-forecasts`. It provides some really encouraging facts about the growth and market for IoT.

The numbers mentioned in the article look quite promising for people or organizations that want to get into the world of Internet of Things, either by building it or supporting it.

In another article published by Louis Columbus, titled *The Era Of Integrated IoT Has Arrived In The Enterprise*: `https://www.forbes.com/sites/louiscolumbus/2017/09/29/the-era-of-integrated-iot-has-arrived-in-the-enterprise`), Louis Columbus talks about the adoption of IoT in enterprises.

You can read more Vodafone fifth annual IoT Barometer report in the previous URL.

Here is an interesting take from my dear friend on IoT and enterprises:

> *It's astonishing to see how the whole IoT phenomenon is picking up but shocking to see more and more IoT product startups and initiatives failing to cater to presumably a fairly absorbent market.*
>
> *The reason behind most of the initiatives not picking up is that we have been using a conventional approach to research and development, which leads most of IoT products to a finish where they become a product, which is costlier than it's worth. Current methods of user or market segmentation are the real bottlenecks. On the other hand, we have products being developed for enterprises and big firms.*
>
> *Enterprises and firms do not have affordability issues so there is undoubtedly a better chance of making good profit; plus it can help produce a blueprint of how the B2C market can be targeted.*
>
> *Currently, I see a trend in IoT initiatives targeted towards enterprise solutions. Well-funded companies and software giants have talented teams rigorously working on developing products, making prototypes, and improvising. But their development process has been more component driven than consumer needs driven, with development teams doing iterations of prototyping, fusing more and more sensors, and then drawing the hypothesis for consumer usage.*
>
> *It's not that the approach is wrong but somehow there is a better approach required.*
>
> *The concept of IoT is in a gestation period and could take about a decade to be fully established in a developing country like India. Were we to have the right research methodologies developed, internet connectivity spanned across corners of consumer-dense countries, and precise market segmentation, that would be the time when real competitive environments would be developed and the usefulness of the IoT products would be tremendous.*

As we can see , the market is huge; there is a lot of potential in terms of opportunities and revenue.

The way I look at it is that all existing enterprise clients are getting into the world of IoT in one way or another. And this is where I see a lot of potential for proposing IoT solutions to clients to make the process, as well as systems, more intelligent and smart with the help of IoT.

With this, we conclude this section on IoT and the market.

IoT technology stack

Before we start building IoT solutions using various out-of-the-box IoT platforms, I would like to talk about the various building blocks of an IoT solution. That includes smart devices, storage, API management, as well as intelligence.

This diagram represents an end-to-end IoT stack:

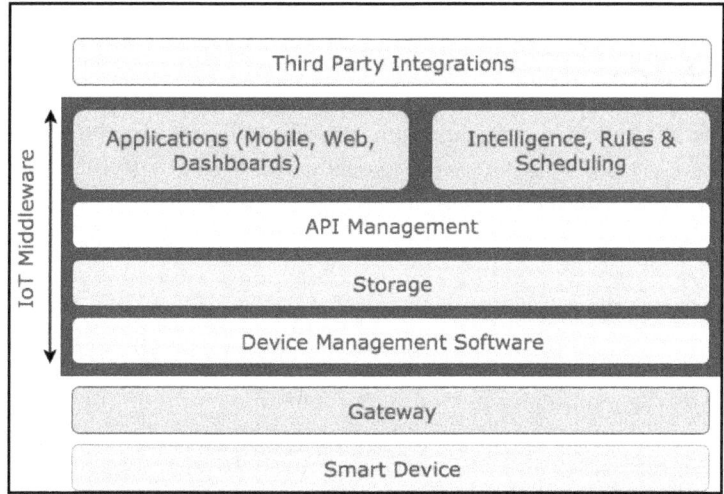

The stack consists of various layers that will be part of any typical IoT solution.

The bottommost layers in the stack are the smart devices or **The Things**. These communicate with the real world and gather the information around them to actuate things. And through the gateway, the smart devices talk to the device management software to keep them integrated with the remaining world.

With the help of the storage layer, the device management software persists the communications and data that arises between the smart devices and the API management layer. The API management layer is responsible for creating an interface between the device, its data, and the applications that want to control and manage these smart devices.

The applications here can be any entity that has the capability of consuming the exposed APIs and managing and monitoring smart devices. Applications here can include a mobile app, a web dashboard, a voice assistant, or an IVR service, to name a few.

On the other hand, rules engines and schedulers can also consume the data exposed by the APIs. Rules here can be simple actions when a certain type of threshold is reached and a schedule is where an action can be performed on a device at a certain configured time.

This data can also be used for analysis as well as for adding intelligence on top of the existing system. Technologies such as big data, machine learning, and artificial intelligence fall under this category.

On top of these layers is where third-party integrations take place.

In the subsequent sections, we will go into each of the layers and explore them further.

Building blocks

As we have seen in the previous section, there are many layers that constitute a typical IoT stack. In this section, we are going to explore each layer. We are going to start with the smart device layer.

Smart devices

Smart devices are the Things present on the face of the earth that can be controlled and monitored. These devices typically have a microcontroller or a microprocessor and these talk to the virtual world using a network communication module. And on the other end, the microcontroller or a microprocessor has various protocols with which it interfaces with a sensor or an actuator.

Microcontroller versus microprocessor

Before we go further, it is good to have an understanding of how a microcontroller and a microprocessor are different:

Microprocessor	Microcontroller
Only CPU; other peripherals are interfaced via the CPU bus	CPU + (Flash) Memory + RAM + ROM + I/O + Timers + UARTS + ADC + DAC and so on on a single chip
General purpose	Single purpose
High processing power	Low processing power

Power hungry	Can work on a battery
Runs an OS (for example, Linux)	Runs on a **tight loop** approach and can support OSs such as **Real Time Operating System (RTOS)**

In a typical IoT scenario, smart devices do only one job, for example reading the door sensor data and sending it to the cloud. For this kind of a solution, a microcontroller with a network module is quite sufficient.

But if we want to run an edge node as a smart device, then we need to have more processing power and that is when we turn to a microprocessor.

The following diagram explains the architecture of a smart device that is driven by a microcontroller:

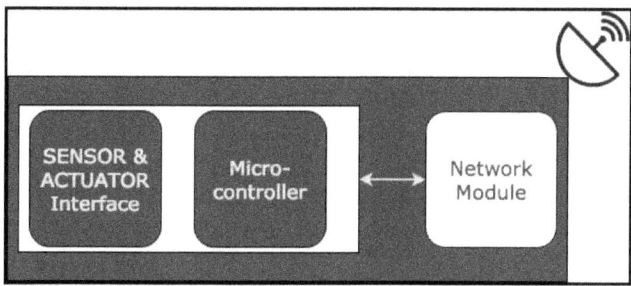

The simplest example of an MCU is Arduino (https://www.arduino.cc/) and a network module example is Espressif ESP8266 (https://www.espressif.com/en/products/hardware/esp8266ex/overview).

This is the most common architecture for hardware in IoT. The three blocks that are shown are replaced as per the solution. We will look at each of the blocks in the next sections.

On the other hand, a microprocessor runs an OS, which has defined network interfaces and a communication module that come on a single board. For example, the Raspberry Pi (https://www.raspberrypi.org/products/).

In this book, we are going to use Raspberry Pi as the smart device for our examples.

Sensors

Sensors and actuators are the backbones of IoT. These are the entities that bridge the gap between the real world and the virtual world. In this section, we are going to look at sensors and in the next section, we are going to look at actuators.

Sensors are devices that can measure a particular property of nature. To simplify things, take a temperature sensor. A temperature sensor generally uses a thermistor. A **thermistor** is an electronic component whose resistance changes with changes in temperature.

In most thermistors, the resistance decreases as the temperature increases. These are called **Negative Temperature Coefficient** (**NTC**) thermistors.

Now, this resistance can either be converted to voltage and be read by a microcontroller or there are *thermistor to digital converters* available that can also do the job of feeding the temperature to a microcontroller.

The previous explanation is an example of how a temperature sensor works. Similarly, other sensors have different mechanisms using which they sense a property.

Examples of a few sensors follow:

Sensor name	Datasheet link
Temperature and humidity sensor (DHT11)	https://akizukidenshi.com/download/ds/aosong/DHT11.pdf
Door sensor or reed switch	https://standexelectronics.com/wp-content/uploads/OKI_Reed_Switch_ORD213.pdf
Passive Infrared (**PIR**) sensor or motion detector	https://cdn-learn.adafruit.com/downloads/pdf/pir-passive-infrared-proximity-motion-sensor.pdf

There are plenty of other sensors that you can explore yourself, right from leak detection to fire detection.

You can find a compiled list of all sensors here: https://en.wikipedia.org/wiki/List_of_sensors.

Actuators

While sensors sense the environment around them, an actuator is responsible for controlling a system by actuating (open/close or on/off). For example, a switch that can be used to turn a light on or off can be controlled via an actuator.

An actuator generally takes a signal which indicates the nature of an operation. For example, if we need to turn a switch on or off, we use a relay.

A relay is an electromagnetic switch that takes in the AC mains power supply at one end and a digital signal at other. The general state of the relay is open and that means there is no power supply flowing through from the mains to our load. Once there is a digital high or a digital low signal (depending on the type of relay), the relay moves to a closed state where the load and mains are short and the power flows through.

To get a better understanding of how a relay works and how to use it, take a look at *How to use a relay, the easy way*: https://www.youtube.com/watch?v=T1fNQjelojs.

A relay is one of several core actuator components, which are then reused in other actuators such as a solenoid valve.

Controllers

In the last section, we looked at what a sensor and an actuator are and how they work. In this section, we look at the controllers that are going to read data from these sensors or control the actuators.

We are going to look at three types of controller:

- Integrated controllers
- Assembled controllers
- System on Chips

The first two types are not industry-standard names. I have used this nomenclature to explain the concepts better.

Integrated controllers

Integrated controllers, also known as **microprocessor-based controllers**, are those pieces of hardware that have the complete landscape needed to interface with a sensor or an actuator and relay it to the outside world.

For instance, Raspberry Pi: `https://www.raspberrypi.org/documentation/`. One single board has all the features that we need to interface with the sensors as well as with the outside world.

Another example is a BeagleBone board: `http://beagleboard.org/bone`.

As you can see, these credit card-sized mini computers can be a simple solution for a remote sensor that needs to be deployed. They have all the built-in capabilities that we need for doing all the tasks. They are for sure overkill and a poor choice if these remote nodes need to run on scarce battery power.

That is where the next type of controller comes in: assembled controllers.

Assembled controllers

Assembled controllers, as you may have guessed, are where we pick and choose the various components that we need to build an efficient and a power-optimized sensor node.

As we have seen earlier, their setup would look like this:

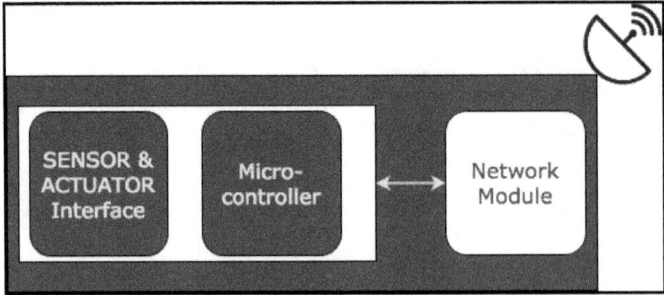

Now, this is where things get interesting. Depending on the compute needed, the power requirements, and the functionality, we can choose a combination of the microcontroller and the network module.

 Here the network module acts as a slave to the microcontroller.

Possible combinations

Some possible combinations are:

- Arduino UNO for microcontroller and Espressif ESP8266 (Wi-Fi) for the network module. You can read more about this setup here: `https://medium.com/@manrick01/arduino-uno-esp8266-esp-12e-uart-wifi-wireless-shield-3a39858e5f25`.
- Arduino UNO for microcontroller and Arduino Ethernet Shield for the network module. You can read more about this setup here: `http://www.instructables.com/id/Arduino-Ethernet-Shield-Tutorial/`.
- Arduino UNO for microcontroller and SIM900A (GSM) for the network module. You can read more about this setup here: `http://www.instructables.com/id/GSM-SIM900A-With-Arduino/`.
- TI MCP430 for microcontroller and TI CC3100 (Wi-Fi) for the network module. More information here: `https://www.youtube.com/watch?v=sCB80DsJfig`.

There can be other possible combinations as well, but these are a few to get you started. Do refer to the datasheets of these ICs to understand how they work and their capabilities and power consumption for a better design of your smart device.

System on Chips

System on Chips (SoCs) are ideal for an IoT solution, where power and processing are very critical. Since they come with their own network module, they are quite self-contained.

You can read more about SoCs here: `https://internetofthingsagenda.techtarget.com/definition/system-on-a-chip-SoC`.

Popular SoCs in market

Here are a few SoCs that are quite popular in the market:

- **Espressif ESP8266**: This module is a Wi-Fi SoC that has the full TCP/IP stack as well as microcontroller capabilities. More about this module here: `https://www.espressif.com/sites/default/files/documentation/0a-esp8266ex_datasheet_en.pdf`.
- **Espressif ESP32**: This module is a low-power SoC that has both Wi-Fi as well as Bluetooth capabilities and has a dual core Xtensa LX6 microprocessor. More about this module here: `https://www.espressif.com/sites/default/files/documentation/esp32_datasheet_en.pdf`.
- **Texas Instruments CC3200**: With an ARM Cortex-M4 processor and a complete Wi-Fi stack, this module is another popular choice in the IoT industry. More about this module here: `http://www.ti.com/lit/ds/symlink/cc3200.pdf`.

There are many other options including the likes of NXP, Qualcomm, or STMicroelectronics in this space. Do explore them.

Hardware communication protocols

Now that we have seen what a sensor, actuator, and controller are, we are going to look at how the sensor/actuator interfaces with the controller.

There are multiple protocols with which communications can happen. The most commonly used ones are:

- GPIO
- Analog/voltage reading
- UART
- SPI
- I²C

Let's get an overview of what each of these are and how they work.

GPIO

General Purpose Input Output (GPIO) is a simple communication mechanism that involves one pin between the controller and the sensor/actuator. This protocol is pretty good for sending a few bits of data.

A relay can be controlled via a GPIO pin. DHT11's temperature can be read using the digital pin.

Analog reading

Sensors sometimes expose their metrics in the form of voltage and a controller can use its internal analog to digital converter to read the data voltage and map it to the datasheet.

For example, the Texas Instruments LM35 temperature sensor works this way. Every 10 millivolts of voltage it generates while sensing, it represents 1 °C in temperature. For instance, if the voltage reading is 235mV, then the ambient temperature is 23.5V. You can read more about LM35 here: `http://www.ti.com/lit/ds/symlink/lm35.pdf`.

UART

The **Universal Asynchronous Receiver and Transmitter** (**UART**) is probably one of the oldest ways to talk to a chip. The transmitter of the controller will be connected to the receiver of the sensor and the receiver of the controller will be connected to the transmitter of the sensor.

This mode supports huge amounts of data being transmitted.

An example of the UART-based sensor is the fingerprint scanner. The data from the fingerprint scanner is sent to the controller over UART for further processing, after a user scans a finger. You can read more about the fingerprint scanner here: `https://cdn-learn.adafruit.com/downloads/pdf/adafruit-optical-fingerprint-sensor.pdf`.

SPI

The **Serial Peripheral Interface** (**SPI**) protocol allows a sensor and a controller to exchange data via two communication lines. SPI is a bus which supports multiple sensors or actuators being controlled on a single bus. The protocol uses three pins connected between the sensor and controller.

For example, the Bosch BME280 temperature humidity pressure sensor supports the SPI protocol to communicate between the controller and sensor. Read more about BME280 here: `https://www.bosch-sensortec.com/bst/products/all_products/bme280`.

I²C

Inter-Integrated Circuit, pronounced as I-Squared-C or I-two-C, uses a single data line and a clock to communicate between multiple sensors connected to the controller. This protocol is very good for on-board or short-range communication.

For example, the BH1750 from the ROHM semiconductor is an ambient light sensor that measures the ambient light around the sensor in Lux. This sensor exposes its data to the controller over the I²C bus. Read more about BH1750 here: http://www.mouser.com/ds/2/348/bh1750fvi-e-186247.pdf.

 This protocol can be used for controller-to-controller communication as well.

This wraps up our exploration of the smart device layer.

In this book, we are going to work with Raspberry Pi 3 as our controller and the DHT11 temperature and humidity sensor as the sensor module.

Gateway and cloud communication

In the last section, we looked at the essentials of hardware or smart devices that form the backbone of the entire IoT solution. In this section, we are going to look at gateways and how the smart device communicates with the cloud over the internet.

Here are the possible ways for a controller connected to a sensor to send data to the cloud over the internet:

- **Ethernet cable**: https://www.lifewire.com/what-is-ethernet-3426740
- **GSM/cellular**: https://www.tutorialspoint.com/gsm/gsm_overview.htm
- **Wi-Fi**: https://www.lifewire.com/what-is-wi-fi-2377430

These three are quite common protocols that we use almost daily.

These communication protocols are more popular in an IoT stack that works using a cloud computing-based approach. If we were using a fog computing-based approach, we would use the following popular protocols to connect to the gateway and then the gateway would relay the data to the cloud using the Ethernet, GSM, or Wi-Fi:

- **Bluetooth Low Energy (BLE)**: https://www.mikroe.com/blog/bluetooth-low-energy-part-1-introduction-ble
- **Z-Wave**: https://www.smarthome.com/sc-what-is-zwave-home-automation
- **Zigbee**: http://www.radio-electronics.com/info/wireless/zigbee/zigbee.php
- **NFC**: https://www.androidauthority.com/what-is-nfc-270730/
- **RFID**: https://www.epc-rfid.info/rfid

We will talk about this more when we discuss cloud computing and fog computing in the later part of this chapter.

Device Management Software

Device Management Software (DMS) is a very crucial piece of software that takes care of device management. Device management includes:

- Device authentication and authorization
- Device connection status
- Device data management
- **Quality of Service (QoS)**

Any TCP/IP-based communication that we make between the smart device and the DMS would satisfy these requirements.

In the next section, we are going to look at the various protocols available for smart devices and cloud communication.

Device to cloud communication protocols

Here are a few popular communication protocols.

Message Queuing Telemetry Transport

The **Message Queue Telemetry Transport** (**MQTT**) protocol is a battery-friendly, small footprint message broker that implements an extremely lightweight publish/subscribe protocol. MQTT is suitable when working with power- and computation-constrained devices.

MQTT for Sensor Networks

MQTT for Sensor Networks (**MQTT-SN**) caters for more non-TCP/IP embedded devices, where MQTT runs using a TCP/IP stack.

 MQTTS and MQTT-SN are different. MQTTS is MQTT over SSL.

Constrained Application Protocol

The **Constrained Application Protocol** (**CoAP**) is a web transfer protocol for use with constrained nodes and constrained networks, which are low-power and lossy. This protocol is designed for **machine-to-machine** (**M2M**) applications, primarily focused on the IoT space.

Simple Text Oriented Messaging Protocol

STOMP is the **Simple** (or **Streaming**) **Text Oriented Messaging Protocol**.

STOMP provides an interoperable wire format so that STOMP clients can communicate with any STOMP message broker to provide easy and widespread messaging interoperability among many languages, platforms, and brokers.

Advanced Message Queuing Protocol

AMQP or **Advanced Message Queuing Protocol** is an open standard for passing messages between applications. This protocol is centered around message management rather than on device management.

Representational state transfer

REST or **Representational state transfer**, or RESTful web services are a methodology using which two systems or one system and a user can exchange information. Using a predefined set of stateless operations, REST-compliant web services allow requesting systems to exchange and manipulate data.

WebSockets

The WebSocket protocol was designed to work well with the existing web infrastructure. As part of this design principle, the protocol specification defines that the WebSocket connection starts its life as an HTTP connection, guaranteeing full backwards compatibility with the pre-WebSocket world. The protocol switch from HTTP to WebSocket is referred to as the WebSocket handshake.

As we can see, there are various options available for communication between smart devices and the cloud. Of them all, MQTT (secure) is the most popular and you would see a lot of platforms and solutions preferring MQTT to other protocols.

Of course, there is always raw TCP/IP communication, but this would mean we would end up implementing the entire device management stack all over again, in our own way.

Storage

So far, we have seen how data originates in a sensor and how the controller reads the data using one of the supported protocols. The controller attempts to transmit that data over any of the communication protocols to the Device Management Software.

Now the data is in the cloud. The basic functionality of connecting the real world with the virtual world ends here and the next level of data processing begins from here.

Storage is a very big part of the IoT Stack that we discussed earlier. The database needs to be scalable, highly available, flexible, secure, fast, and highly optimized to process thousands of reads/writes per second.

Here are a few options for storage software.

MongoDB

MongoDB is a document database with the scalability and flexibility that you want along with the querying and indexing that you need. MongoDB is a distributed database at its core, so high availability, horizontal scaling, and geographic distribution are built in and easy to use. MongoDB is free and open source, published under the **GNU Affero General Public License**.

Apache Cassandra

Apache Cassandra is one of the best highly scalable and highly available databases, without compromising on performance. Its linear scalability and proven fault tolerance on any kind of hardware makes this a perfect database for mission-critical applications.

Time series databases

A **time series database** (**TSDB**) represents a data point as a time and value, the value being the sensor value and the time being the time of record origination. Time series databases are pretty fast at data filtering and executing aggregation functions. In IoT, a lot of activity starts after the data is persisted in the database. Most of these activities involve generating dashboards and running queries to analyze the data and that is where a TSDB plays a major role.

Some of the popular time series databases are outlined next.

InfluxDB

InfluxDB is one of the most popular TSDBs and is one of the ideal solutions for use cases involving large amounts of time-stamped data, including DevOps monitoring, application metrics, IoT sensor data, and real-time analytics. InfluxDB also offers an SQL-like query language for interacting with data.

KairosDB

KairosDB is a fast time series database on Cassandra. The API provides operations to list existing metric names, list tag names and values, store metric data points, and query for metric data points. Aggregators perform an operation on data points and down samples. Standard functions such as `min`, `max`, `sum`, `count`, `mean`, and more are available.

Netflix Atlas

Atlas was developed by Netflix to manage dimensional time series data for near real-time operational insight. It has in-memory data storage, allowing it to gather and report very large numbers of metrics very quickly. Atlas captures operational intelligence and provides a picture of what is currently happening within a system.

RIAK TS

RIAK TS is an enterprise-grade NoSQL time series database optimized specifically for IoT and time series data. It can transform, store, and analyze massive amounts of time series data and claims to be faster than Apache Cassandra.

This wraps up the section on data storage and the choices we have.

In the next section, we will move one layer above storage into the API management layer.

API management

Once the data is persisted, the next step is to expose the data to the virtual world, where other applications and interfaces can consume it.

Technologies such as Node.js, Go, and Python are a good choice for exposing APIs. But gone are the days where one needed to sit and stitch together APIs to expose secure data. There are ready-made **Backend as a Service** (**BaaS**) available in the market that one can deploy quite easily.

API gateway administration

Once our microservice to expose data has been set up, the next step is to make sure the data is secured and that only the intended applications get the access to the data.

That is where software such as Kong (`https://github.com/Kong/kong`), Istio (`https://istio.io/`), or Tyk (`https://tyk.io/`) take the burden away from you. They provide an entire API gateway where things related to security—authorization and authentication, rate limiting, audit, and logging—can be done quite easily at the same time as monitoring the entire API microservice layer.

This is pretty good solution in modern times, not only for IoT-related stacks.

This concludes our section on API management. In the next section, we are going to look at applications that consume the APIs exposed.

Applications

Now that the data is exposed in the form of APIs, it can be consumed by an interface such as a mobile app, a web dashboard, or a smart watch.

Since the data is exposed over REST APIs or WebSockets, any client that is capable of interfacing with these web technologies can extract the data/metrics and provide an overview of what is happening on the device.

The purpose of these applications is to represent sensor data and provide an interface to control the actuator.

Intelligence

The powerful part of IoT is its ability to read data provided by various sensors, make sense of it, and then act on it. This is where intelligence comes into picture.

A typical flow would be as follows:

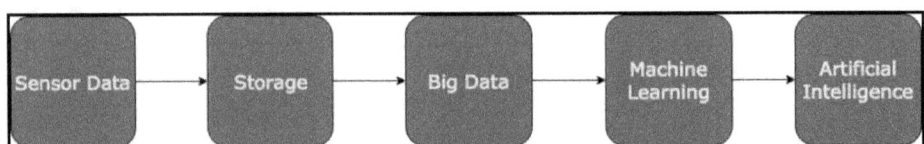

The data originates at the sensors and then is saved to the **Storage**. The huge sets of data in **Storage** are then cleaned and normalized and put into a **Big Data** system. Then **Machine Learning** is done on top of this data and, based on the derived data models, we act on the results using **Artificial Intelligence**.

Using technologies such as machine learning, we perform various analyses on the data. Analysis can range from simple predictions to understanding users, behavior based on their interaction with the sensors. Then, using these predictions, we can propose possible automations to the user. Apart from pattern recognition, we can also perform cross-sectional data analysis, such as the time versus power consumption of a specific device. If we see any anomaly in that data, we can alert the users.

Rules and alerts

Now that we have the setup to get the sensor data into the cloud, we can show it in a dashboard or run intelligence on top of that data as well as execute certain user-defined rules on the incoming data.

The rule here can be as simple as: if the temperature sensor data is greater than 25 °C, send me a notification on my mobile or if the temperature sensor data is less than 18 °C, turn off the air conditioner.

These rules can be created by the user and automate a lot of things based on context and needs.

Inspired by this thought, a popular service named IFTTT came to life.

IFTTT

If This Then That (**IFTTT**) provides an interface to chain events. Events can be data coming into the system or a certain schedule that has been fired or any such activity. Using an applet, one can chain various events to perform automation.

For instance, if movement is detected in the hallway then turn on the lights: a simple If This Then That scenario.

The IFTTT service can be used for non-IoT activities as well. You can read more about IFTTT here: `https://ifttt.com/discover`.

Scheduling

There may be times when you want certain activities to happen at certain times of the day and you are not always available to execute them.

For instance, every day at 6 P.M. turn on the backyard light and at 5 A.M. turn it off. A very mundane task and a human presence is really not required.

That is where a scheduling engine comes into picture. You set up a schedule, similar to a wake-up alarm, defining when the schedule should fire and what action should happen at that time. This will take care of getting the job done.

There are services such as cron-job.org (`https://cron-job.org/en/`), EasyCron (`https://www.easycron.com/`), or Getcron (`http://www.getcron.com/index_EN.html`) that can be leveraged to run jobs.

You can always build your own scheduler in any of the popular programming language as well; you can find plenty of libraries for this.

This concludes our section on utilizing data exposed by the API management layer.

In the next section, we will look at how the data as well as intelligence can be consumed by third-party services.

Third-party integration

So far, we have seen how to consume data and make sense of it, and how to work with manual automation using rules and schedules. In this section, we are going to look at how third-party services can integrate with our stack.

Imagine you want to have Amazon Alexa or Google Assistant as one of the interfaces to the smart devices that we built. These third-party services do not play well with our APIs directly and that is where this integration layer comes into the picture.

This is a custom layer that we will be using to write wrapper functions that act as a bridge between our API management layer and the third-party service. All this layer does is massage and accept data from Amazon Alexa APIs, and then it converts it to a format the API management layer understands; it then reads the response from the API management layer and converts it to a format Amazon Alexa API understands. This way, the core of the stack need not change for every integration with other services.

In IoT, integrating with third-party services is bound to happen at some point or another because one entity/organization cannot build everything needed for IoT.

For instance, in a smart home, you may have built a smart device that can sense the temperature along with a few other parameters. Now you want your customer/user to able to integrate their Nest thermostat with your temperature sensor values. We set up a rule to control their thermostat from our stack.

This layer makes sure that our stack is scalable and integratable with other services as well.

With this, we wrap up the section on building blocks. We have seen various layers, their components, and how all of them form a complete IoT stack when stitched together.

In the next section, we will be looking at the security aspects of IoT.

IoT and security

Did you know that the first IoT murder was supposed to happen in 2014? Don't believe me, check out: *First IoT-mediated murder could occur in 2014, experts warn* http://www.itpro.co.uk/hacking/23242/first-iot-mediated-murder-could-occur-in-2014-experts-warn.

Security is a very important part of IoT, be it as simple as stealing data or monitoring your door sensor to know when you have left your home or spoofing a data record to indicate an unwanted event to create havoc. Security is essential.

Now we need to invest in a firewall for our toaster.

IoT devices are being used to perform DDoS attacks on other entities. Stealing data from a sensor is one thing, but reprogramming/hacking a smart device to think it is something else is a new level of disaster.

Mirai bot attack

On Friday October 21, 2016 there was a **Distributed Denial of Service (DDoS)** attack that took place on a DNS provider named Dyn, bringing down major websites such as Etsy, GitHub, Netflix, Twitter, and Spotify.

This was a Mirai bot attack (https://www.corero.com/resources/ddos-attack-types/mirai-botnet-ddos-attack.html). All this malware does is convert devices running Linux into remotely controlled Bots that can be used as part of the botnet for performing large-scale network attacks.

Old router and IP cameras were the major source of devices that were used in the attack that brought down part of the USA.

You can read more about the attack from Dyn here: https://dyn.com/blog/dyn-analysis-summary-of-friday-october-21-attack/.

This is just one of a few attacks that have happened in the recent past. You can find plenty more on the internet.

Ransomware

The new trend in IoT hacking is ransomware. Hackers get into IoT systems or software and block it or disrupt it. In order for the device or the system to work properly again, the owners need to pay a ransom (mostly through cryptocurrency such as Bitcoin).

Imagine a world where your coffee machine blackmails you into paying money or it will brew only decaf.

In this time and age, what is the best way to be secure? Just turn things off?

Jokes aside, this is a pretty serious issue. Do remember that systems are built to be hacked. So, what might seem a security solution today may be a new attack name tomorrow.

In the world of IoT, our primary goal is to keep data safe and the secondary goal is to keep our devices and servers updated.

For data communication security, we can use a standard such as X.509, where we encrypt the transported data using public/private keys. If needed, the data that is being transmitted can be scrambled and encrypted.

All of the data stored in databases needs to be encrypted. This definitely causes overhead but will save us from attacks.

Check out this article on how MongoDB databases were attacked and how ransoms were required to get them back: `https://www.networkworld.com/article/3157766/linux/mongodb-ransomware-attacks-and-lessons-learned.html`.

In the next section, we will start looking at the two types of IoT stacks that the world is moving towards: cloud computing and fog computing.

End-to-end architecture

Now that we are aware of the building blocks for a typical IoT solution, we will look at the two different types of architecture for building solutions, their pros and cons, and which setup is suitable for what application.

Using cloud computing

Microsoft Azure defines cloud computing as:

> *Simply put, cloud computing is the delivery of computing services-servers, storage, databases, networking, software, analytics, and more-over the internet (the cloud).*

In IoT, cloud computing is used when the devices talk directly to the cloud. Take a look at this IoT stack built using cloud computing:

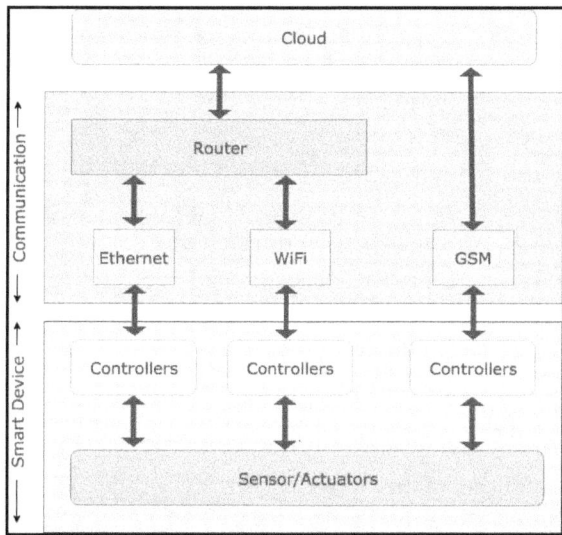

The sensor data needs to reach the cloud finally. So, what means do we have? We can connect an Ethernet cable to our controller to talk to a router and then send the data via the router or use a Wi-Fi module to interface with a local router access point. We can also use a GSM module to send the data via a GSM network.

Pros and cons of using cloud computing in the IoT

Now let's quickly look at the pros and cons of this approach:

- **Pros**:
    - If we have only one or two devices in an environment (for router-based communication)
    - If devices are closely positioned to each router (for wireless and router-based communication)

- If the network strength of the SIM/GSM is better than good (for GSM-based communication)
- If the battery life of the smart device is not a factor, as both GSM and Wi-Fi modules consume high power (for wireless-based communication)

- **Cons:**

  - If there is no internet access, these devices are literally dumb devices. No rules or schedules can be run on these devices if they are offline. No intelligence can be gathered.
  - If more devices are connected in the same environment, then we may not have enough Ethernet ports on a router or the router capability to access more devices as Wi-Fi clients (for router-based communication).
  - If the devices are far away from the router, they cannot contact the router or may struggle to keep their connection alive (for wireless and router-based communication).
  - If a particular GSM network is patchy in an area, the connectivity with the cloud is a major issue, again making this device a dumb device till the internet comes on.
  - GSM and Wi-Fi modules consume a lot of power and are not capable of running on a battery for long (not even 6 months).

The biggest issue among all this is the necessity for these devices to be always connected to the internet. If the network goes down, these devices will still function but the data they gather will be quite useless.

Imagine a smart home with about 40 to 50 smart devices deployed; here, all of them need to be connected to power at all times and moving them around might not be an option. Placing them at remote places where there is no power is a breaking factor. The distance between the Wi-Fi router and the device needs to be small.

In developing nations, both internet connectivity and power may be a challenge. This approach may not be a suitable approach for those nations.

These are some of the key challenges when working with cloud computing and IoT.

Now, let us look at fog computing.

Using fog computing

Fog computing, fog networking, or fogging is a computation paradigm where the cloud comes closer to the earth or the **fog layer**. This layer has the computational infrastructure needed to run most essential operations and has all the features that a typical cloud would have but runs locally.

The primary difference between cloud computing and fog computing is that the sensor/actuator network does not heavily rely on the internet to work.

Take a look at this IoT stack built using fog computing:

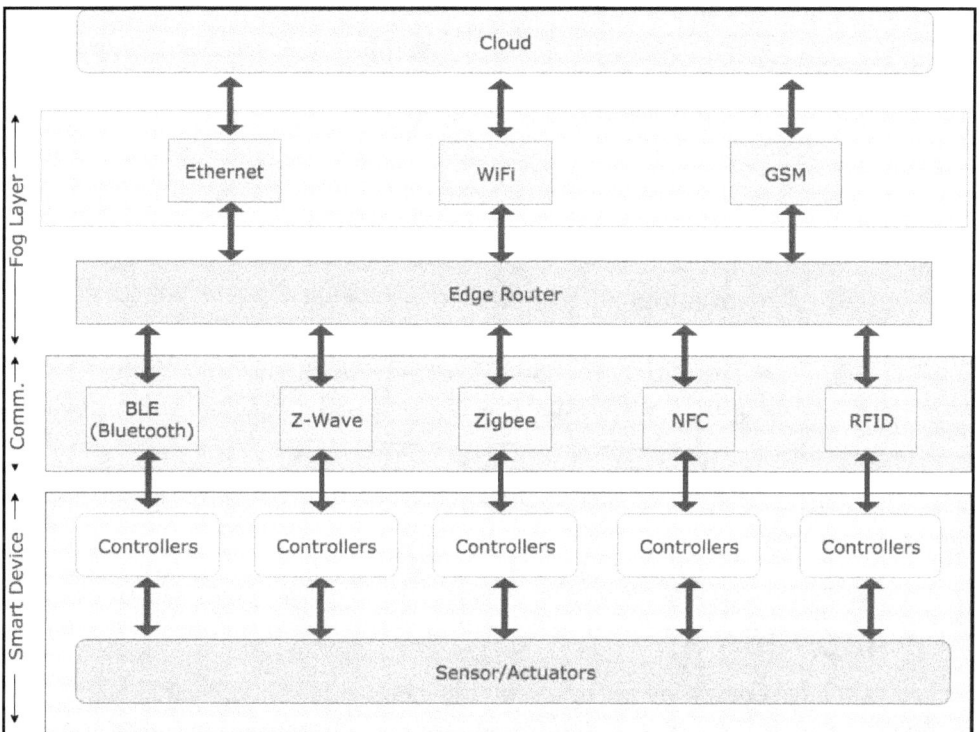

In the stack, the sensor nodes do not directly talk to the gateway. Instead, they talk to an **Edge Router**, which is responsible for locally collecting all the data from various sensors, and this **Edge Router** sends the data to the **Cloud** when the network is available.

We can think of the edge router as a *mini-cloud* which can execute almost all basic functions such as storing data, running rules, executing schedules, and managing the devices offline if the internet is not available.

Pros and cons of using fog computing in the IoT

Now let's quickly look at the pros and cons of this approach.

- **Pros:**
    - Ideal for multiple devices connected to a network.
    - The range between the edge router and hub is not a factor because these smart devices or edge nodes use long range or mesh-based communication.
    - All the edge nodes run a protocol such as Bluetooth, Zigbee, or Z-Wave, which are power-efficient and can run a CR2032 battery for years together.
    - The availability of the internet is not a factor for this smart network to work. The edge router is capable of taking on the role of a mini-cloud to emulate all its features.

- **Cons:**
    - The biggest con in a system like this is the necessity for a consumer to buy an edge router even though they would like to use just one node
    - Inventory management for an organization would be higher because they need to maintain multiple devices now
    - The initial purchasing cost is on the higher side as the user needs to purchase the edge router along with the actual smart device

If we are looking at building a system where there are plenty of devices connected close to each other and they need to work seamlessly irrespective of the internet connection, then fog computing is better.

Edge computing

Do take a look at *Edge Computing vs Fog Computing* here: `https://medium.com/@rshariffdeen/edge-computing-vs-fog-computing-5b23d6bb049d`. This article talks about the subtle differences between fog- and edge-based computing.

Which is better?

Fog computing pushes intelligence towards the smart devices, reducing the amount of data that needs to go to the cloud and decreasing operational latency between the user and the smart device. Cloud computing is a centralized system that can scale on demand and can perform on-demand analysis in real time, among other things.

Here is a table from Cisco's blog, written by Maher Abdelshkour, explaining the differences between cloud and fog computing:

Table 1		
Requirements	**Cloud Computing**	**Fog Computing**
Latency	High	Low
Delay Jitter	High	Very low
Location of Service	Within the Internet	At the edge of the local network
Distance between client and server	Multiple hops	One hope
Security	Undefined	Can be defined
Attack on data enroute	High probability	Very low probability
Location awareness	No	Yes
Geo-distribution	Centralized	Distributed
No. of server nodes	Few	Very large
Support for Mobility	Limited	Supported
Real time interactions	Supported	Supported
Type of last mile connectivity	Leased Line	Wireless

Another table with a high-level comparison follows:

Table 2	
Cloud Computing	**Fog Computing**
Data and applications are processed in a cloud, which is time consuming task for large data.	Rather than presenting and working from a centralized cloud, fog operates on network edge. So it consumes less time.
Problem of bandwidth, as a result of sending every bit of data over cloud channels.	Less demand for bandwidth, as every bit of data's were aggregated at certain access points instead of sending over cloud channels.
Slow response time and scalability problems as a result of depending servers that are located at remote places.	By setting small servers called edge servers in visibility of users, it is possible for a fog computing platform to avoid response time and scalability issues.

 You can read more about this here: `https://blogs.cisco.com/ perspectives/iot-from-cloud-to-fog-computing`.

To summarize, depending on the scale, cost, and real-time nature of the application you are planning to deploy, you can pick between cloud computing and fog computing.

IoT standards

We have covered almost all topics related to IoT and its technology stack. The final topic in this chapter is going to be about standards in IoT.

As we have seen so far, there are way too many ways in which one can build their IoT solution stack and there are plenty of masters in this field who think their approach is better. This leads to multiple ways of implementing solutions in IoT.

Be it hardware standards, software standards, communication standards, or data computation standards, there are plenty of options available. As we start looking at various platforms in the book, you will come to realize how each of them is different from the other internally, but that they end up with a similar solution stack.

Take a look at this excellent article named *IoT Standards and Protocols - An overview of protocols involved in Internet of Things devices and applications. Help clarify with IoT layer technology stack and head-to-head comparisons* here: `https://www.postscapes.com/internet- of-things-protocols/`. It will give you a high-level understanding of all the possible protocols and standards in each layer.

Summary

In this chapter, we have gone through all the key building blocks of an IoT stack. Then we looked at security, the differences between cloud computing and fog computing, and finally we talked a bit about IoT standards.

In the next chapter, we are going to look at the real-world applications of IoT.

Further reading

- Internet Coke Machine: `http://knowyourmeme.com/memes/internet-coke-machine`
- Internet Toaster: `https://www.livinginternet.com/i/ia_myths_toast.htm`
- The Trojan Room coffee pot from Quentin Stafford-Fraser himself: `https://www.cl.cam.ac.uk/coffee/qsf/coffee.html`
- You can find a compiled list of all sensors here: `https://en.wikipedia.org/wiki/List_of_sensors`
- SoCs: `https://internetofthingsagenda.techtarget.com/definition/system-on-a-chip-SoC`
- GPIO: `https://techterms.com/definition/gpio`
- ADC: `https://wiki.analog.com/university/courses/electronics/text/chapter-20`
- UART: `http://www.circuitbasics.com/basics-uart-communication/`
- SPI: `https://www.allaboutcircuits.com/technical-articles/spi-serial-peripheral-interface/`
- I^2C protocol: `https://learn.sparkfun.com/tutorials/i2c`
- MQTT: `http://mqtt.org/`
- MQTT-SN: `http://mqtt.org/2013/12/mqtt-for-sensor-networks-mqtt-sn`
- STOMP: `https://datatracker.ietf.org/doc/rfc7252/`
- AMQP: `http://www.amqp.org/about/what`
- REST: `https://www.codecademy.com/articles/what-is-rest`
- WebSocket: `https://websocket.org/aboutwebsocket.html`
- MongoDB: `https://www.mongodb.com/what-is-mongodb`
- Apache Cassandra: `http://cassandra.apache.org/`
- InfluxDB: `https://www.influxdata.com/time-series-platform/influxdb/`
- KairosDB: `https://kairosdb.github.io/`
- Atlas: `https://github.com/Netflix/atlas/wiki`
- RiakTShere: `http://basho.com/products/riak-ts/`
- IoT, from Cloud to Fog Computing: `https://blogs.cisco.com/perspectives/iot-from-cloud-to-fog-computing`

Applications of IoT 2

In the last chapter, we defined IoT, looked at its history, and finally went through all the key building blocks of an IoT application. In this chapter, we are going to take a step back and understand the real-world applications of IoT before we start working with the building blocks.

The topics covered in this chapter are:

- IoT and its value proposition
- The healthcare domain and IoT
- The industrial domain and IoT
- Other IoT application areas

IoT and its value proposition

From the examples we have looked at in the previous chapter, we have seen how IoT helps us achieve a world of connected devices. But is that all there is to IoT? Well, no. The world of connected devices is step zero in the process of human evolution.

In a few years from now, IoT will be as integral as the internet itself.

Having a world of connected devices is all about convenience in terms of the ability to monitor and manage these devices remotely. Next comes the world of smart devices. Smart devices are the next generation of IoT, where the devices not only talk to a centralized entity, such as the cloud, but also talk to each other, keeping you in the loop.

Taking a smart home scenario, take a look at the following WhatsApp group chat for **Arvind's Home**:

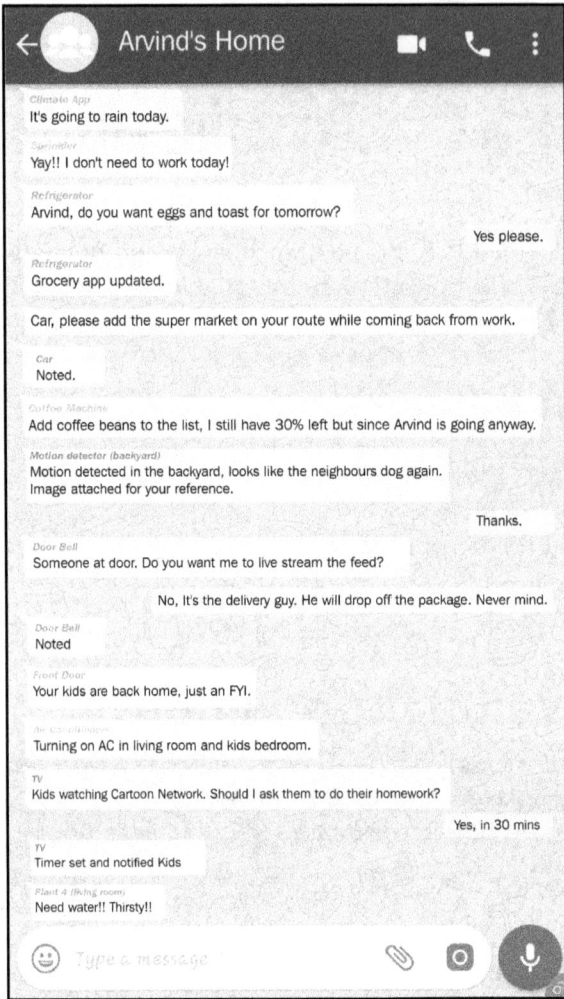

Take a look at another WhatsApp group chat for **Super Market X**:

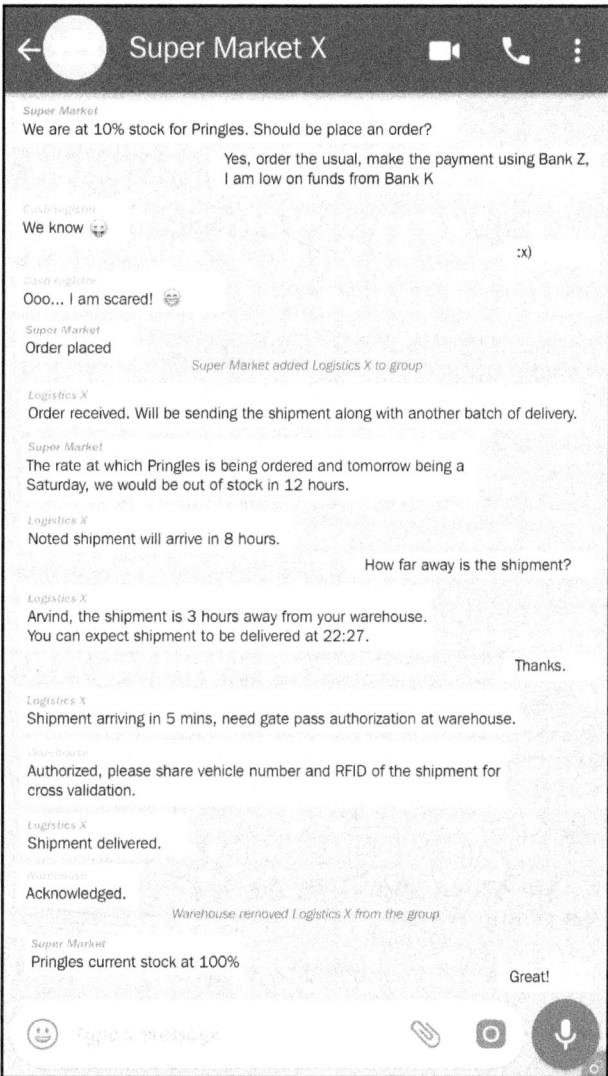

The previous two conversations paint a good picture as to what I mean by smart devices. These devices are not only connected, but can use the power of machine learning and artificial intelligence to make predictions, enable automation, and bring intelligence to life.

For us to achieve this, we are looking at two major categories:

- Connected devices
- Smart devices

Connected devices

A world where anything is connected to the internet and can be remotely monitored and managed is a connected device. From TVs to chairs, everything can be connected and monitored.

"Ericsson predicts there will be a total of approximately 28B connected devices worldwide by 2021, with nearly 16B related to IoT."

Source: https://www.forbes.com/sites/louiscolumbus/2016/07/09/internet-of-things-on-pace-to-replace-mobile-phones-as-most-connected-device-in-2018

16 billion IoT devices; imagine what could be part of it. And this is only until 2021. In another 10 years, with a **compound annual growth rate** (**CAGR**) of at least 5%, you can imagine the number of connected devices. These devices can either be connected directly via a GSM/cellular network or use various other long-range communication systems, such as LoRaWAN, to achieve this.

Smart devices

Now that all the devices are connected, we are going to feed data from these devices to our intelligence systems that can derive actionable outcomes from them.

This is where the world of artificial intelligence comes into the picture.

Artificial intelligence

The world where machines can take action on their own, without being programmed, is artificial intelligence.

There was a time when we used to write chatbots using a set of rules similar to a rules engine. Something along the lines of, if the incoming message consists of these keywords, respond this way. But this produced monotonous results.

Eliza was one of the oldest chatbots that was invented, and ran on pattern recognition and string substitution. It was developed by Joseph Weizenbaum at the MIT Computer Science and Artificial Intelligence Laboratory between 1964 and 1966. More than a chatbot, Eliza was a **Rogerian psychotherapist**.

Chat with Eliza in real time by visiting this URL: `http://www.manifestation.com/ neurotoys/eliza.php3`.

Times have changed; no developer is sitting and programming these chatbots. They define the bare minimum of conversational skills and then leave these bots to the real world for them to learn by themselves by correlating information across various conversations. This brings in a larger vocabulary and contextual conversational skills.

For instance, as of February 2018, if I launch Google Assistant and converse with it, it would look like this:

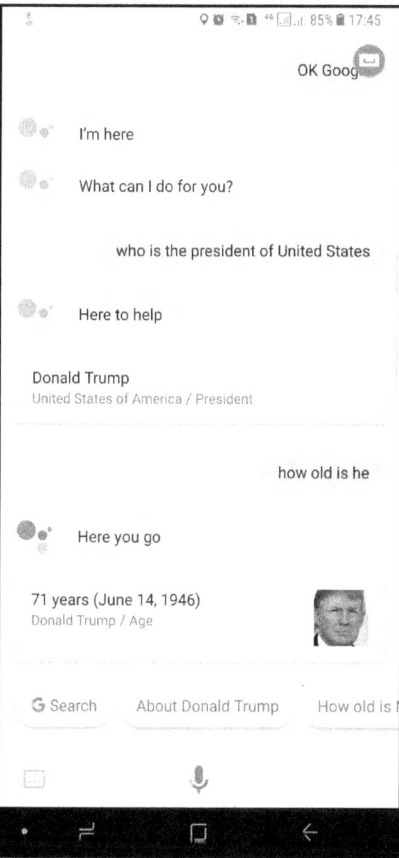

I asked who the president of United States is, and I got a correct reply, and then I asked how old he is, and I got 71 years back.

Do note that I have not mentioned to whom I was referring, but the assistant was able to understand the conversation and keep up with me.

This is what I meant by *contextual conversational skills* and this is going to slowly redefine what machines can do for us.

AI doesn't come with one technology. It is a combination of multiple skills that help a system to make a decision, depending on what you want to achieve.

For instance, take a robot: a combination of computer vision, motor skills and a bit of intelligence prevents the robot from colliding with objects.

Here is a representation of various technologies that come together to produce AI:

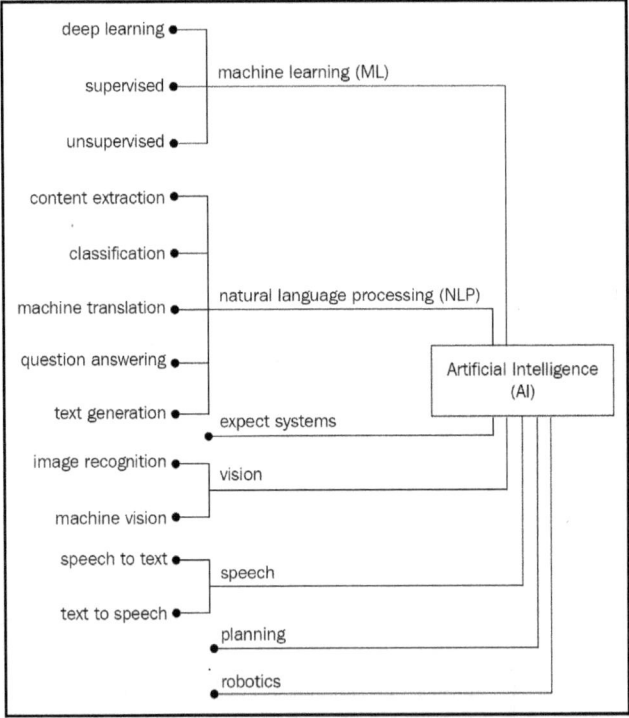

Source: http://www.remakinglawfirms.com/artificial-intelligence-law-state-play-2016/

As we can see from the diagram, machine learning forms one key source of learning for AI. In `Chapter 9`, *IoT and Machine Learning*, we are going to look at the world of machine learning and see how to work with it in IoT applications and realize the true value of IoT.

This summarizes what AI is and how we can achieve it at a high level.

In the next section, we are going to talk about healthcare and IoT.

Healthcare and IoT

In my humble opinion, IoT, and healthcare are match made in heaven. The value that comes from integrating seamless connectivity and smartness between living beings and their health is priceless.

Things such as postoperative care, elderly monitoring, and remote diabetes monitoring are only a few areas of impact.

Before we proceed further, I would recommend you to watch this video, *Scott Hanselman's best demo! IoT, Azure, Machine Learning & more* at `https://www.youtube.com/watch?v=u5oTz1e5qqE` to understand the true power of real-time healthcare.

In 2018, we are defining smart healthcare, but the sad truth is that something as trivial as healthcare and its intelligence component should have been the primary focus from the beginning.

As a side note, if you want to see how these disruptive technologies might turn out from the eyes of *Charlie Brooker* (`http://www.imdb.com/name/nm0111765/`), I would recommend watching a TV series named *Black Mirror*: `http://www.imdb.com/title/tt2085059/`.

Let's look at possible applications of healthcare in IoT.

Remote diagnosis

The remote diagnosis of patients, mainly in the case of postoperative care, is essential. Spending huge amounts of money to stay in the **Intensive Care Unit (ICU)** of a hospital, just for observation, is not really ideal. Instead, the patient might be discharged from the ICU and sent home. Using the world of smart devices, we can monitor the patient remotely, since that is the premise of the IoT.

Remote monitoring is not only efficient for postoperative care; it can be highly effective for older people who are prone to more health issues than others. Things such as fall detection and remote heart monitoring are no longer a myth. Take a look at these products:

- **Medical guardian**: `https://www.medicalguardian.com`
- **Medical care alert**: `https://www.medicalcarealert.com/Fall-Detection-Medical-Alert-System-s/1850.htm`
- **Philips lifeline**: `https://www.lifeline.philips.com/safety-solutions/homesafe`
- **Medical alert system**: `https://www.amazon.com/Medical-Systems-Seniors-Monthly-medical/dp/B018DJ428A/`
- **Scosche RHYTHM+ heart rate monitor armband**: `https://www.amazon.com/Scosche-RHYTHM-Heart-Monitor-Armband/dp/B00XIT788C`
- **Wahoo TICKR heart rate monitor**: `https://www.amazon.com/Wahoo-TICKR-Monitor-iPhone-Android/dp/B00INQVYZ8`

 Neither Packt Publications nor the author is endorsing any of the listed products in this chapter or the book. These are only for reference and awareness.

AI doctors

When I think of AI doctors, I think of *Baymax* from the *Walt Disney* movie *Big Hero 6* (`http://www.imdb.com/title/tt2245084/`). Here is a video demonstrating *Baymax* in action: `https://www.youtube.com/watch?v=FmaJPV1okPo`.

Are bots going to replace doctors? Well, yes, someday, and someday soon. With today's technology advancements in the domain of healthcare and machine learning, it is easy for a machine to perform a predictive health diagnosis and treat a patient.

We are talking about a world of WebMD, but with contextual intelligence. What do I mean by this?

I went to *WebMD Symptom Checker Beta* (`https://symptoms.webmd.com/default.htm`) and I entered dizziness, fatigue, headache, and cough as symptoms, and provided an age and gender without any history. You can see a list of possible conditions that I could have here:

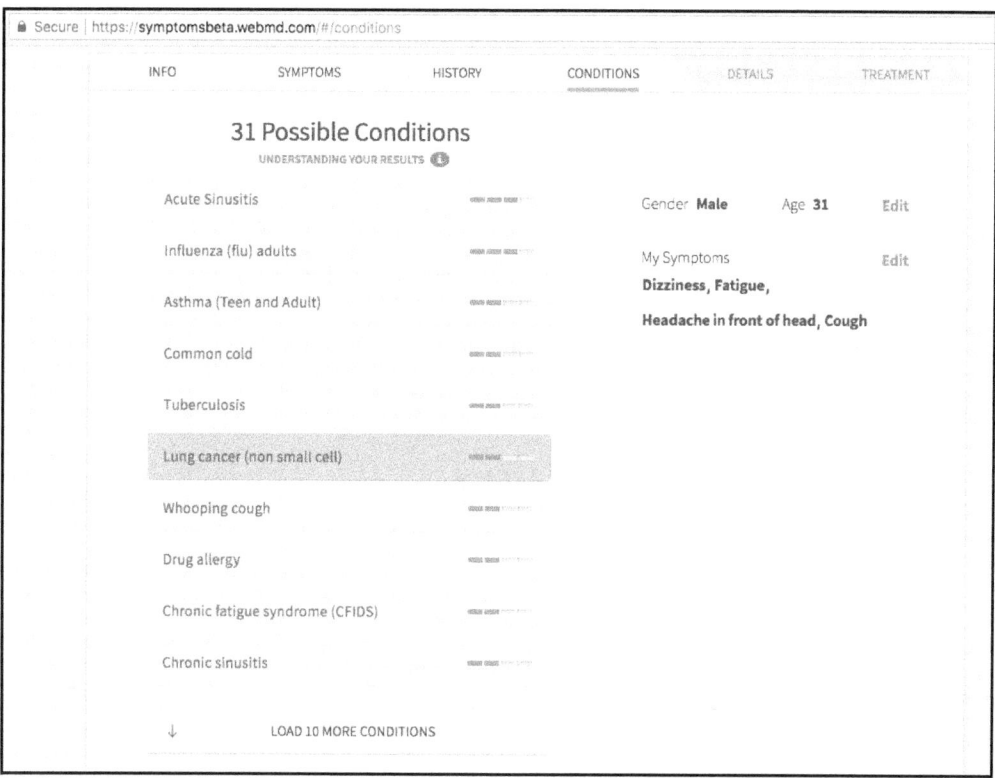

Anyone who sees the list of predictions would have new symptoms increasing the severity of the disease.

Nothing against WebMD, but there may be a virtual intelligent doctor soon that can predict better as it keeps learning from various sources.

One day, you might even get a push notification saying that you will fall sick by 3.42 P.M. today and that the antibiotics are on the way. How cool would that be? Of course, not for the patient, but for the technology.

Here is another AI doctor in the making, *IBM Watson Health*: `https://www.ibm.com/watson/health/`.

So, as I said earlier, AI doctors are not as far away as we think.

This concludes our subsection on AI doctors.

In this section, we have seen the impact of IoT on healthcare. But there are things in healthcare that can also be part of the smart healthcare ecosystem.

For instance, there could be sound sensors placed around nurse stations in a hospitals and corridors outside the ICU and patient wards. If the sound levels in those areas cross a certain threshold, there could be a notification such as the light flickering to let the people around know that they are being loud. This is just one example among many to show you how IoT can contribute to healthcare in areas that are not really healthcare centric.

Take a look at this video by Anixter titled *What is a Smart Hospital?* at `https://www.youtube.com/watch?v=nHH1TzDRiqc` and this *Advantech Intelligent Hospital Solution Video, Advantech(EN)*: `https://www.youtube.com/watch?v=LIafbX_JXHE`. This will help you understand what other things could be part of a smart healthcare system.

In the next section, we are going to look at industrial IoT.

Industrial IoT

Industrial IoT or, as it's more popularly known, **IIoT**, is one of the key impact areas of IoT. With the power of industrial sensors, as well as a world of smart devices, we can achieve and automate a lot more.

The following diagram is from an article by Greg Cline on *Industry 4.0 and Industrial IoT in Manufacturing: A Sneak Peek*, at `http://www.aberdeenessentials.com/opspro-essentials/industry-4-0-industrial-iot-manufacturing-sneak-peek/`:

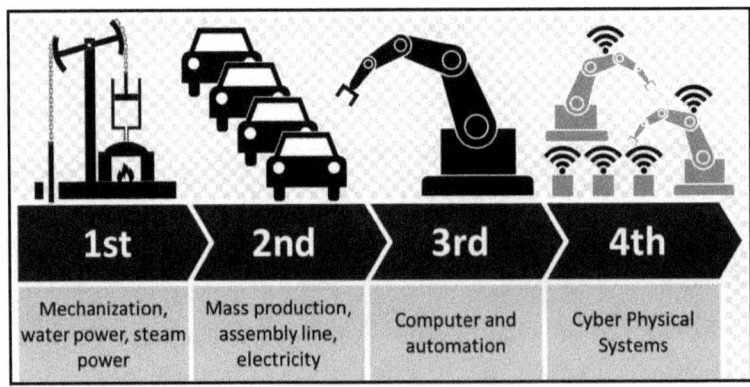

As we can see from the diagram, we are currently in the era of industry 4.0, where, with the power of smart devices, we could change the way a manufacturing process runs.

Take a look the following videos to get a better idea as to what industry 4.0 is all about:

- **Industrie 4.0 - The Fourth Industrial Revolution (Siemens)**: `https://www.youtube.com/watch?v=HPRURtORnis`
- **Industry 4.0 in the Volkswagen Group (Volkswagen)**: `https://www.youtube.com/watch?v=JT18w6yAjds`
- **Genius of Things: Advancing Industry 4.0 with AI and IoT (IBM Watson)**: `https://www.youtube.com/watch?v=9hjgoC1heiI`

IIoT has two ways of being realized:

1. Through the manufacturing process of a product
2. Through the product itself

Imagine a car's manufacturing process, **#1**, defined how IIoT can contribute to optimizing and maximizing the throughput of the manufacturing process of the cars. The second method monitors sensors inside cars, which can help improve the life of a car as well as maximize the experience for the driver.

For instance, establishing that a certain type of windshield has a higher failure rate than others, via the user's feedback received from **#2**, can be directly be fed back into **#1** to increase the overall quality of the final product.

Now, let's take a look how IIoT is being realized.

Optimization

The first step towards realizing IIoT is optimization.

Let's look at an on-floor manufacturing process, where we are automating systems and getting maximum efficiency in terms of equipment and also maximizing their life.

Take a look at the following example of a conveyor belt system that moves a load from point **A** to point **B**:

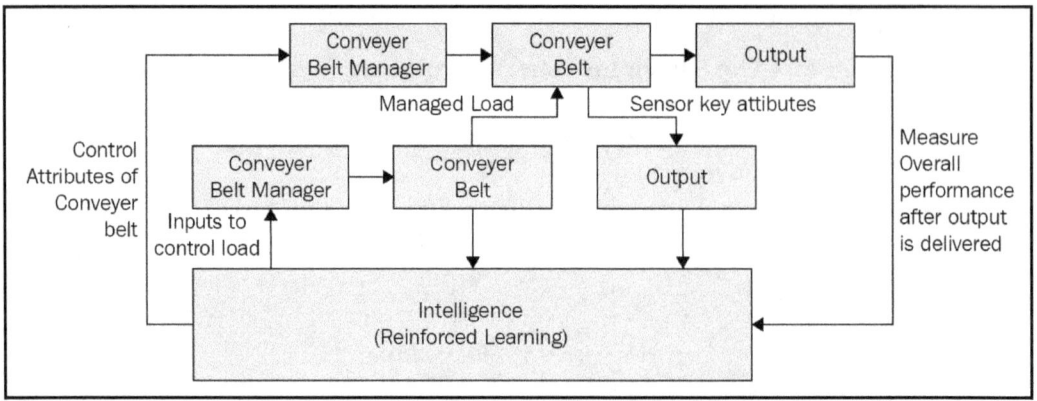

It may look quite confusing, but the diagram represents this: a conveyor belt carries loads, and the load can be bottles or cases or anything that we are processing. Then there are sensors attached to this conveyor belt that keep monitoring the belt in terms of power consumption, efficiency, throughput, wear and tear, and so on. And finally, there is the actual output. How well was the conveyor belt doing its job?

The sensor data, applied load, and the output performance are fed into an intelligence system which considers various things and decides on the optimal load and operating attributes of the conveyor belt. Based on that, the conveyor belt adjusts itself for long life, lower power consumption, and higher throughput.

This is a very simple example of how IIoT is going to change the way we are going to do things in the industrial sector.

Predictive maintenance

Scheduled maintenance is something that has been happening for a long time. Most of the equipment that we see is maintained on a schedule rather than on the basis of its actual working life. This is where IoT comes in with a concept of predictive maintenance.

Imagine if you could predict a machine failure even before it happened. Isn't that what every business wants: to have literally zero downtime in their manufacturing process?

Imagine a factory that needs to manufacture 1 million ice-cream sandwiches per day and the factory throughput is exactly 1 million ice-cream sandwiches per day. What is percentage of error allowed? ZERO! Right?

This is where the world of predictive maintenance comes into the picture by continuously monitoring various parameters of all the machines on the floor, including the life cycle and efficiency. The moment it sees a machine's efficiency going down, it raises an alert to personnel on the floor, who can then decide the optimal time to replace the machine without major impact.

As of today, there are various service providers, such as Microsoft Azure, that offer out-of-the-box predictive maintenance. Take a look at the following two videos, which demonstrate predictive maintenance in action, from the Azure platform:

- **Dive into Predictive Maintenance using Cortana Intelligence Suite**: https://www.youtube.com/watch?v=qS1SZPDK9WU
- **Predictive Maintenance in the IoT Era**: https://www.youtube.com/watch?v=s4HU8JynyFY

Predictive maintenance also entails gathering other critical data that can be valuable by itself, and that may or may not have an impact on the end results, but that will be useful in overall analysis.

You can continue to explore IIoT or industry 4.0 on the internet. Here are a few links that can get you started:

- **Everything You Need to Know About the Industrial Internet of Things**: https://www.ge.com/digital/blog/everything-you-need-know-about-industrial-internet-things
- **Industrial Internet of Things (IIoT)**: http://internetofthingsagenda.techtarget.com/definition/Industrial-Internet-of-Things-IIoT
- **The Industrial Internet of Things (IIoT)**: the business guide to Industrial IoT: https://www.i-scoop.eu/internet-of-things-guide/industrial-internet-things-iiot-saving-costs-innovation/
- **A comprehensive guide to enterprise IoT project success**: http://internetofthingsagenda.techtarget.com/essentialguide/A-comprehensive-guide-to-enterprise-IoT-project-success

Other applications of IoT

In this chapter, we have dwelled on the world of healthcare and industry. Now, at a high level, let's take a look at other potential areas of impact.

Agriculture

Smart agriculture is all about finding optimal farming methodologies to increase the final yield, as well as to preserve natural resources. This is more beneficial to commercial farmers than anybody else.

Crops that yield cotton, cocoa, sugar, oranges, and so on would have a greater impact on the ability of smart and controlled farming.

Greenhouses can also benefit from the technologies of smart farming.

Here is an overview of this domain:

- **Solutions for Smart Farming**: https://www.kaaproject.org/agriculture/
- **An In-Depth Look At IoT In Agriculture & Smart Farming Solutions**: https://www.link-labs.com/blog/iot-agriculture
- **IoT in agriculture – a way towards smart farming**: http://www.softwebiot.com/iot-use-cases/iot-solutions-for-agriculture-industry/
- **IoT Applications in Agriculture**: https://www.iotforall.com/iot-applications-in-agriculture/

Smart city

Not much introduction is needed about this domain. We have all been part of it already on a small or large scale, be it CCTV traffic surveillance or smart garbage management systems.

Here is an overview of this domain:

- **What is a smart city?**: https://www.youtube.com/watch?v=Br5aJa6MkBc
- **Smart city solutions with Kaa IoT Platform**: https://www.kaaproject.org/smart-city/
- **IoT for Smart Cities: A Fully Integrated approach maximizes the possibilities**: https://networks.nokia.com/innovation/iot-smart-cities

- **Smart Cities Start with smart utilities**: `https://sensus.com/internet-of-things/smart-cities/`
- **Smart Cities: Solving Urban Problems Using Technology**: `https://www.youtube.com/watch?v=nnyRZotnPSU`

Smart retail

Here is an overview of this domain:

- **Introducing Amazon Go and the world's most advanced shopping technology**: `https://www.youtube.com/watch?v=NrmMk1Myrxc`
- **Inside The First Amazon Go Store**: `https://www.youtube.com/watch?v=zdbumR6Bhd8`
- **Internet of Things Solutions in Retail Industry**: `https://www.kaaproject.org/retail/`
- **Internet of Things (IoT): Smart Retail Solutions**: `https://www.intel.com/content/www/us/en/internet-of-things/smart-retail-solutions.html`
- **Smart Retail**: `https://iot.telefonica.com/smart-retail/smart-retail`

Smart logistics

The ability to track and manage assets and maintain real-time inventory is a dream of any multi-million dollar organization that deals with **supply chain management**.

The more effective inventory and asset management is, the better it can be automated to increase the efficiency of the process.

Here is an overview of this domain:

- **Inside Alibaba's smart warehouse staffed by robots**: `https://www.youtube.com/watch?v=FBl4Y55V2Z4`
- **IoT platform for smart supply chain solutions**: `https://www.kaaproject.org/logistics/`
- **Internet of Things in Logistics**: `https://www.dpdhl.com/content/dam/dpdhl/presse/pdf/2015/DHLTrendReport_Internet_of_things.pdf`
- **Logistics 4.0 and smart supply chain management in Industry 4.0**: `https://www.i-scoop.eu/industry-4-0/supply-chain-management-scm-logistics/`

In this section, I have outlined only the key areas. IoT fits in every single area that we are interacting with today, from toilet papers to robots!

This chapter was designed to give you an idea as to where an enterprise can fit in the world of IoT.

I hope you got a sense of various possible applications involving IoT.

Summary

In this chapter, we have gone through various domains where IoT can add value. We have specifically dwelled on the healthcare and industry domains. Next, we looked at other possible domains that could be impacted by IoT.

In the next few chapters, we are going to look at various IoT platforms that can bring the previous visions to reality.

Getting Started with IoT Platforms

3

In the previous chapter, we saw the various domain specific use cases and application areas. In this chapter, we are going to put that knowledge to use by building our sample IoT solution using Raspberry Pi 3, DHT11 temperature and humidity sensor, and the ThingSpeak platform. We are going to start off by developing an understanding of what an IoT platform is and how one can easily use them to build an IoT solution without much hassle.

The topics covered in this chapter are as follows:

- Introduction to IoT platforms
- Getting started with Raspberry Pi 3
- Getting started with the ThingSpeak IoT platform
- Building an IoT solution that shows the temperature and humidity in real time on the ThingSpeak dashboard

IoT platform or IoT middleware

As we have seen saw in `Chapter 1`, *Introduction to IoT*, there are plenty of pieces that go into an IoT stack. Building all of them and managing them in real time is a huge, daunting, time- and money-consuming task.

This is where the ready-made IoT platforms play an important role.

In a nutshell, IoT platforms are support software that connect smart devices and the entities that use the data from these smart devices (such as humans, other systems, and so on).

IoT platforms are also known as the **IoT middleware**, as these are the middleman between the data collected on the edge and the user-facing application.

A typical IoT platform will have the following layers, as we have seen in Chapter 1, *Introduction to IoT*:

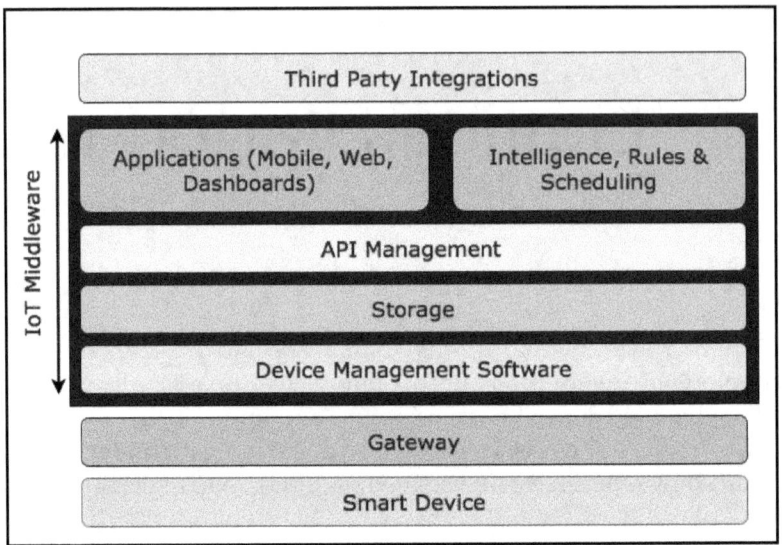

Why platforms?

Why do we need these platforms? Why can't we build one of our own?

We can; however, first we have to consider the following points:

- How long does it take for one to build a piece of end-to-end, bug free IoT middleware?
- Your resources' time versus money spent on building this middleware.
- Your in-house team's ability to build an IoT middleware.
- How generic can you build it? Will this IoT middleware scale for all types of applications?

Since almost all IoT platforms have a similar set of features, using a continuously improving, community contributed platform is always better than building one on your own.

But do note that if you are planning to build a platform for creating a piece of **intellectual property (IP)** for your organization, I would recommend doing a great deal of research before starting the design. As mentioned in the `Chapter 1`, *Introduction to IoT*, there are plenty of options and standards out there in the market, and a lot of them become obsolete very fast.

 If you are planning to build your own IoT platform, take a look at my other book, *Practical Internet of Things with JavaScript*, here: `https://www.packtpub.com/hardware-and-creative/advanced-iot-java script`.

IoT platforms

Now that we have a sense of why we are using an existing IoT platform for our IoT solutions, let us look at the options we have for these platforms. The following are a few popular IoT platforms.

You can visit the site links next to the provider to read more about the offerings:

- **AWS IoT**: `https://aws.amazon.com/iot/`
- **Microsoft Azure IoT**: `https://www.microsoft.com/en-in/internet-of-things/azure-iot-suite`
- **IBM Watson**: `https://www.ibm.com/internet-of-things`
- **Google Cloud IoT**: `https://cloud.google.com/solutions/iot/`
- **Cisco IoT Cloud Connect**: `https://www.jasper.com/`
- **Salesforce IoT cloud**: `https://www.salesforce.com/eu/iot-cloud/`
- **Bosch IoT Suite**: `https://www.bosch-si.com/iot-platform/bosch-iot-suite/homepage-bosch-iot-suite.html`
- **Kaa IoT**: `https://www.kaaproject.org/`
- **ThingSpeak**: `https://thingspeak.com/`
- **DeviceHive**: `https://devicehive.com/`
- **ThingsBoard**: `https://thingsboard.io/`

In this book, we are going to explore five IoT platforms, namely:

- AWS IoT
- Microsoft Azure IoT
- Google IoT Core
- IBM Watson IoT
- Kaa IoT

In the previous list, all other platforms are commercial, except Kaa IoT which is an open source platform.

After exploring the aforementioned five platforms, we will do a comparison among them to help you choose the appropriate platform for a specific use case.

Example implementation

To better understand these five platforms, we will build a sample end-to-end IoT application on each of the platforms, and then perform the same task on each to see how it differs from the others.

On each of the platforms, we are going to perform following tasks:

- Integrate the DHT11 sensor with Raspberry Pi 3
- Send the sensor data to the platform
- Visualize the data
- Set thresholds on the data and receive alerts
- Perform data analysis

To get started, we are going to first setup Raspberry Pi 3 to talk to the internet, then integrate the DHT11 sensor with the Raspberry Pi 3.

In this chapter, to get a feel for the end-to-end data flow, we will transmit data to the ThingSpeak platform.

So let's get started.

Setting up the Raspberry Pi 3

If you do not have a Raspberry Pi 3, you can purchase one from a local electronics store or you can order one from Amazon:
`https://www.amazon.com/Raspberry-Pi-Desktop-Starter-White/dp/B01CI58722`.

Make sure you order a kit that has a power cord, microSD card, and casing (optional).

Most of the hobby-kit stores that sell the Raspberry Pi 3 kit sell the microSD card with Raspbian OS preloaded.

If you are new to Raspberry Pi 3, here are a few things to get you started.

Raspberry Pi 3 is a single-board computer, designed and developed by The Raspberry Pi Foundation. Raspberry Pi 3 is the third generation Raspberry Pi.

In this book, we are going to use Raspberry Pi 3 Model B. Some of the specifications of Raspberry Pi 3 Model B are as follows:

Feature	Specification
Generation	3
Release date	February 16
Architecture	ARMv8-A (64/32-bit)
System on a Chip	Broadcom BCM2837
CPU	1.2 GHz 64-bit quad-core ARM Cortex-A53
Memory (SDRAM)	1 GB (shared with GPU)
USB 2.0 ports	Four (via the on-board 5-port USB hub)
On-board network	10/100 Mbit/s Ethernet, 802.11n wireless, Bluetooth 4.1
Low-level peripherals	17 x GPIO plus the same specific functions and HAT ID bus
Power ratings	300 mA (1.5 W) average when idle, 1.34 A (6.7 W) maximum under stress (with monitor, keyboard, mouse, and Wi-Fi connected)
Power source	5 V via Micro-USB or GPIO header

For more information on the specification, please refer to Raspberry Pi 3 specifications, which can be found at:
`https://www.raspberrypi.org/magpi/raspberry-pi-3-specs-benchmarks/.`

For us to continue forward smoothly, make sure Raspberry Pi 3 is set up, and is connected to the internet either over Wi-Fi or Ethernet.

If you are new to setting up Raspberry Pi 3, refer to the *Beginner's Guide to Installing Node.js on a Raspberry Pi*:
`http://thisdavej.com/beginners-guide-to-installing-node-js-on-a-raspberry-pi/.`
We will, cover the Node.js part, until then you can start the Pi and configure the Wi-Fi.

Once the OS has been installed, boot up the Raspberry Pi 3 and log into it. At this point in time, it will be connected to the Internet over your own access point or Ethernet, and you should be able to browse the internet without issues.

I access my Raspberry Pi 3 from my Apple MacBook Pro using VNC Viewer (`https://www.realvnc.com/en/connect/download/viewer/`). This way, I am not always connected physically to the Raspberry Pi 3.

In the first example, we are going to connect Raspberry Pi 3 to the ThingSpeak platform, and interface with the DHT11 temperature and humidity sensor connected to the Raspberry Pi 3.

For this example, we will use Node.js as the programming language.

Setting up Node.js on the Raspberry Pi 3

Log into your Raspberry Pi 3, either via VNC or SSH, or directly connecting it to a monitor.

We will start off by downloading Node.js. Open a new Terminal and run the following commands:

```
$ sudo apt update

$ sudo apt full-upgrade
```

This will upgrade all the packages that need upgrades. Next, we will install the latest version of Node.js. We will be using the Node 7.x version:

```
$ curl -sL https://deb.nodesource.com/setup_7.x | sudo -E bash -
$ sudo apt install nodejs
```

This will take a moment to install and once your installation is done you should be able to run the following commands to see the version of Node.js and npm:

```
$ node -v
$ npm -v
```

You should see something like this:

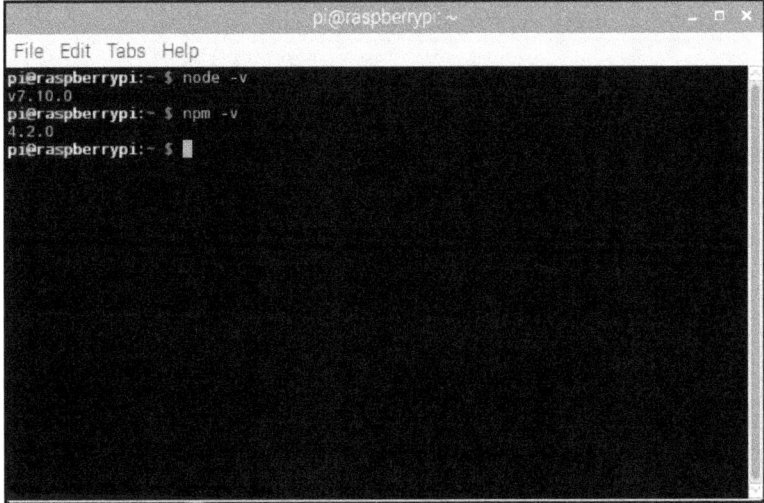

With this, we are done with setting up the required software for running our example on a Raspberry Pi 3.

Setting up ThingSpeak

Now that we have setup Raspberry Pi 3, we will setup ThingSpeak.

ThingsSpeak is an IoT platform, as discussed earlier, that can collect data and help us run analytics on top of it. We will be using ThingSpeak in this example to load data into the cloud using a simple HTTP API and view the data in real time using charts.

This platform is super easy to use and the best way to get started with IoT exploration. Hence, ThingSpeak has been chosen to explore the basics.

If you are new to ThingSpeak, refer to this: `https://thingspeak.com/pages/learn_more`.

Creating an account

If you do not have an account already, you can visit `https://thingspeak.com/users/sign_up` to create one. Once you have created the account, activate it, and log in.

Once you have logged in, you will see an interface like this:

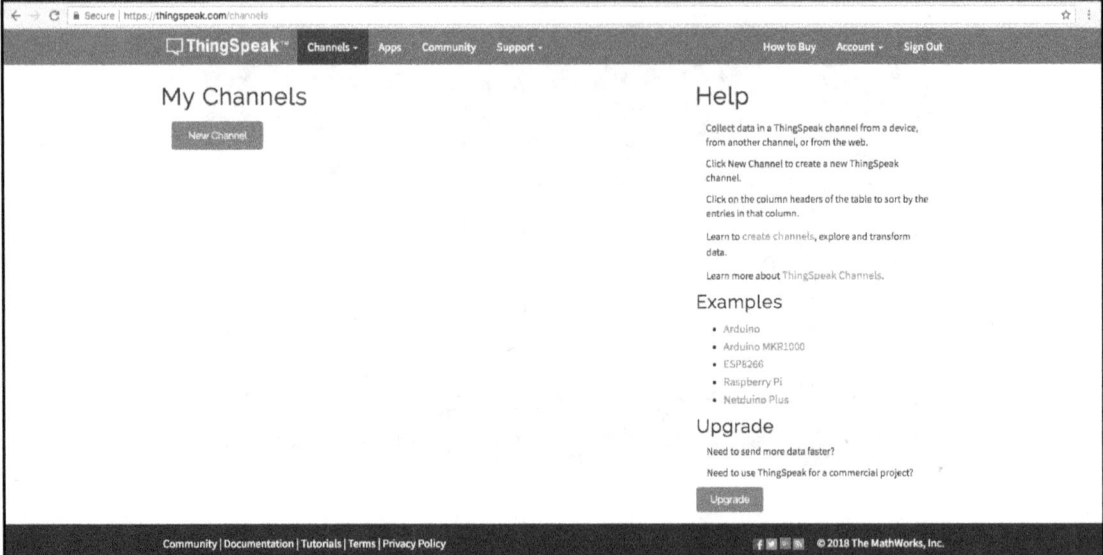

Creating a channel

Now we need a new channel to store all our data. From the home page, click on **New Channel** and fill in the form as shown here:

Field	Value
Name	Pi3 DHT11 Node

Description	A Raspberry Pi 3, DHT11 node to log the temperature and humidity of the surroundings
Field 1	Temperature
Field 2	Humidity

Then click on **Save Channel**.

Now we have our own dashboard with two charts, one for temperature and another for humidity. These are empty as we have not posted any data to this platform.

Sending test data

To send data to ThingSpeak, we must do the following:

1. We construct an HTTP request that specifies the write API key for the channel and what data needs to be posted.
2. Once the channel has been created, click on the channel name and then click on the **API Keys** tab. You should see two keys, as shown here:

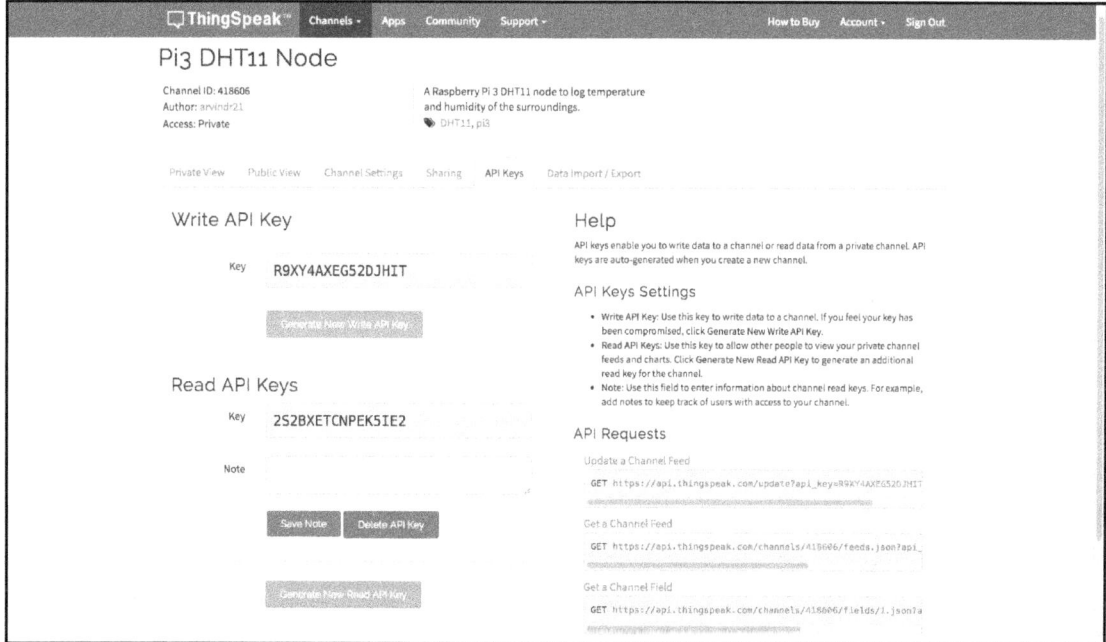

3. Make a note of the **Write API Key**. This key is used when we want to perform write operations.

4. Now, we will construct the GET URL that we will use to send the data: `https://api.thingspeak.com/update?api_key=R9XY4AXEG52DJHIT&field1=25&field2=30`.

5. Update the previous URL with your **Write API Key**. The first URL field corresponds to temperature value and second one corresponds to humidity.

6. Now, navigate to this URL in the browser and you should see the following response:

7. Next, head back to the **Private View** tab in your ThingSpeak channel and you should see the following:

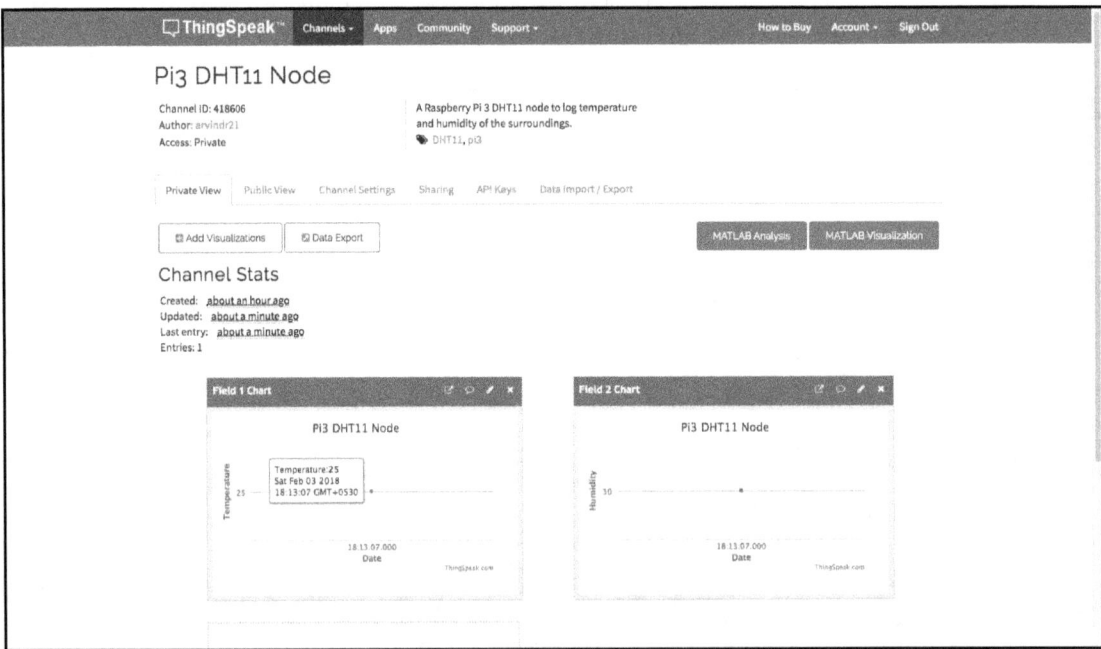

The data we have posted is logged into the dashboard. Isn't it simple?

In the next section, we are going to integrate DHT11 with Raspberry Pi 3 and then send that data over to ThingSpeak using an HTTP request.

Building the solution

Now that we have all the essentials set up, we will get started with the electronics.

Things needed

The things you will need for this are as follows:

- **One Raspberry Pi 3**:
  https://www.amazon.com/Raspberry-Pi-Desktop-Starter-White/dp/B01CI5872
  2
- **One
  breadboard**: https://www.amazon.com/Solderless-Breadboard-Circuit-Circbo
  ard-Prototyping/dp/B01DDI54II
- **One DHT11 sensor**:
  https://www.amazon.com/HiLetgo-Temperature-Humidity-Arduino-Raspberry/
  dp/B01DKC2GQ0
- **Three male-to-female jumper cables**:
  https://www.amazon.com/RGBZONE-120pcs-Multicolored-Dupont-Breadboard/d
  p/B01M1IEUAF/

 If you are new to the world of Raspberry Pi GPIO's interfacing, take a look at *Raspberry Pi GPIO Tutorial: The Basics Explained*:
https://www.youtube.com/watch?v=6PuK9fh3aL8.

Schematic

We will now set this up using the following schematic:

1. Connect the Raspberry Pi 3 and DHT11 sensor as shown in the following diagram:

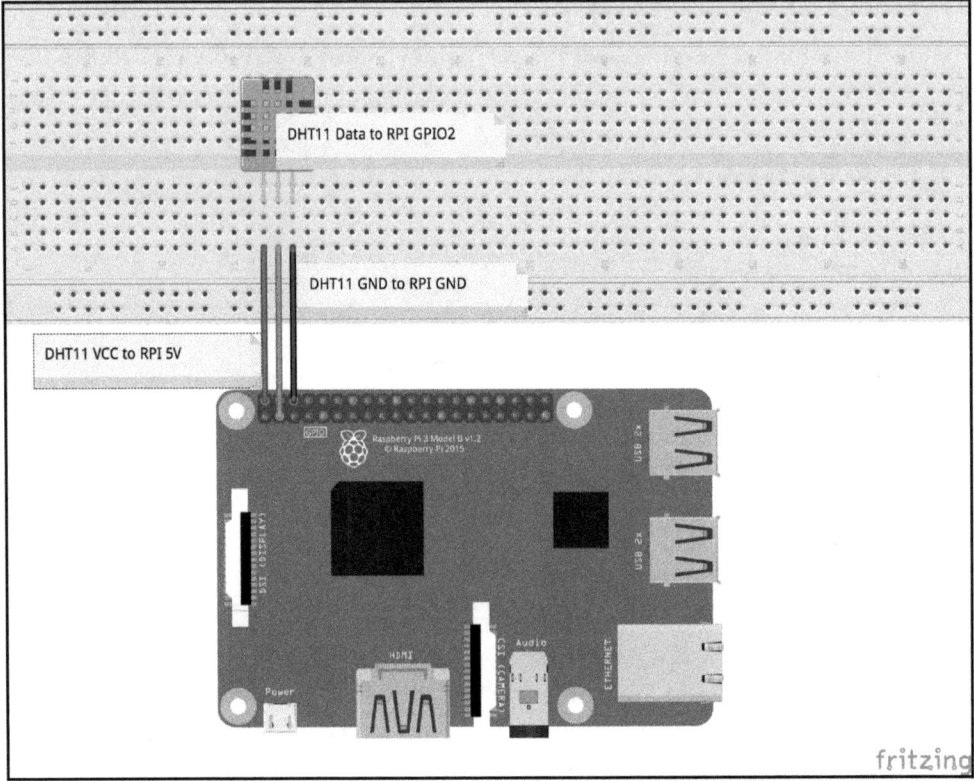

2. Once this has been done, power on the Raspberry Pi 3 and log into it.
3. Next, on the desktop of your Pi, create a folder named DHT11. Open a new Terminal, and cd into the DHT11 folder.
4. Now, as mentioned earlier, we are going to use Node.js as the programming language for building the client application that will interact with the DHT11 and ThingSpeak platform. Run the following command:

```
$ npm init -y
```

5. This will generate a `package.json` with default values. Next, we need two node package modules to complete the solution:

   - `rpi-dht-sensor`: To read the temperature value from the DHT11 sensor. More information on the module can be found at:
     `https://www.npmjs.com/package/rpi-dht-sensor`.
   - `request`: To send an HTTP request from the Raspberry Pi 3 to the ThingSpeak platform to update our sensor data. More information on the module can be found at:
     `https://www.npmjs.com/package/request`.

6. From inside the `DHT11` folder, run the following command:

   ```
   $ npm install request rpi-dht-sensor --save
   ```

7. This will install the required modules. Now create a new file named `index.js` and update it as shown here:

   ```
   var request = require('request');
   var rpiDhtSensor = require('rpi-dht-sensor');

   var API_KEY = 'Z76XNSBNRH34DNMS'; // ThingSpeak 'write' API key
   var dht = new rpiDhtSensor.DHT11(2); // `2` => GPIO2

   function read() {
       var readout = dht.read();
       var t = readout.temperature.toFixed(2);
       var h = readout.humidity.toFixed(2);

       console.log(new Date(), 'Temperature: ' + t + 'C, ' +
   'humidity: ' + h + '%');
       // Post data only if temperature and humidity are > `0`
       if (t > 0 && h > 0) {
           uploadData({
               t: t,
               h: h
           });
       }
       setTimeout(read, 30000); // 30 seconds gap between reads
   }

   // inti read
   read();

   function uploadData(data) {
   ```

```
        var options = {
            method: 'POST',
            url: 'https://api.thingspeak.com/update',
            headers: {
    'Content-Type': 'application/x-www-form-urlencoded'
            },
            form: {
                field1: data.t,
                field2: data.h,
                api_key: API_KEY
            }
        };

        request(options, function(error, response, body) {
            if (error) { console.log(error) };
        });
    }
```

8. Save the file and go back to the Terminal and run the following command:

    $ sudo node index.js

    You should see the following data:

Ignore the first record. It takes the sensor some time to start reading the data. Till then, we get 0 as the temperature and humidity value.

9. Now, if we head back to the **Private View** tab, we should see this:

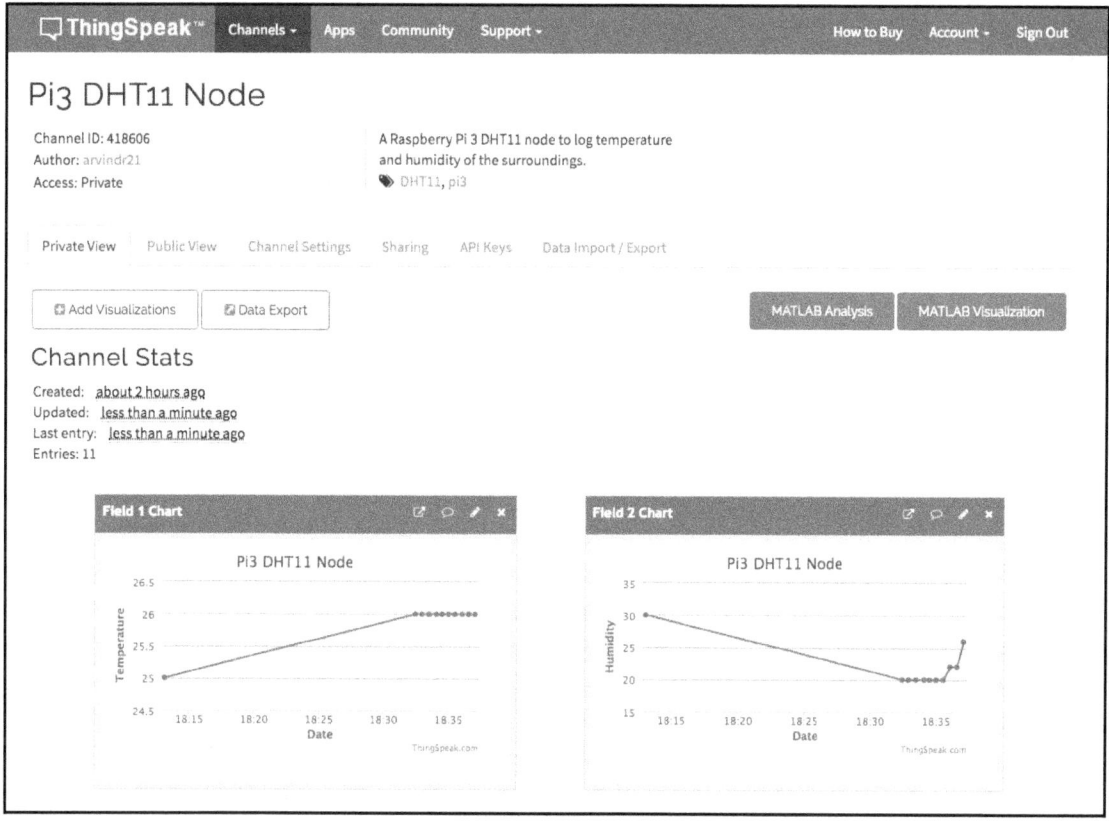

Isn't this simple? Your first end-to-end IoT solution!

We will execute a similar example on the other five platforms as well and compare how each is different.

Summary

In this chapter, we have talked about platforms, what they are, and why we need one. We then discussed a few popular platforms. Following that, we set up Raspberry Pi 3 and the ThingSpeak platform, and built a solution where we posted the DHT11 sensor data to the cloud and visualized it.

In the next chapter, we are going to build the same sample solution, but using the AWS IoT platform to explore how that is done.

4
AWS IoT

In the last chapter, we looked at how to build an end-to-end IoT solution using Raspberry Pi 3, a DHT11 temperature and humidity sensor, and the ThingSpeak platform. In this chapter, we are going to implement the same solution using the AWS IoT platform. Along with that, we are going to work on building a visualization dashboard and setup rules.

Topics covered in this chapter are:

- AWS IoT architecture
- Setting up an end-to-end solution using AWS IoT
- Setting up a visualization dashboard for the solution

AWS IoT

AWS IoT is the most comprehensive and popular IoT platform as of today. It has all the building blocks needed to work with a smart device as well as work on the output of that smart device (such as metrics, AI, and so on).

As part of the AWS IoT suite, there are many services offered. Some of them are listed in the following sections.

AWS IoT Core

AWS IoT Core is a managed cloud service that enables IoT solutions to be built easily with the power of AWS infrastructure. AWS IoT Core has all the essential components needed to build an end-to-end IoT middleware. IoT Core is secure and scalable—any kind of device that is capable of connecting to the internet can talk to AWS IoT Core and be managed. IoT Core can support billions of devices and trillions of messages.

AWS IoT Device Management

The AWS IoT Device Management service makes device onboarding and managing very simple and easy, especially when we are dealing with millions of devices.

AWS Greengrass

The AWS Greengrass software helps us run local computations on edge nodes in a secure way. It can also run AWS Lambda functions. It can also help us communicate with other devices and keep device data in sync, even when not connected to the internet.

AWS IoT Analytics

One of the value propositions of IoT data gathering is analytics. AWS IoT Analytics helps us to run sophisticated analytics on top of huge volumes of data. AWS IoT Analytics takes care of all the infrastructure and required scalability.

Amazon FreeRTOS

Amazon FreeRTOS is an OS for microcontrollers that runs on less power and is remotely deployed as a node or a gateway. Amazon FreeRTOS has all the essential stacks needed to manage a remote device securely.

The above mentioned services were some of the key services from AWS IoT. You can read more at https://aws.amazon.com/iot/.

Now that we are aware of some of the key services from AWS, we are going to make use of them to build our sample application.

Designing the sample application

In this section, we are going to build the same sample application using the **AWS IoT Stack**.

Solution

The solution we are going to build is going to be similar to the one from `Chapter 3`, *Getting Started with IoT Platforms*. We are going to connect a DHT11 sensor to Raspberry Pi 3 and then transmit the data over to the AWS IoT platform using MQTT-S. Then we'll take that data and pass it on to Elasticsearch and Kibana to build visualization.

In the next section, we are going to look at the overall architecture of the solution.

Architecture

The following diagram explains the architecture of the solution:

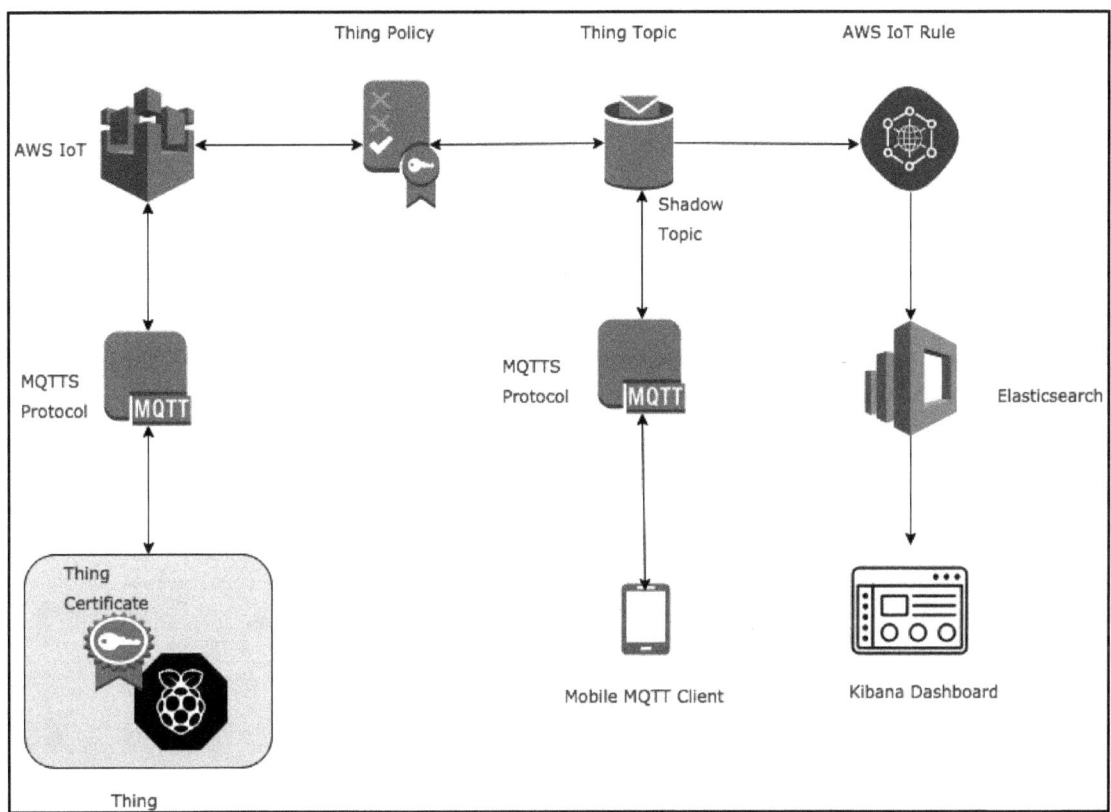

The Things or smart devices connect over MQTT-S with AWS IoT Core. Then the device is authenticated, authorized, and validated and the connection gets established. For authentication, we are using a device certificate that we generated while registering a device. Once the connection is established, the device can create its own MQTT topics and then publish or subscribe to them.

But in our example, we are not going to create new topics. Instead, we are going to work with a concept named **Device Shadow** provided by AWS IoT Core.

All the data that goes through the AWS IoT cloud is not persisted. Assume that if a smart device goes offline because it lost its power or connectivity and we want to see the latest data, that would be a challenge. Hence, we use Device Shadows to send the data that we want to persist. This way, the client who is requesting the data need not wait for it. Device Shadow is a replica of the device present on the cloud, with the latest states and attributes that were persisted by the device.

AWS IoT provides a few reserved topics and a mechanism to read the data. We will work with that in our example.

Now, using another MQTT client, we are going to request the data on-demand.

Once we see the data updating in real time, we will start work on visualization. Since there is no specific dashboard provided to visualize data, like we have seen in the ThingSpeak platform, we are going to use Elasticsearch and Kibana to do this.

To achieve this, we are going to create a rule to send incoming data to an Elasticsearch cluster. From there, we will use Kibana to visualize the data.

This is an overview of the solution that we are going to build.

End-to-end communication

Following are the steps we are going to follow to achieve the solution.

First, set up the Thing and publish data to AWS IoT:

1. Create a new AWS and AWS IoT Thing account
2. Create a new AWS IoT type
3. Create a new AWS IoT certificate
4. Create a new AWS IoT policy
5. Associate the policy with the certificate
6. Associate the certificate with the Thing

7. Set up Raspberry Pi 3 and DHT11
8. Set up the AWS IoT client on Raspberry Pi 3
9. Start reading the sensor data and publish it to the shadow Thing topic
10. Subscribe to the Thing shadow from another client to visualize the data

Data visualization

Next, set up rules to send the real-time data to the Elasticsearch cluster for data visualization:

1. Create a new Elasticsearch cluster
2. Create a new IoT rule to send data to the Elasticsearch cluster
3. Set up Kibana
4. Visualize the data in Kibana

So, now that we are clear as to what we want to do, let's get started.

Pricing

Do check the pricing before you start experimenting with AWS IoT. You can find more information at `https://aws.amazon.com/iot-core/pricing/`.

Building the sample application

We will start off by implementing the end-to-end solution, where we take the data from the DHT11 sensor and post it to the AWS IoT Thing topic.

End-to-end communication

To get started with AWS IoT, we need to have an AWS account. If you do not have an AWS account, you can create one by navigating to this URL: `https://aws.amazon.com/free/`.

Once you have created your account, you can log in and navigate to the AWS IoT Console. Or you can follow the `https://console.aws.amazon.com/iot/home` URL to reach the page.

Setting up the IoT Thing

Once you are on the AWS IoT Console page, make sure you have selected a region that is close to your location. I have selected the **US East (N. Virginia)** region as shown in the following screenshot:

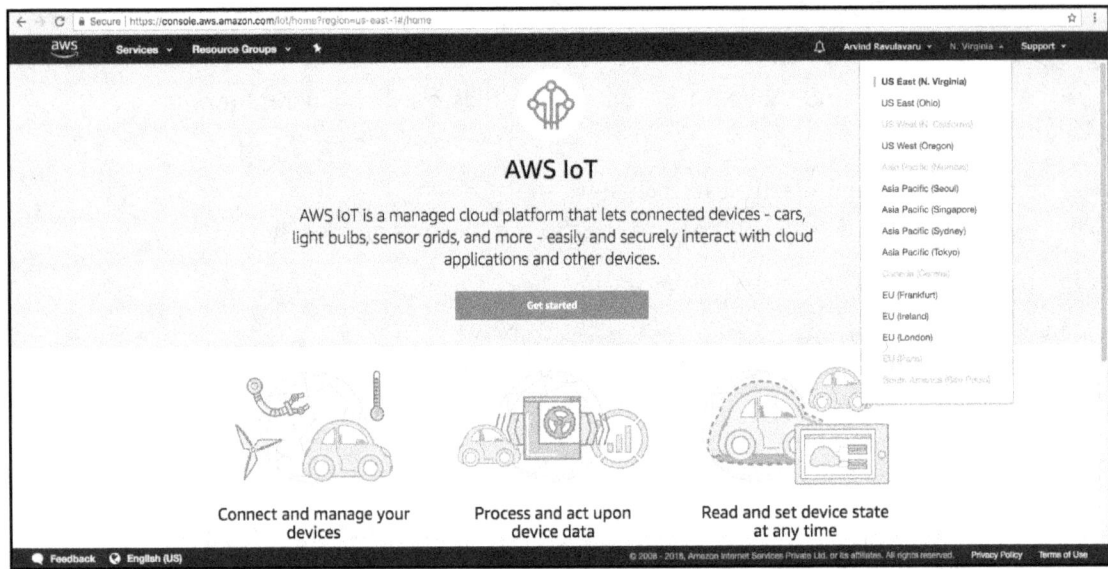

1. Now, click on the **Get started** button in the center of the page. From the side menu, navigate to **Manage** | **Things** and you should see a screen as shown here:

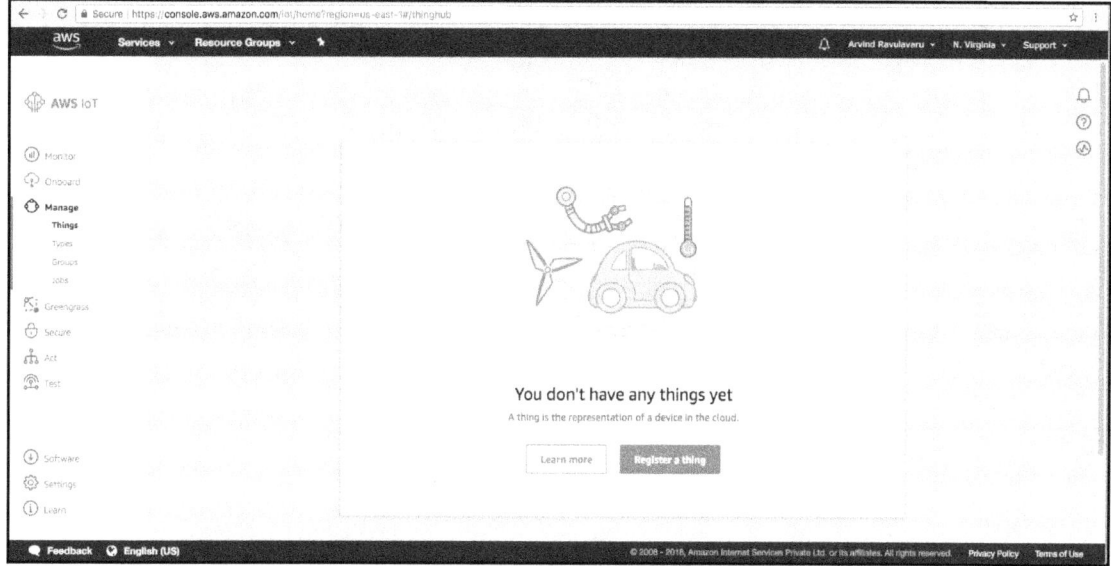

2. Next, click on the **Register a thing** button and you should see a screen as shown here:

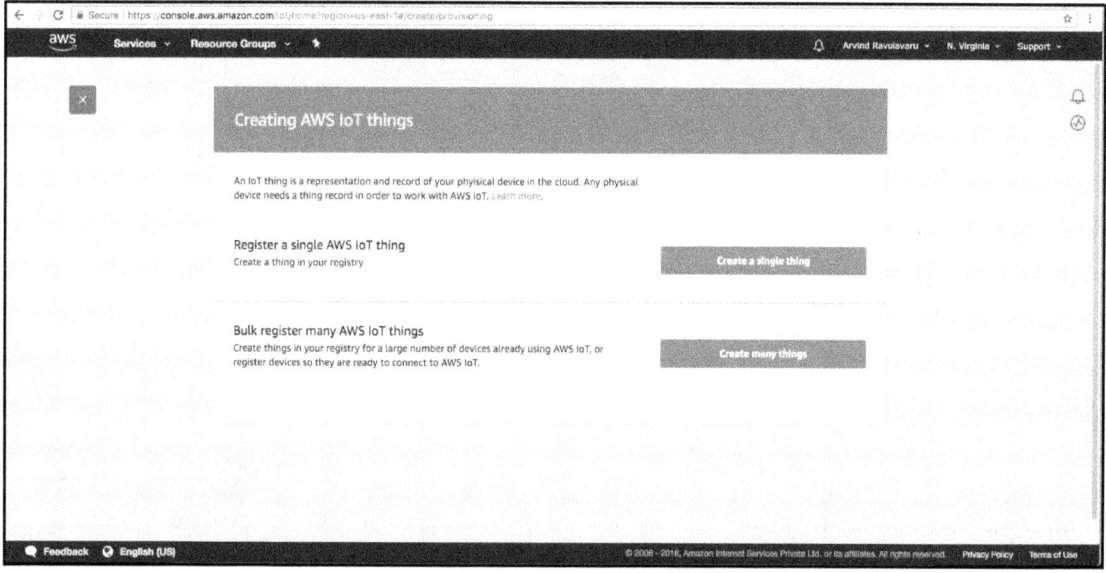

3. Right now, we are going to onboard only one Thing. So, click on **Create a single thing**.

4. On the next screen, we will start filling in the form by naming the device. I have called my device `Pi3-DHT11-Node`. You can give your Thing any name but do remember to update the code where applicable.

5. Next, we are going to apply a Type. Since this is our first device, we are going to create a new Type. Click on **Create a thing type** and fill in the form as shown in the following screenshot:

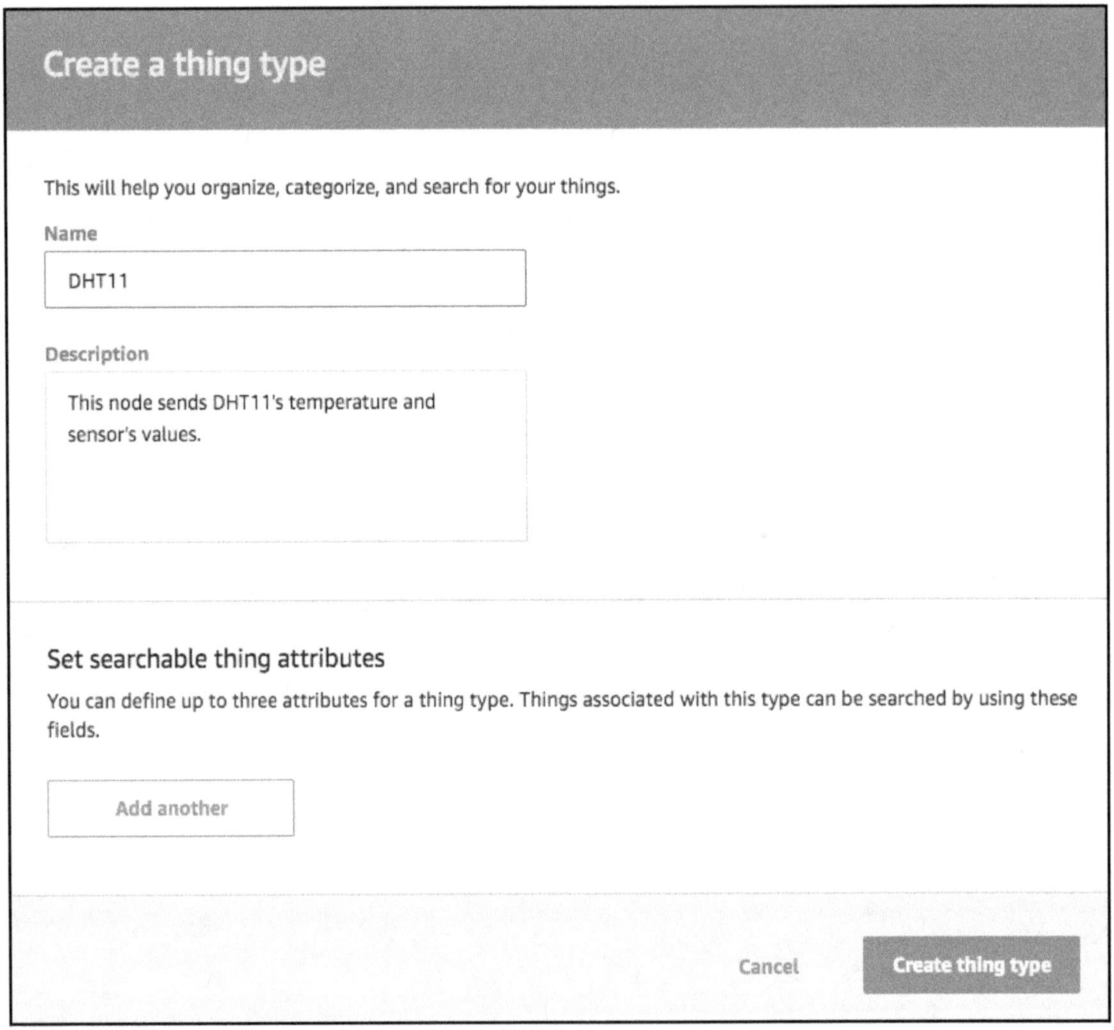

Create a thing type

This will help you organize, categorize, and search for your things.

Name

DHT11

Description

This node sends DHT11's temperature and sensor's values.

Set searchable thing attributes

You can define up to three attributes for a thing type. Things associated with this type can be searched by using these fields.

Add another

Cancel   **Create thing type**

6. If we have different types of devices, such as motion sensors, door sensors, or DHT11 sensors, we can create a Type to easily group our nodes.

7. Click on the **Create thing type** button and this will create a new type; select that value as the default.

8. Next, we are going to add this device to a group—a group of Raspberry Pi 3, DHT11 nodes. You can group your devices as per your requirements and classification.

9. Now, click on **Create group** and create it with the following values:

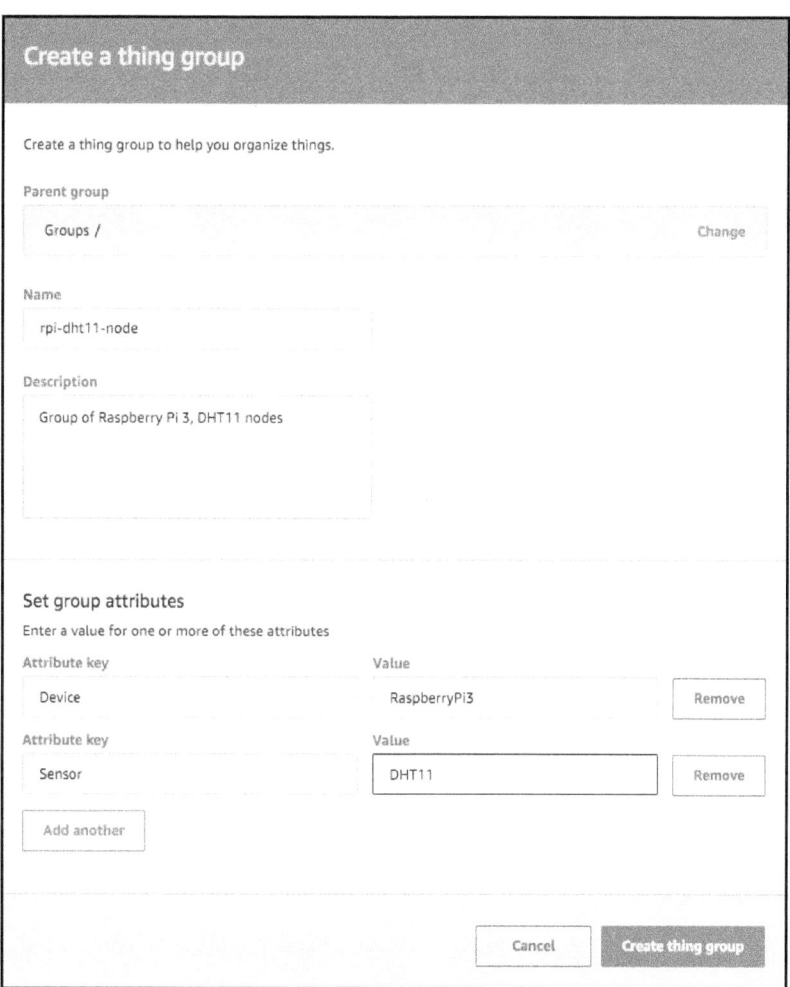

We have added two attributes to identify this group easily, as shown in the previous screenshot.

10. Click on the **Create thing group** and this will create a new group—select that value as the default. These are the only Things we are going to set up in this step. Your form should look something like this:

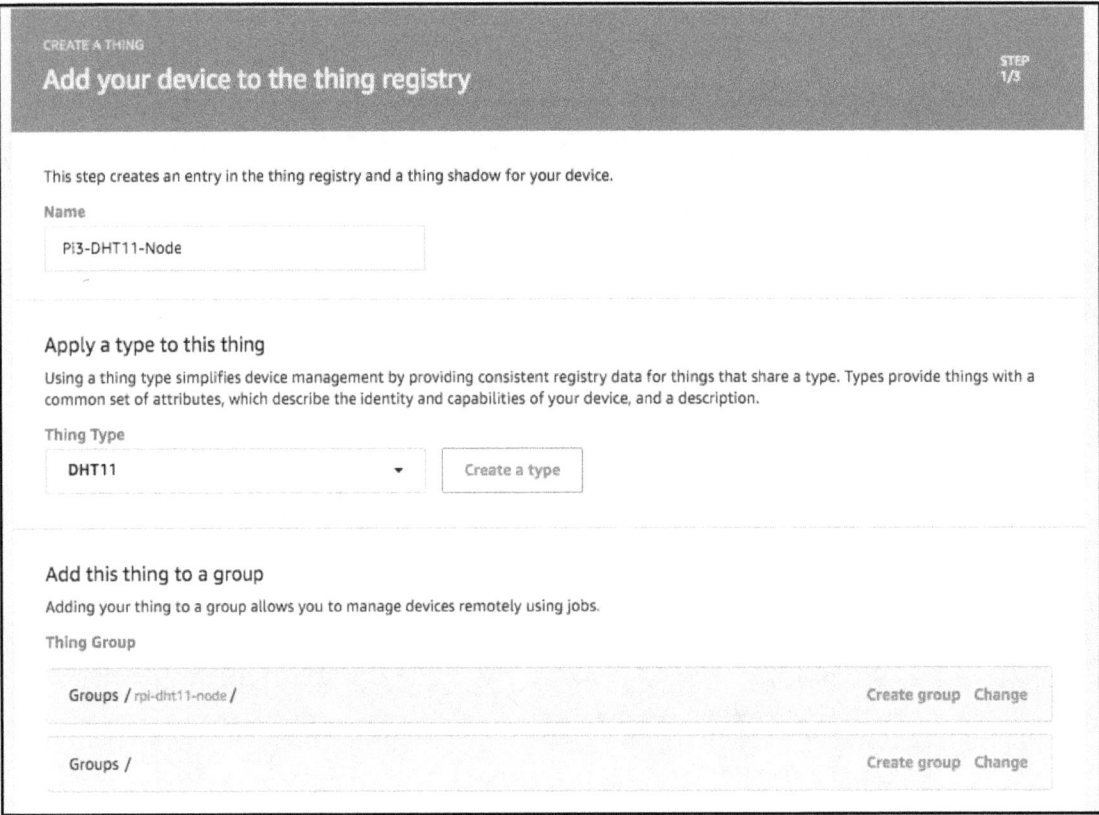

11. At the bottom of the page, click on the **Next** button.
12. Now, we need to create a certificate for the Thing. AWS uses certificate-based authentication and authorization to create a secure connection between the device and AWS IoT Core.

For more information, refer to *MQTT Security Fundamentals: X509 Client Certificate Authentication*:
`https://www.hivemq.com/blog/mqtt-security-fundamentals-x509-clie` `nt-certificate-authentication`.

The current screen should look as shown here:

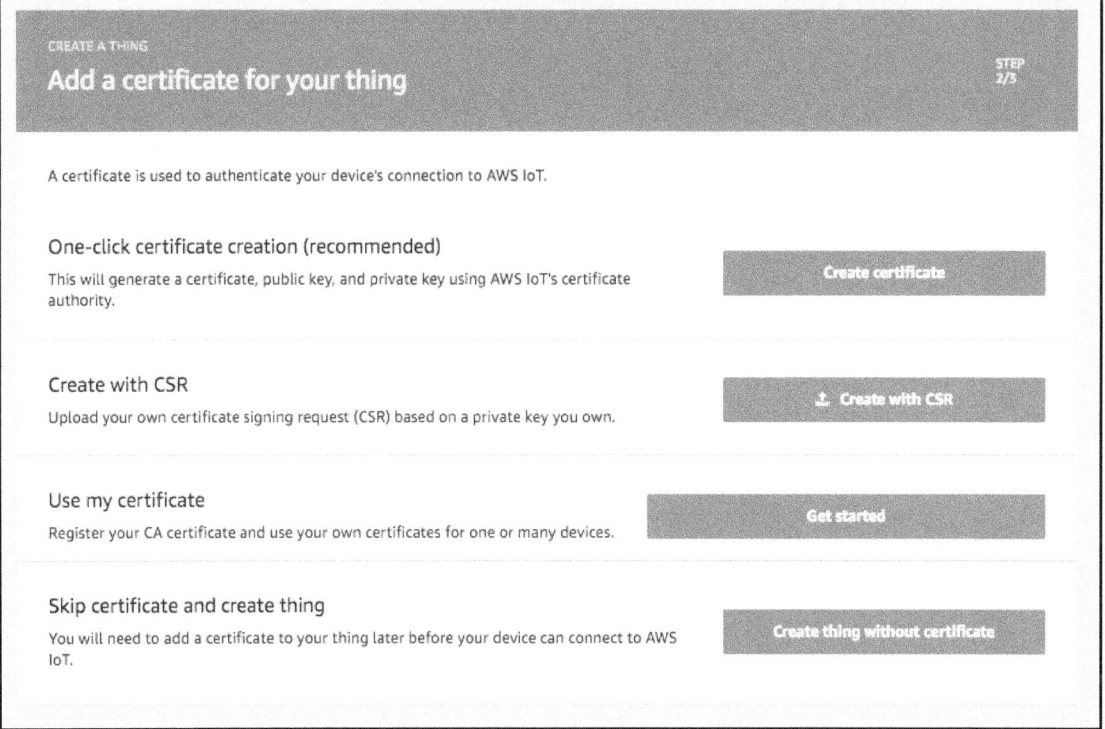

13. Under **One-click certificate creation (recommended)**, click on the **Create certificate** button. This will create three certificates as illustrated in the following screenshot:

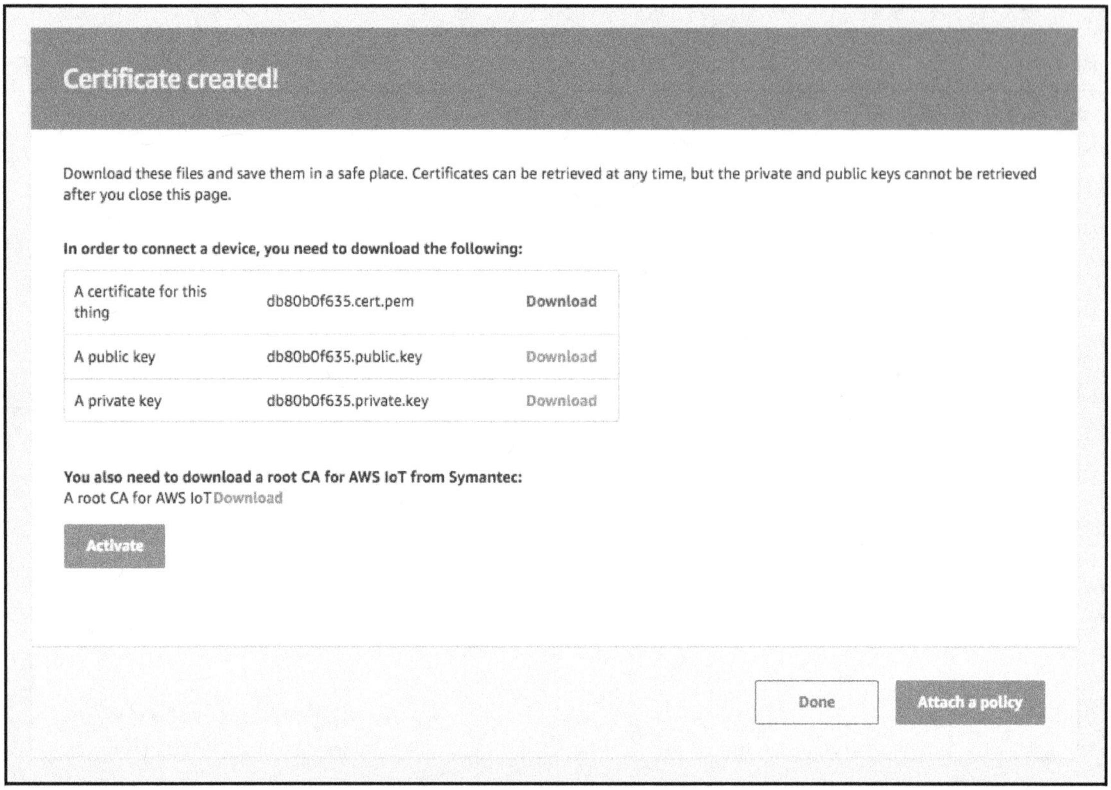

Certificate created!

Download these files and save them in a safe place. Certificates can be retrieved at any time, but the private and public keys cannot be retrieved after you close this page.

In order to connect a device, you need to download the following:

A certificate for this thing	db80b0f635.cert.pem	Download
A public key	db80b0f635.public.key	Download
A private key	db80b0f635.private.key	Download

You also need to download a root CA for AWS IoT from Symantec:
A root CA for AWS IoT Download

Activate

Done   Attach a policy

Do not share these certificates with anyone. These are as good as the username and password of your device to post data to AWS IoT.

14. Once the certificates are created, download the following:

- **Client certificate**: `db80b0f635.cert.pem`
- **Public Key**: `db80b0f635.public.key`
- **Private Key**: `db80b0f635.private.key`
- **Root CA**: From this URL you can download or copy the text:
  `https://www.symantec.com/content/en/us/enterprise/verisign
  /roots/VeriSign-Class%203-Public-Primary-Certification-
  Authority-G5.pem`

 My keys start with `db80b0f635`. Yours may start with something else.

15. Once you have downloaded the keys, click on the **Activate** button.
16. Once the activation is successful, click on **Attach a policy**. Since we did not create any policies, you will see a screen similar to as what is shown here:

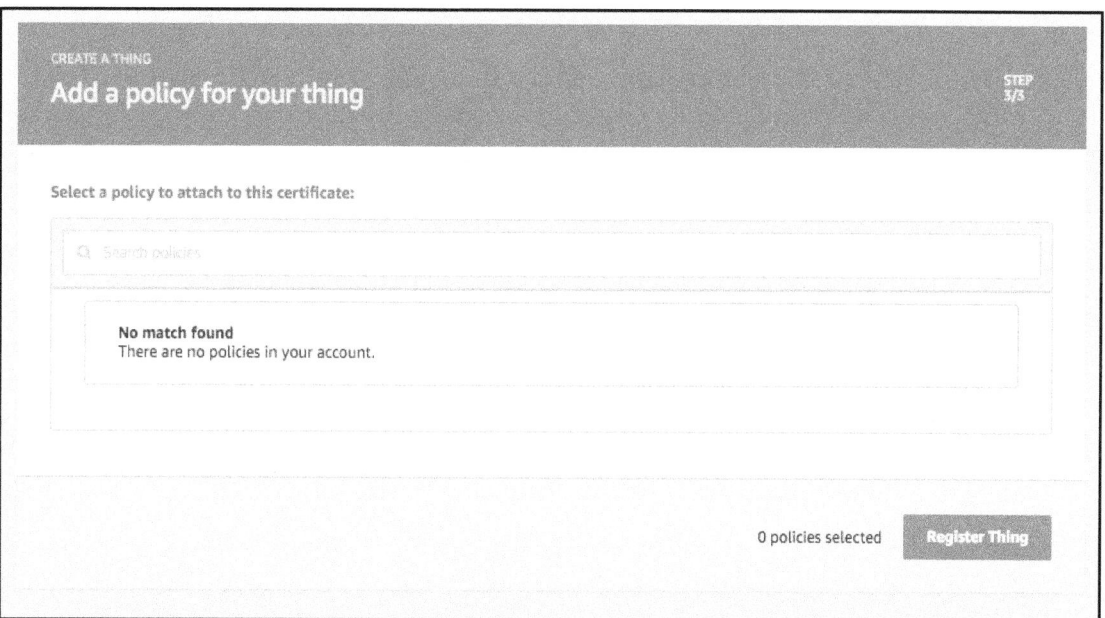

No issues with that. We will create a policy manually and associate it with this certificate in a moment.

17. Finally, click on the **Register Thing** button and a new Thing named **Pi3-DHT11-Node** will be created. Click on **Pi3-DHT11-Node** and you should see something like this:

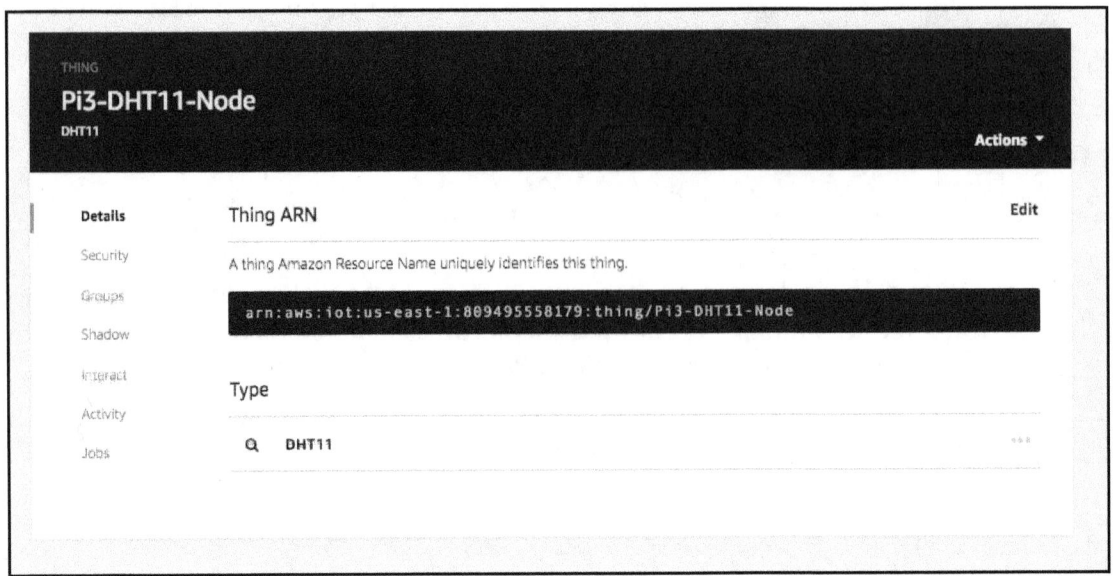

18. We are not done with the setup yet. We still need to create a policy and attach it with a certificate to proceed.

19. Navigate back to the **Things** page, and from the side menu on this page, select **Secure** | **Policies**:

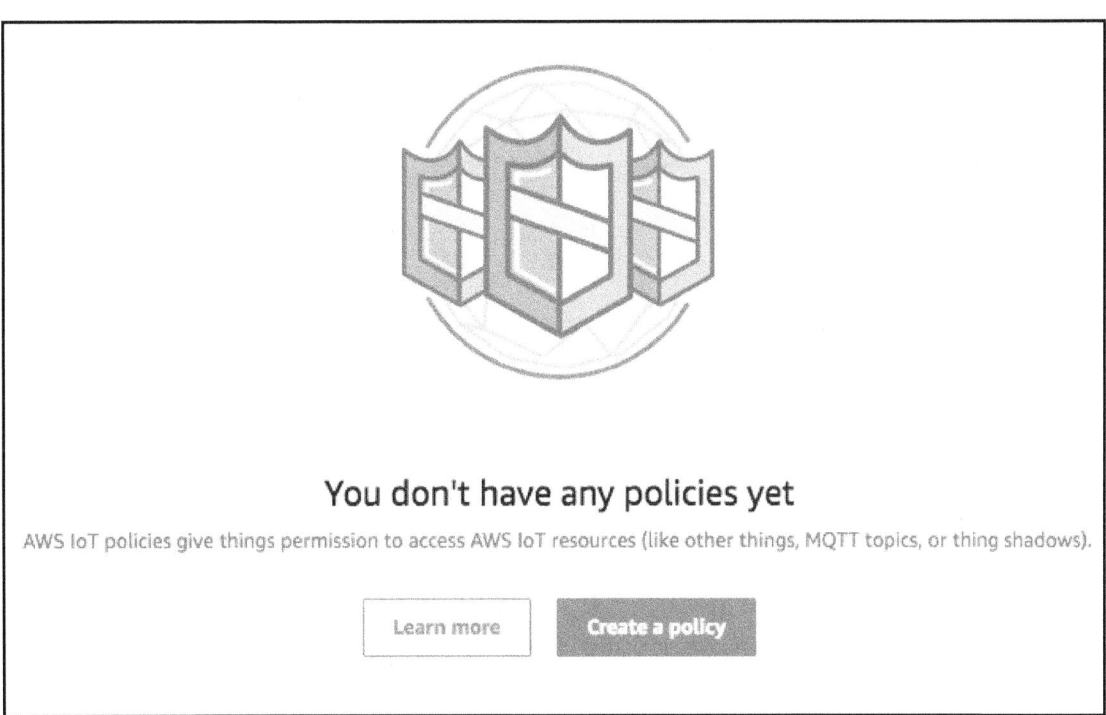

You don't have any policies yet

AWS IoT policies give things permission to access AWS IoT resources (like other things, MQTT topics, or thing shadows).

Learn more   Create a policy

20. Now, click on **Create a policy** and fill in the form as demonstrated in the following screenshot:

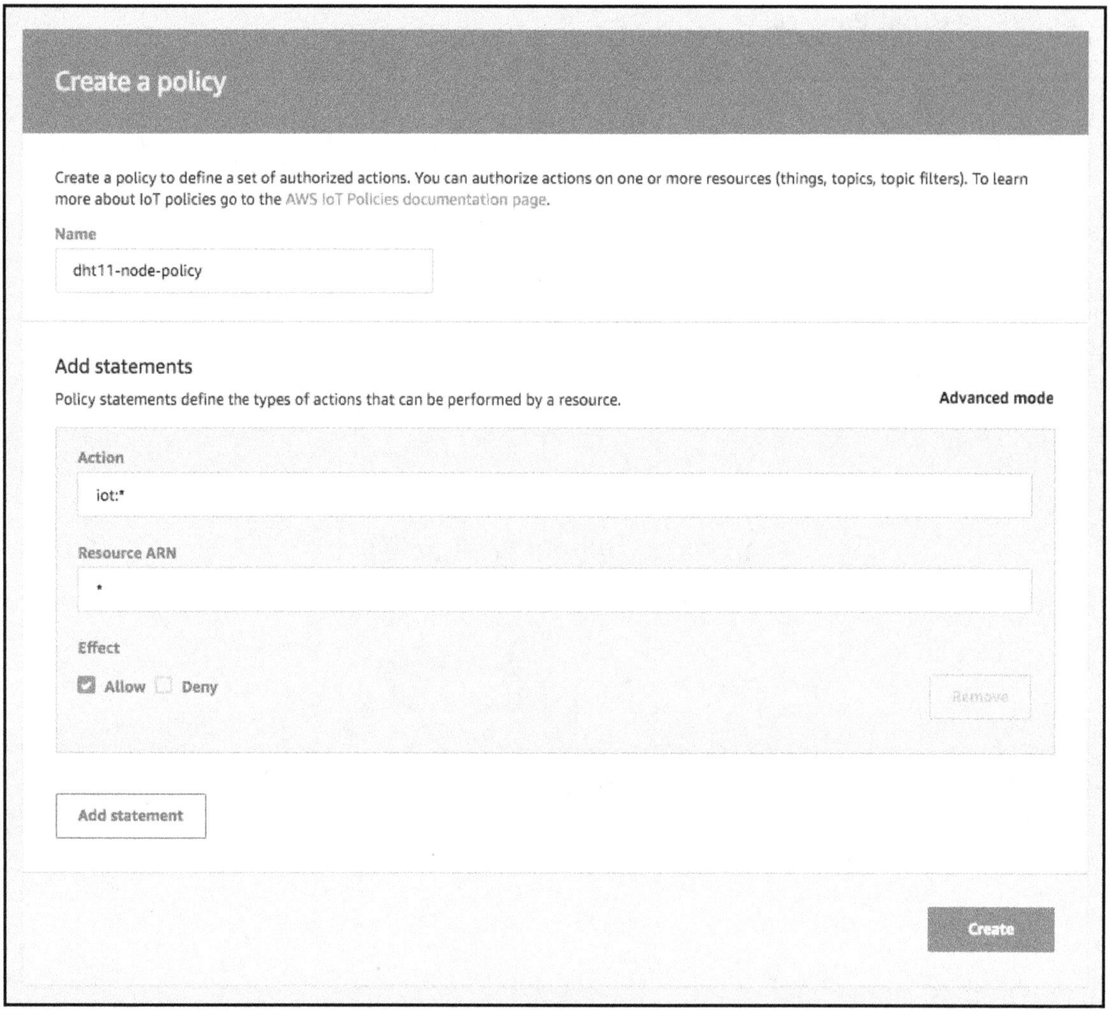

Create a policy

Create a policy to define a set of authorized actions. You can authorize actions on one or more resources (things, topics, topic filters). To learn more about IoT policies go to the AWS IoT Policies documentation page.

Name

dht11-node-policy

Add statements

Policy statements define the types of actions that can be performed by a resource.   **Advanced mode**

Action

iot:*

Resource ARN

*

Effect

☑ Allow ☐ Deny   Remove

Add statement

Create

In the previously demonstrated policy, we are allowing any kind of IoT operation to be performed by the device that uses this policy and on any resource. This is a dangerous setup, mainly for production; however, this is okay for learning purposes.

21. Click on the **Create** button and this will create a new policy. Now, we are going to attach this policy to a certificate.

22. Navigate to **Secure | Certificates** and, using the options available at the top-right of the certificate we created, we are going to attach the policy:

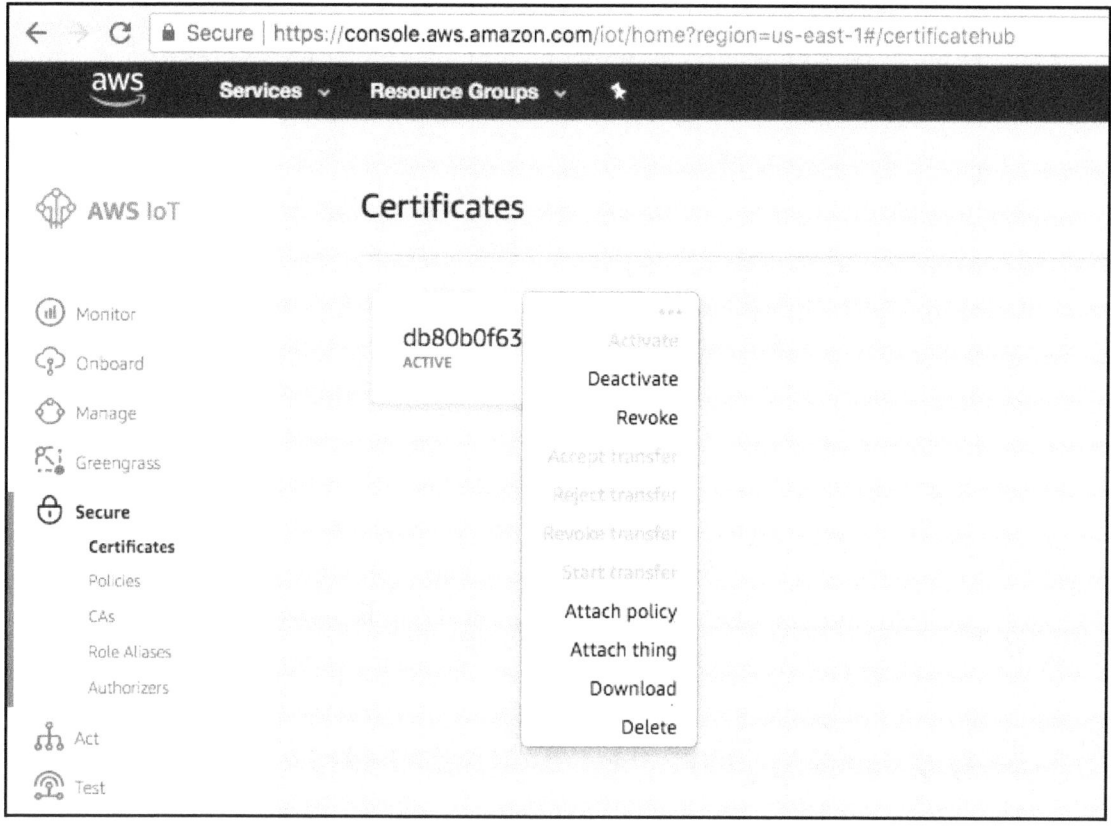

23. Click on **Attach policy** on the previous screen and select the policy we have just created:

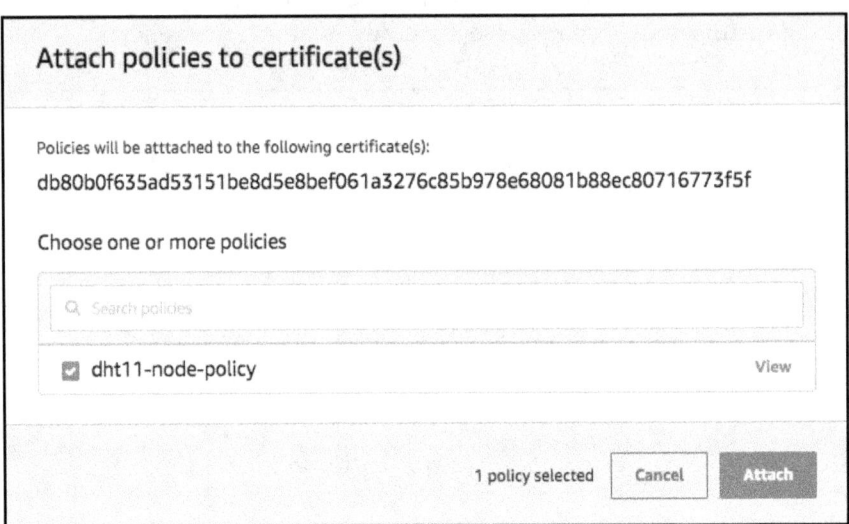

24. Now, click on **Attach** to complete the setup.

With this, we are done with the setup of a Thing.

In the next section, we are going to use Node.js as a client on Raspberry Pi 3 to send data to the AWS IoT.

Setting up Raspberry Pi 3 on the DHT11 node

Now that we have our Thing set up in AWS IoT, we are going to complete the remaining operation in Raspberry Pi to send data.

Things needed

You will need the following hardware to set up Raspberry Pi 3 on the DHT11 node:

- **One Raspberry Pi 3**:
  https://www.amazon.com/Raspberry-Pi-Desktop-Starter-White/dp/B01CI5872
  2
- **One breadboard**:
  https://www.amazon.com/Solderless-Breadboard-Circuit-Circboard-Prototy
  ping/dp/B01DDI54II/
- **One DHT11 sensor**:
  https://www.amazon.com/HiLetgo-Temperature-Humidity-Arduino-Raspberry/
  dp/B01DKC2GQ0
- **Three male-to-female jumper cables**:
  https://www.amazon.com/RGBZONE-120pcs-Multicolored-Dupont-Breadboard/d
  p/B01M1IEUAF/

 If you are new to the world of Raspberry Pi GPIO's interfacing, take a look at this *Raspberry Pi GPIO Tutorial: The Basics Explained* video tutorial on YouTube, at: https://www.youtube.com/watch?v=6PuK9fh3aL8.

Connect the DHT11 sensor to Raspberry Pi 3 as shown in the following diagram:

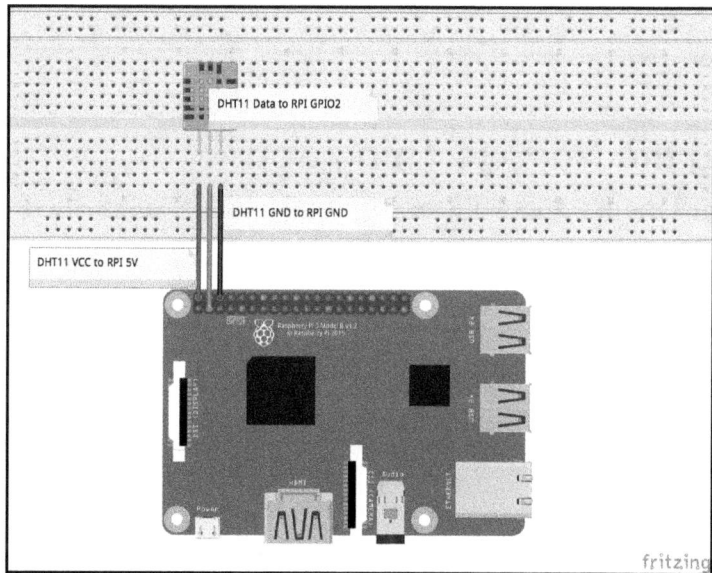

Next, start Raspberry Pi 3 and log in to it. On the desktop, create a new folder named `AWS-IoT-Thing`. Open a new Terminal and `cd` into this folder.

Setting up Node.js

Assuming that this is the same Raspberry Pi 3 that was used in `Chapter 3`, *Getting Started with IoT Platforms*, it should have Node.js installed. If Node.js is not installed, please refer to the following steps:

1. Open a new Terminal and run the following commands:

```
$ sudo apt update
$ sudo apt full-upgrade
```

2. This will upgrade all the packages that need upgrades. Next, we will install the latest version of Node.js. We will be using the Node 7.x version:

```
$ curl -sL https://deb.nodesource.com/setup_7.x | sudo -E bash -
$ sudo apt install nodejs
```

3. This will take a moment to install, and once your installation is done, you should be able to see the version of Node.js and NPM after running the following commands:

```
$ node -v
$ npm -v
```

Developing the Node.js Thing app

Now, we will set up the app and write the required code:

1. From the Terminal, once you are inside the `AWS-IoT-Thing` folder, run the following command:

```
$ npm init -y
```

2. Next, we will install `aws-iot-device-sdk`
   (`http://npmjs.com/package/aws-iot-device-sdk`) from NPM. This module has
   the required client code to interface with AWS IoT. Execute the following
   command:

   ```
   $ npm install aws-iot-device-sdk --save
   ```

3. Next, we will install `rpi-dht-sensor`
   (`https://www.npmjs.com/package/rpi-dht-sensor`) from NPM. This module
   will help in reading the DHT11 temperature and humidity values. Let's run the
   following command:

   ```
   $ npm install rpi-dht-sensor --save
   ```

4. Your final `package.json` file should look like this:

   ```
   {
     "name": "AWS-IoT-Thing",
     "version": "1.0.0",
     "main": "index.js",
     "scripts": {
       "test": "echo "Error: no test specified" && exit 1"
     },
     "keywords": [],
     "author": "",
     "license": "ISC",
     "description": "",
     "dependencies": {
       "aws-iot-device-sdk": "^2.2.0",
       "rpi-dht-sensor": "^0.1.1"
     }
   }
   ```

Now that we have the required dependencies installed, let's continue:

5. Create a new file named `index.js` at the `root` of the `AWS-IoT-Thing` folder. Next, create a folder named `certs` at the `root` of the `AWS-IoT-Thing` folder and move the four certificates we have downloaded there. Your final folder structure should look something like this:

```
pi@raspberrypi: ~/Desktop/AWS-IoT-Thing                        _  □  ×

File  Edit  Tabs  Help
pi@raspberrypi:~/Desktop/AWS-IoT-Thing $ tree -I 'node_modules'
.
├── certs
│   ├── db80b0f635-certificate.pem.crt
│   ├── db80b0f635-private.pem.key
│   ├── db80b0f635-public.pem.key
│   └── RootCA-VeriSign-Class 3-Public-Primary-Certification-Authority-G5.pem
├── index.js
└── package.json

1 directory, 6 files
```

6. Open `index.js` in any text editor and update it as shown in the following code snippet:

```
var awsIot = require('aws-iot-device-sdk');
var rpiDhtSensor = require('rpi-dht-sensor');

var dht = new rpiDhtSensor.DHT11(2); // `2` => GPIO2
const NODE_ID = 'Pi3-DHT11-Node';
const INIT_DELAY = 15;
const TAG = '[' + NODE_ID + '] >>>>>>>>> ';

console.log(TAG, 'Connecting...');

var thingShadow = awsIot.thingShadow({
  keyPath: './certs/db80b0f635-private.pem.key',
  certPath: './certs/db80b0f635-certificate.pem.crt',
  caPath: './certs/RootCA-VeriSign-Class 3-Public-Primary-
Certification-Authority-G5.pem',
  clientId: NODE_ID,
  host: 'a1afizfoknpwqg.iot.us-east-1.amazonaws.com',
  port: 8883,
  region: 'us-east-1',
  debug: false, // optional to see logs on console
});
```

```
thingShadow.on('connect', function() {
  console.log(TAG, 'Connected.');
  thingShadow.register(NODE_ID, {}, function() {
    console.log(TAG, 'Registered.');
    console.log(TAG, 'Reading data in ' + INIT_DELAY + '
seconds.');
    setTimeout(sendData, INIT_DELAY * 1000); // wait for
`INIT_DELAY` seconds before reading the first record
  });
});

function fetchData() {
  var readout = dht.read();
  var temp = readout.temperature.toFixed(2);
  var humd = readout.humidity.toFixed(2);

  return {
    "temp": temp,
    "humd": humd
  };
}

function sendData() {
  var DHT11State = {
    "state": {
      "desired": fetchData()
    }
  };

  console.log(TAG, 'Sending Data..', DHT11State);

  var clientTokenUpdate = thingShadow.update(NODE_ID, DHT11State);
  if (clientTokenUpdate === null) {
    console.log(TAG, 'Shadow update failed, operation still in
progress');
  } else {
    console.log(TAG, 'Shadow update success.');
  }

  // keep sending the data every 30 seconds
  console.log(TAG, 'Reading data again in 30 seconds.');
  setTimeout(sendData, 30000); // 30,000 ms => 30 seconds
}

thingShadow.on('status', function(thingName, stat, clientToken,
stateObject) {
  console.log('received ' + stat + ' on ' + thingName + ':',
stateObject);
```

```
});

thingShadow.on('delta', function(thingName, stateObject) {
  console.log('received delta on ' + thingName + ':', stateObject);
});

thingShadow.on('timeout', function(thingName, clientToken) {
  console.log('received timeout on ' + thingName + ' with token:',
clientToken);
});
```

In the previous code, we are using `awsIot.thingShadow()` to connect to our AWS Thing that we have created. To the `awsIot.thingShadow()`, we pass the following options:

- `keyPath`: This is the location of `private.pem.key`, which we have downloaded and placed in the `certs` folder.
- `certPath`: This is the location of `certificate.pem.crt`, which we have downloaded and placed in the `certs` folder.
- `caPath`: This is the location of `RootCA-VeriSign-Class 3-Public-Primary-Certification-Authority-G5.pem`, which we have downloaded and placed in the `certs` folder.
- `clientId`: This is the name of the Thing we have created in AWS IoT **Pi3-DHT11-Node**.
- `host`: This is the URL to which the Thing needs to connect to. This URL is different for different Things. To get the host, navigate to your Thing and click the **Interact** tab as shown in the following screenshot:

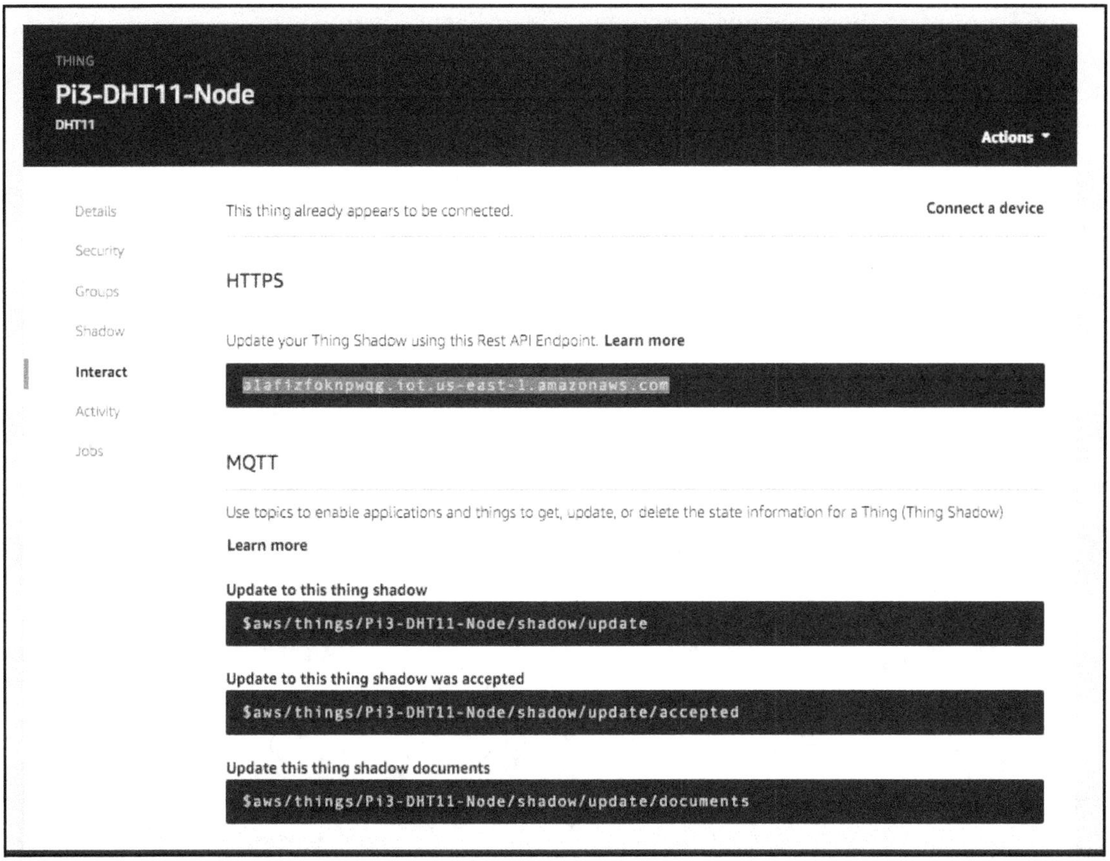

THING

Pi3-DHT11-Node

DHT11

Actions ▼

Details	This thing already appears to be connected.
Security	
Groups	**HTTPS**
Shadow	
Interact	Update your Thing Shadow using this Rest API Endpoint. **Learn more**
Activity	`a1afizfoknpwqg.iot.us-east-1.amazonaws.com`
Jobs	

Connect a device

MQTT

Use topics to enable applications and things to get, update, or delete the state information for a Thing (Thing Shadow)

Learn more

Update to this thing shadow

`$aws/things/Pi3-DHT11-Node/shadow/update`

Update to this thing shadow was accepted

`$aws/things/Pi3-DHT11-Node/shadow/update/accepted`

Update this thing shadow documents

`$aws/things/Pi3-DHT11-Node/shadow/update/documents`

The highlighted URL is the host.

- `port`: We are using SSL-based communication, so the port will be `8883`.
- `region`: The region in which you have created the Thing. You can find this in the URL of the page. For example,
  `https://console.aws.amazon.com/iot/home?region=us-east-1#/thing/Pi3-DHT11-Node`.
- `debug`: This is optional. If you want see some logs rolling out from the module during execution, you can set this property to `true`.

We will connect to the preceding host with our certificates. In the `thingShadow.on('connect')` callback, we call `thingShadow.register()` to register. We need to register only once per connection. Once the registration is completed, we will start to gather the data from the DHT11 sensor and, using `thingShadow.update()`, we will update the shadow. In the `thingShadow.on('status')` callback, we will get to know the status of the update.

Save the file and execute the following command:

```
$ sudo node index.js
```

We should see something like this:

As you can see from the previous logs on the console screen, the device first gets connected then registers itself. Once the registration is done, we will wait for 15 seconds to transmit the first record. Then we wait for another 30 seconds and continue the process.

We are also listening for status and delta events to make sure that what we have sent has been successfully updated.

Now, if we head back to the AWS IoT Thing page in the AWS Console and click on the **Shadow** tab, we should see the last record that we have sent update here:

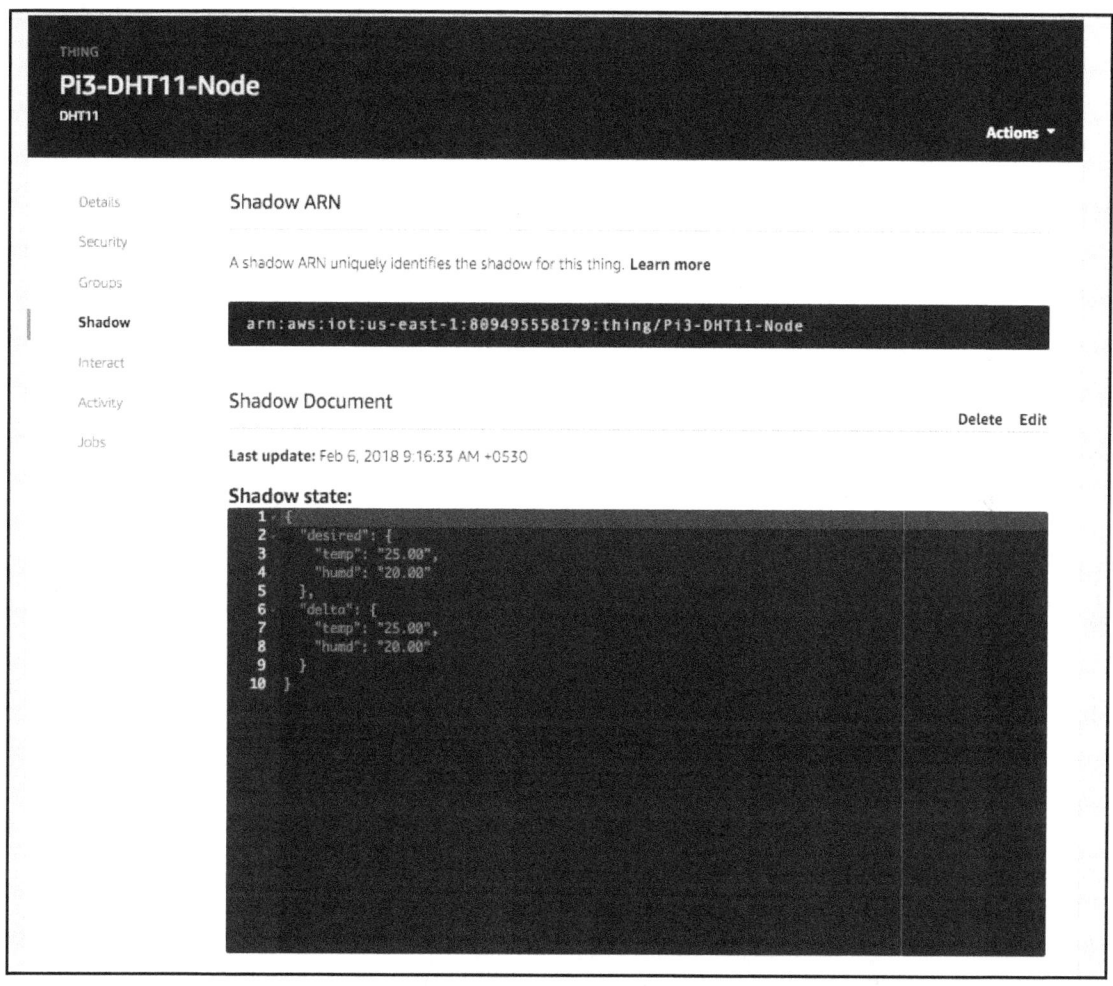

Underneath that, you can see the metadata of the document, which should look something like:

```
{
  "metadata": {
   "desired": {
    "temp": {
     "timestamp": 1517888793
    },
    "humd": {
     "timestamp": 1517888793
    }
   }
  },
  "timestamp": 1517888794,
  "version": 16
}
```

The preceding JSON represents the data structure of the Thing's data, assuming that the Thing keeps sending the same structure of data at all times.

Now that the Thing is sending data, let us actually read the data coming from this Thing.

Reading the data from the Thing

There are two approaches as to how you can get the shadow data:

- **Using the REST API:**
  https://docs.aws.amazon.com/iot/latest/developerguide/device-shadow-rest-api.html
- **Using MQTT-SNL:**
  https://docs.aws.amazon.com/iot/latest/developerguide/device-shadow-mqtt.html

The following example used the MQTTS approach to fetch the shadow data. Whenever we want to fetch the data of a Thing, we publish an empty packet to the $aws/things/Pi3-DHT11-Node/shadow/get topic. Depending on whether the state was accepted or rejected, we will get a response on $aws/things/Pi3-DHT11-Node/shadow/get/accepted or $aws/things/Pi3-DHT11-Node/shadow/get/rejected, respectively.

For testing the data fetch, you can either use the same Raspberry Pi 3 or another computer. I am going to use my MacBook as a client that is interested in the data sent by the Thing.

In my local machine, I am going to create the following setup, which is very similar to what we have done in Raspberry Pi 3:

1. Create a folder named test_client. Inside the test_client folder, create a folder named certs and get a copy of the same four certificates we have used in Raspberry Pi 3.

2. Inside the test_client folder, run the following command on the Terminal:

   ```
   $ npm init -y
   ```

3. Next, install the aws-iot-device-sdk module using the following command:

   ```
   $ npm install aws-iot-device-sdk --save
   ```

4. Create a file inside the test_client folder named index.js and update it as shown here:

   ```
   var awsIot = require('aws-iot-device-sdk');

   const NODE_ID = 'Pi3-DHT11-Node';
   const TAG = '[TEST THING] >>>>>>>>> ';

   console.log(TAG, 'Connecting...');

   var device = awsIot.device({
     keyPath: './certs/db80b0f635-private.pem.key',
     certPath: './certs/db80b0f635-certificate.pem.crt',
     caPath: './certs/RootCA-VeriSign-Class 3-Public-Primary-
   Certification-Authority-G5.pem',
     clientId: NODE_ID,
     host: 'a1afizfoknpwqg.iot.us-east-1.amazonaws.com',
     port: 8883,
     region: 'us-east-1',
     debug: false, // optional to see logs on console
   });

   device.on('connect', function() {
     console.log(TAG, 'device connected!');
     device.subscribe('$aws/things/Pi3-DHT11-
   Node/shadow/get/accepted');
     device.subscribe('$aws/things/Pi3-DHT11-
   Node/shadow/get/rejected');
     // Publish an empty packet to topic `$aws/things/Pi3-DHT11-
   Node/shadow/get`
     // to get the latest shadow data on either `accepted` or
   `rejected` topic
   ```

```
device.publish('$aws/things/Pi3-DHT11-Node/shadow/get', '');
});

device.on('message', function(topic, payload) {
    payload = JSON.parse(payload.toString());
    console.log(TAG, 'message from ', topic, JSON.stringify(payload,
null, 4));
});
```

 Update the device information as applicable.

5. Save the file and run the following command on the Terminal:

```
$ node index.js
```

We should see something similar to what is shown in the following console output:

```
→ test_client node index.js
[TEST THING] >>>>>>>>>  Connecting...
[TEST THING] >>>>>>>>>  device connected!
[TEST THING] >>>>>>>>>  message from  $aws/things/Pi3-DHT11-Node/shadow/get/accepted {
    "state": {
        "desired": {
            "temp": "25.00",
            "humd": "20.00"
        },
        "delta": {
            "temp": "25.00",
            "humd": "20.00"
        }
    },
    "metadata": {
        "desired": {
            "temp": {
                "timestamp": 1517889793
            },
            "humd": {
                "timestamp": 1517889793
            }
        }
    },
    "version": 22,
    "timestamp": 1517889904
}
```

This way, any client that is interested in the data of this Thing can use this approach to get the latest data.

You can also use an MQTT library in the browser itself to fetch the data from a Thing. But do keep in mind this is not advisable as the certificates are exposed. Instead, you can have a backend microservice that can achieve the same for you and then expose the data via HTTPS.

With this, we conclude the section on posting data to AWS IoT and fetching it. In the next section, we are going to work with rules.

Building the dashboard

Now that we have seen how a client can read the data of our Thing on demand, we will move on to building a dashboard, where we show data in real time.

For this, we are going to use Elasticsearch and Kibana.

Elasticsearch

Elasticsearch is a search engine based on Apache Lucene. It provides a distributed, multi-tenant capable, full-text search engine with an HTTP web interface and schema-free JSON documents.

Read more about Elasticsearch at
`http://whatis.techtarget.com/definition/ElasticSearch`.

Kibana

Kibana is an open source data visualization plugin for Elasticsearch. It provides visualization capabilities on top of the content indexed on an Elasticsearch cluster. Users can create bar, line, and scatter plots, or pie charts and maps on top of large volumes of data.

Read more about Kibana at `https://www.elastic.co/products/kibana`.

As we have seen in the architecture diagram, we are going to create a rule in AWS IoT. The job of the rule is to listen to an AWS topic and then send the temperature and humidity values from that topic to an Elasticsearch cluster that we are going to create using the AWS Elasticsearch Service (`https://aws.amazon.com/elasticsearch-service/`).

The cluster we are going to provision on AWS will also have a Kibana setup for easy visualizations.

We are going to use Kibana and build the visualization and then a dashboard from that visualization.

We are going to use Elasticsearch and Kibana for a basic use case.

The reason I have chosen to use Elasticsearch instead of building a simple web application that can display charts is because we can do way more than just building dashboards in Kibana using Elasticsearch. This is where the IoT Analytics comes in.

We are not going to explore IoT analytics per se, but this setup should give you an idea and get you started off.

Setting up Elasticsearch

Before we proceed further, we are going to provision a new Elasticsearch cluster.

Do note that the cluster we are going to provision is under free tier and has a limitation of resources. Read more about the limitations at
`https://aws.amazon.com/about-aws/whats-new/2017/01/amazon-elasticsearch-service`
`-free-tier-now-available-on-t2-small-elasticsearch-instances/`.

> Neither Packt Publishing nor me is in any way responsible for any billing that happens as a by-product of running any example in this book. Please read the pricing terms carefully before continuing.

To set up Elasticsearch, head over to the **Amazon Elasticsearch Service** console or use the services menu on the of AWS console page to reach the Amazon Elasticsearch Service console page. You should see a screen similar to what is shown here:

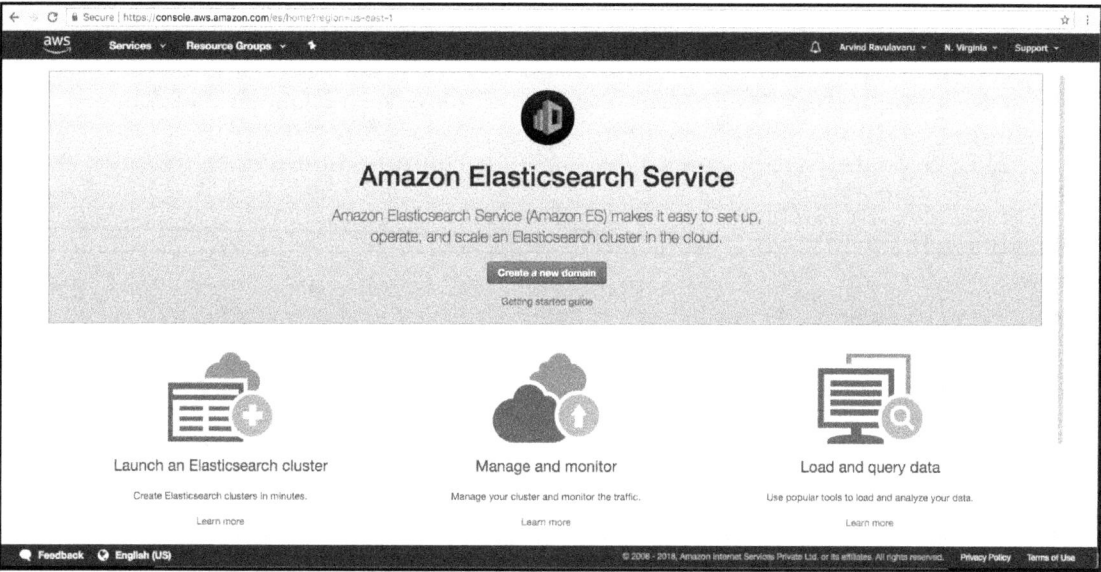

1. Click on the **Create a new domain** button and fill in the next screen, as shown in the following screenshot:

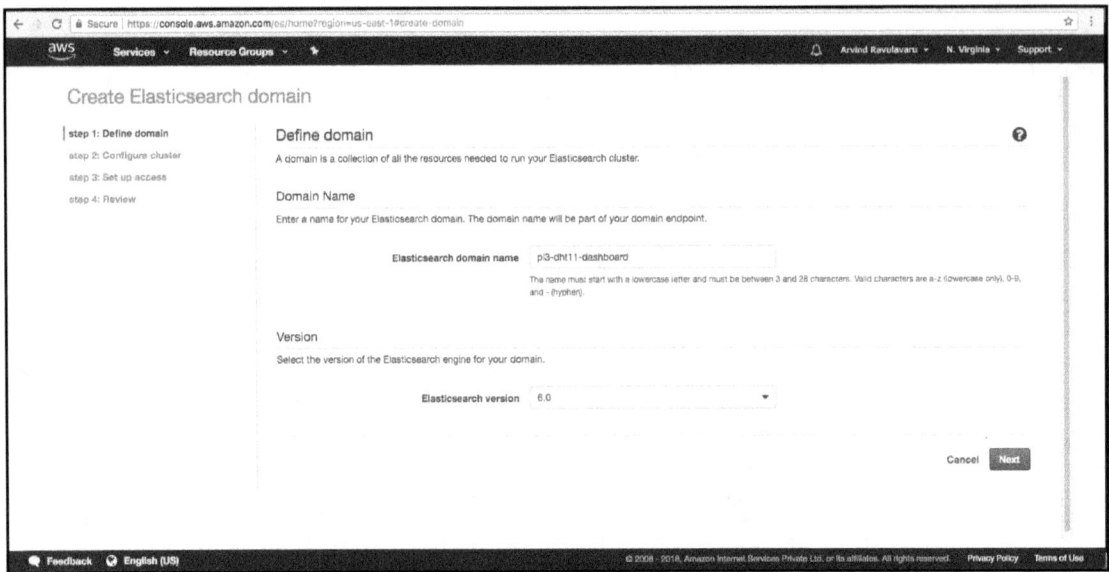

2. Click on the **Next** button. Under the **Node configuration** section, update it as illustrated here:

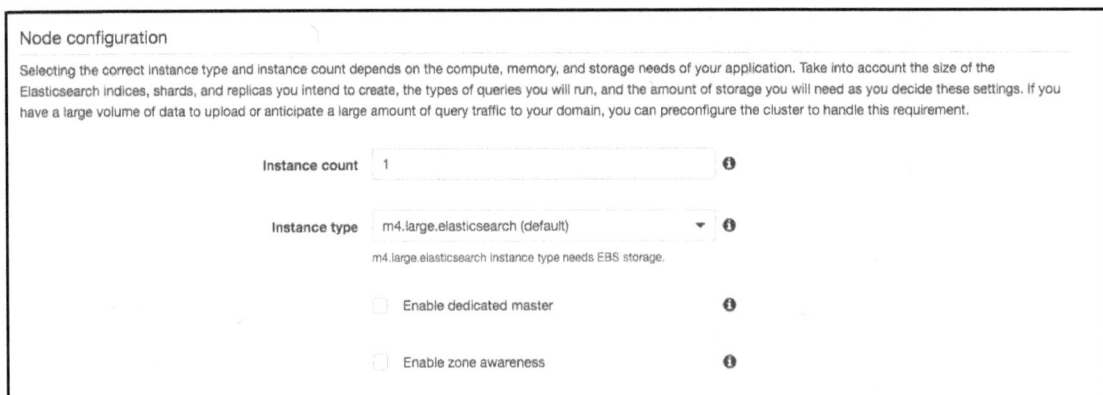

If you are planning to run bigger queries, I would recommend checking **Enable dedicated master** and setting it up.

3. Under the **Storage configuration** section, update it as illustrated in the following screenshot:

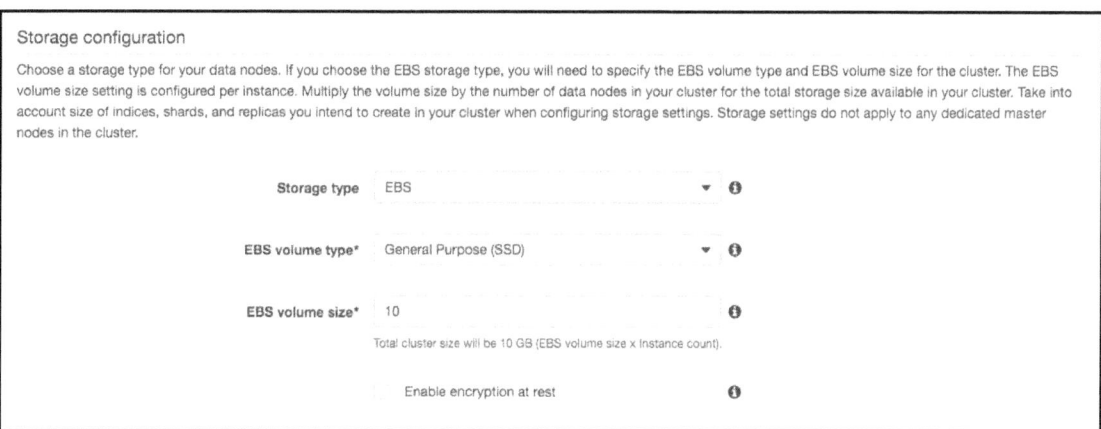

4. Leave the remaining sections as the defaults and click **Next** to continue.
5. On the **Setup access** screen, under **Network configuration**, select **Public access**, and for the access policy, select **Allow open access to the domain** and accept the risks associated with this configuration.

We are using this setup to quickly work with services and to not worry about credentials and security. DO NOT use this setup in production.

6. Finally, click **Next**, review the selections we have made, and click **Confirm**.

Once the process has started, it will take up to 10 minutes for the domain to be provisioned.

Once the domain is provisioned, we should see a similar screen to what is illustrated here:

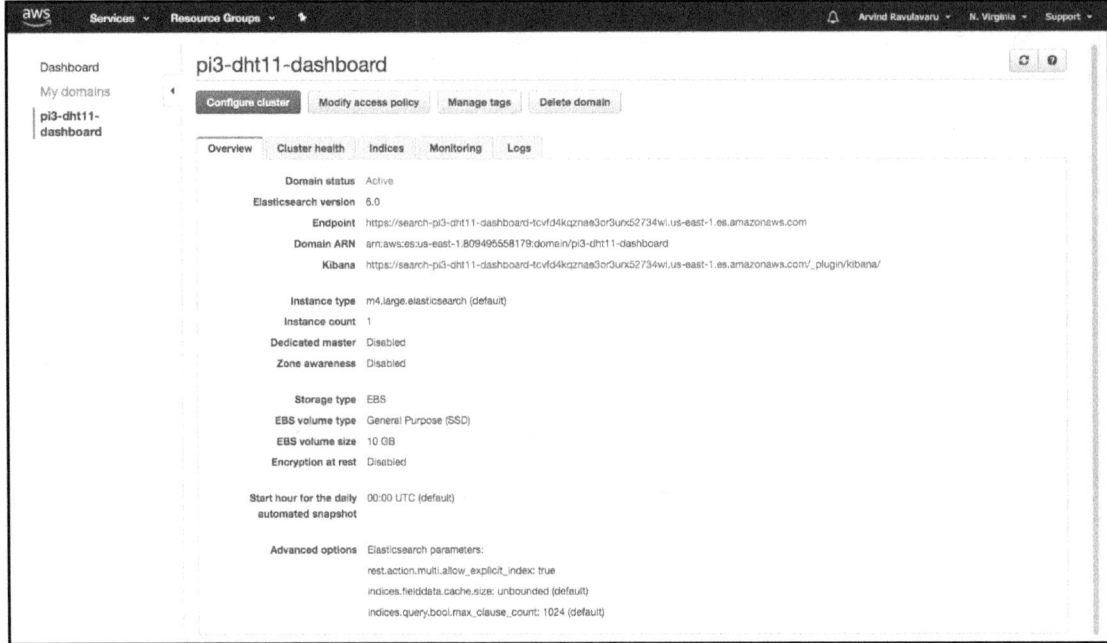

Here we have our **Endpoint**, to which data will be sent for indexing. And we also have the URL for Kibana.

When we click on the Kibana URL, after it loads, you will be presented with the following screen:

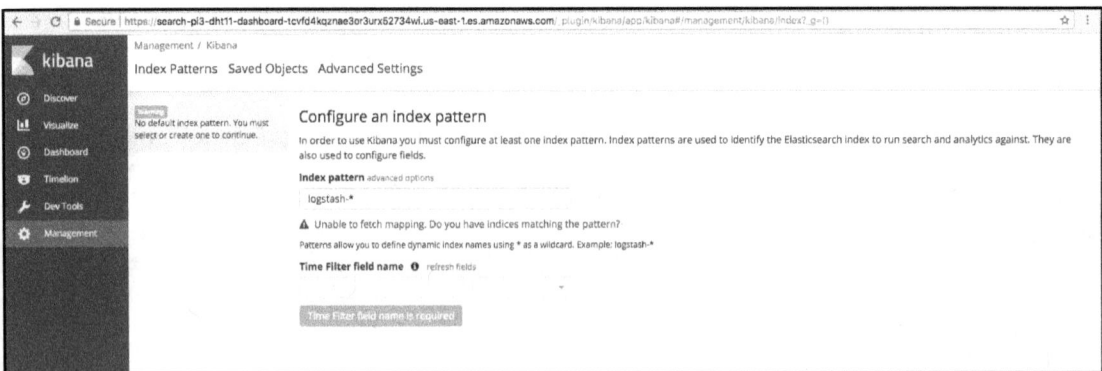

The previous screen will change once we start indexing data. In the next section, we are going to create an IAM role.

Setting up an IAM Role

Now that we have Elasticsearch and Kibana up and running, we will get started with setting up an IAM role. We will be using this role for the IoT rule and to put data into Elasticsearch:

1. To get started, head over to `https://console.aws.amazon.com/iam`. From the side menu, click on the **Roles** link and you should see a screen like this:

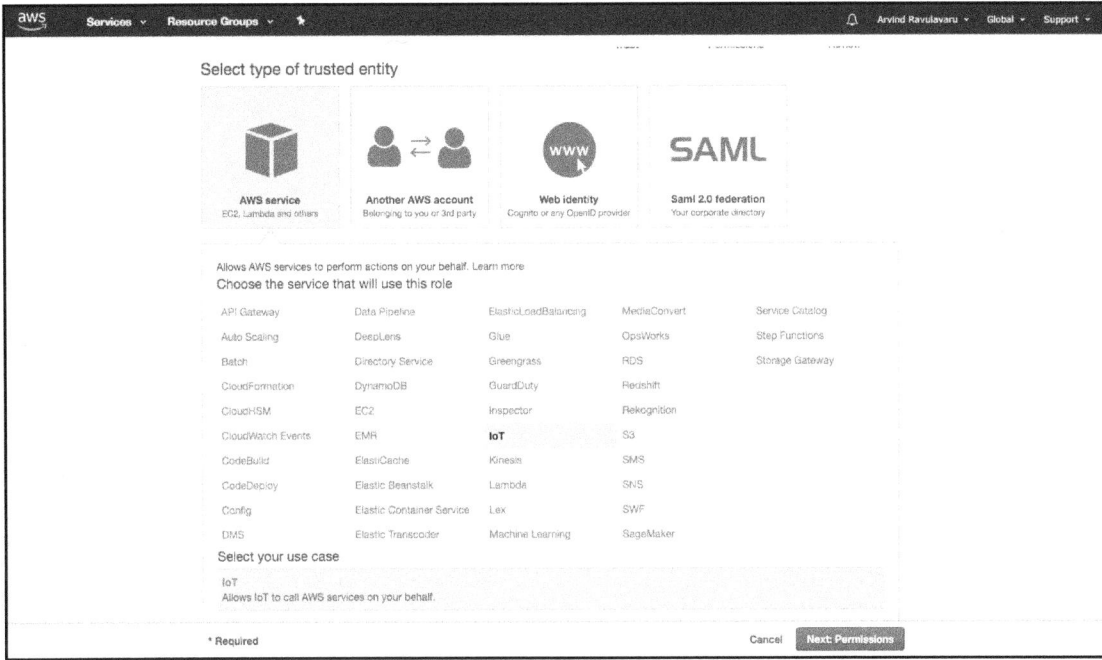

2. Select **AWS service** from the top row and then select **IoT**. Click **Next: Permissions** to proceed to the next step:

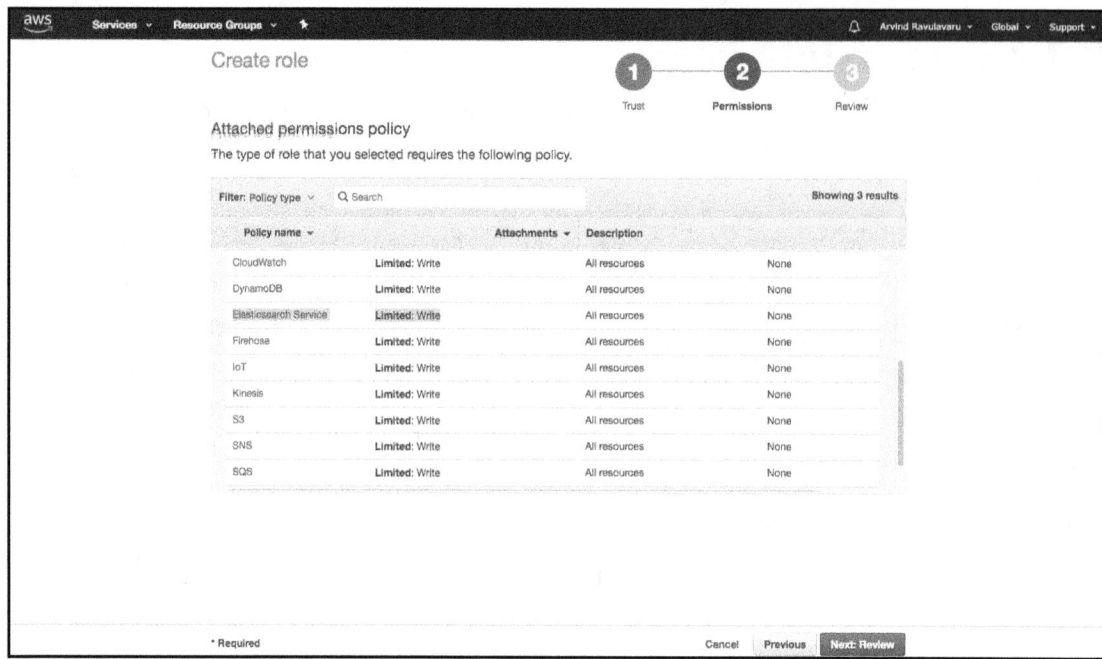

3. All the policies needed for AWS IoT access resources across AWS are preselected. The one we are interested in is under `AWSIoTRulesActions` and **Elasticsearch Service**. All we need here is the `ESHttpPut` action.

4. Finally, click the **Next: Review** button and fill in the details as shown in the following screenshot:

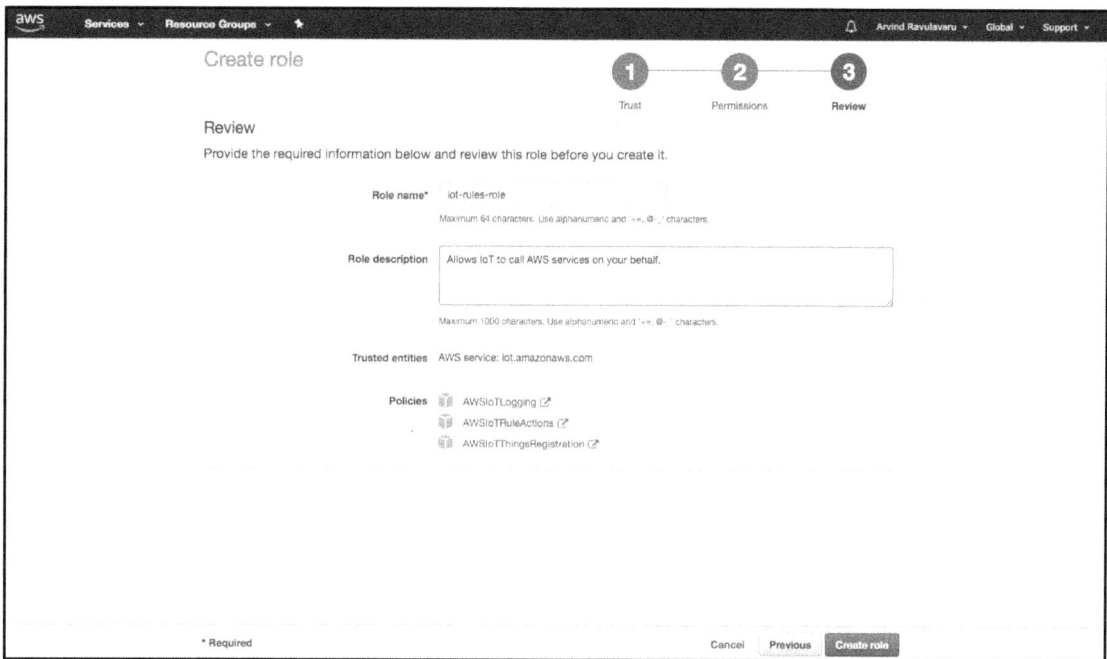

5. Once we click **Create role**, a new role with the name provided will be created.

Now that we have Elasticsearch up and running, as well as the IAM role needed, we will create the IoT Rule to index incoming data into Elasticsearch.

Creating an IoT Rule

To get started, head over to AWS IoT and to the region where we have registered our Thing:

1. From the menu on the left-hand side, click on **Act** and then click the **Create a rule** option. On the **Create rule** screen, we will fill in the details as shown in the following table:

Field	Value
Name	ES_Indexer
Description	Index AWS IoT topic data to Elasticsearch service
SQL version	2016-03-23
Attribute	cast(state.desired.temp as decimal) as temp, cast(state.desired.humd as decimal) as humd, timestamp() as timestamp
Topic filter	$aws/things/Pi3-DHT11-Node/shadow/update
Condition	

2. Once we fill the form in with the information mentioned in the previous table, we should see the rule query statement as demonstrated here:

```
SELECT cast(state.desired.temp as decimal) as temp,
cast(state.desired.humd as decimal) as humd, timestamp() as
timestamp FROM '$aws/things/Pi3-DHT11-Node/shadow/update'
```

3. This query selects the temperature and humidity values from the `$aws/things/Pi3-DHT11-Node/shadow/update` topic and casts them to a decimal or float data type. Along with that, we select the timestamp.

4. Now, under **Select one or more actions**, click **Add action**, and then select **Send messages to the Amazon Elastic Service**. Click on **Configure action**.

5. On the **Configure action** screen, fill in the details as illustrated here:

Field	Value
Domain Name	`pi3-dht11-dashboard`
Endpoint	Will get auto selected
ID	`${newuuid()}`
Index	`sensor-data`
Type	`dht11`
IAM role name	`iot-rules-role`

6. Once the details mentioned in the table are filled in, click on the **Create action** button to complete the setup.
7. Finally, click on **Create rule** and a new rule should be created.

Elasticsearch configuration

Before we continue, we need to configure Elasticsearch to create a mapping. The timestamp that we generate in AWS IoT is of the type long. So, we are going to create a mapping field named `datetime` with the type `date`.

From a command line with cURL (`https://curl.haxx.se/`) present, execute the following command:

```
curl -XPUT
'https://search-pi3-dht11-dashboard-tcvfd4kqznae3or3urx52734wi.us-east-1.es
.amazonaws.com/sensor-data?pretty' -H 'Content-Type: application/json' -d'
    {
      "mappings" : {
        "dht11" : {
          "properties" : {
            "timestamp" : { "type" : "long", "copy_to": "datetime" },
            "datetime" : {"type": "date", "store": true }
          }
        }
      }
    }
    '
```

Replace the URL of Elasticsearch in the previous command as applicable. This will take care of creating a mapping when the data comes in.

Running the Thing

Now that the entire setup is done, we will start pumping data into the Elasticsearch:

1. Head back to Raspberry Pi 3, which was sending the DHT11 temperature and humidity data, and run our application. We should see the data being published to the shadow topic:

```
pi@raspberrypi: ~/Desktop/AWS-IoT-Thing                                    _ □ ×
File  Edit  Tabs  Help
pi@raspberrypi:~/Desktop/AWS-IoT-Thing $ sudo node index.js
[Pi3-DHT11-Node] >>>>>>>>>  Connecting...
[Pi3-DHT11-Node] >>>>>>>>>  Connected.
[Pi3-DHT11-Node] >>>>>>>>>  Registered.
[Pi3-DHT11-Node] >>>>>>>>>  Reading data in 15 seconds.
[Pi3-DHT11-Node] >>>>>>>>>  Sending Data.. { state: { desired: { temp: '0.00', humd: '0.00' } } }
[Pi3-DHT11-Node] >>>>>>>>>  Shadow update success.
[Pi3-DHT11-Node] >>>>>>>>>  Reading data again in 30 seconds.
received delta on Pi3-DHT11-Node: { version: 218,
  timestamp: 1517976309,
  state: { temp: '0.00', humd: '0.00' },
  metadata:
   { temp: { timestamp: 1517976309 },
     humd: { timestamp: 1517976309 } } }
received accepted on Pi3-DHT11-Node: { state: { desired: { temp: '0.00', humd: '0.00' } },
  metadata: { desired: { temp: [Object], humd: [Object] } },
  version: 218,
  timestamp: 1517976309 }
```

2. Head over to the Elasticsearch page, to the **pi3-dht11-dashboard** domain, and to the **Indices** tab, and you should see the screen illustrated here:

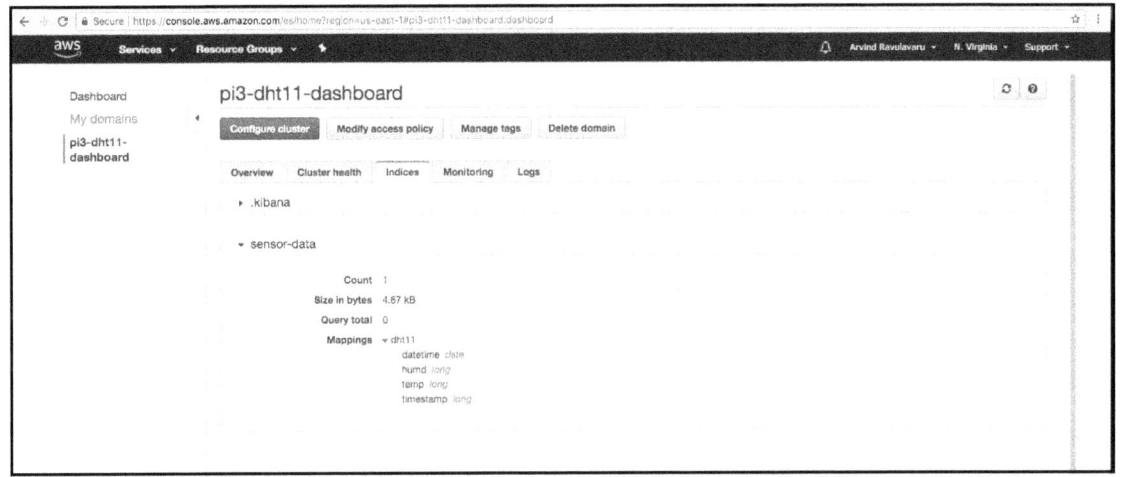

3. Next, head over to the **Kibana** dashboard. Now we will configure the **Index pattern** as shown in the following screenshot:

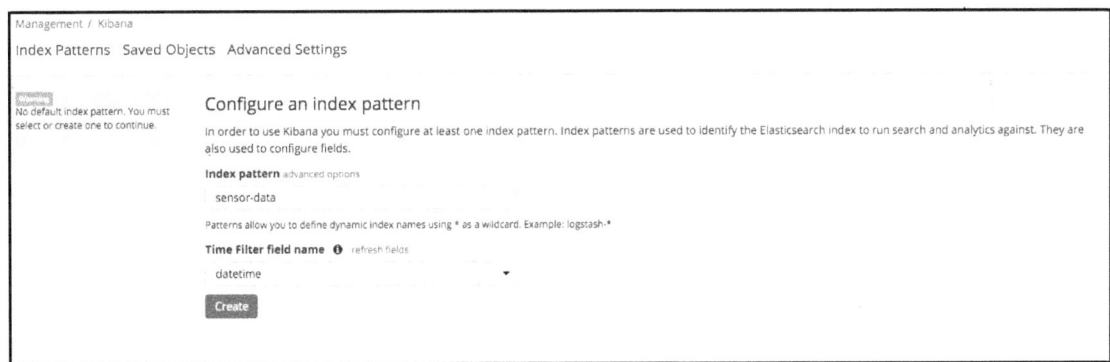

4. Do not forget to select the time filter. Click on **Create** and you should see the fields on the next screen, as shown here:

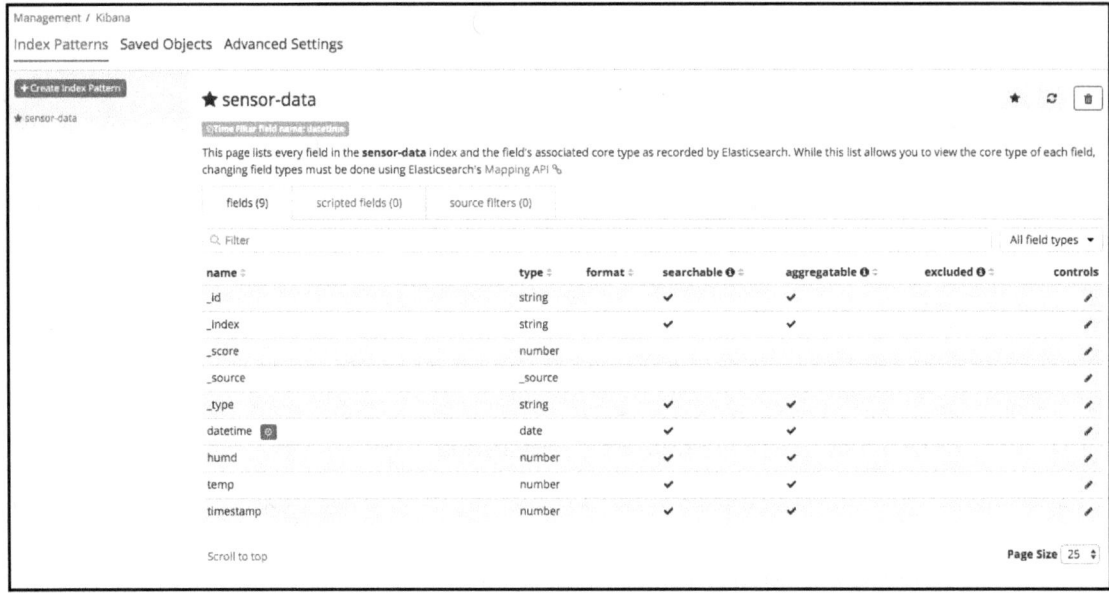

5. Now, click on the **Discover** tab on the left-hand side of the screen and you should see the data coming in, as shown in the following screenshot:

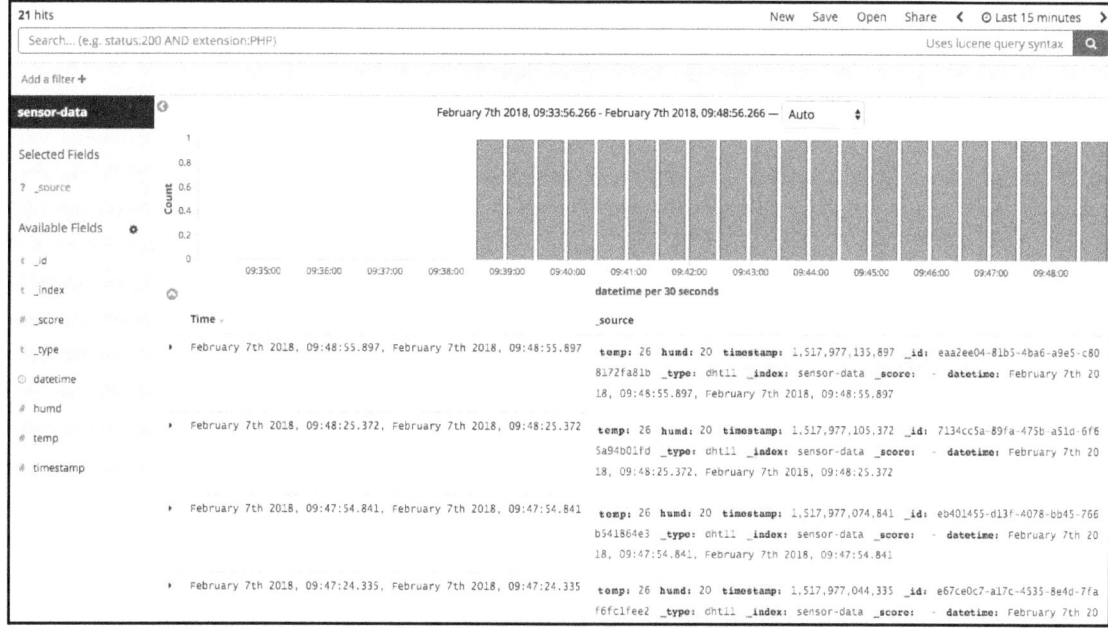

Building the Kibana dashboard

Now that we have the data coming in, we will create a new visualization and then add that to our dashboard:

1. Click on the **Visualize** link from the side menu and then click on **Create a Visualization**. Then under **Basic Charts** select **Line**.

2. On the **Choose search source** screen, select **sensor-data** index and this will take us to the graph page.

3. On the **Metrics** section in the **Data** tab, set the following as the first metric:

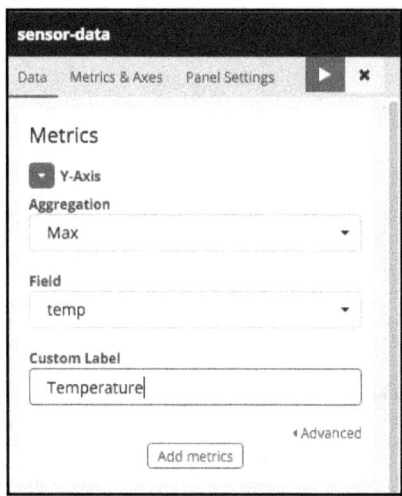

4. Click on the **Add metrics** button and set up the second one as follows:

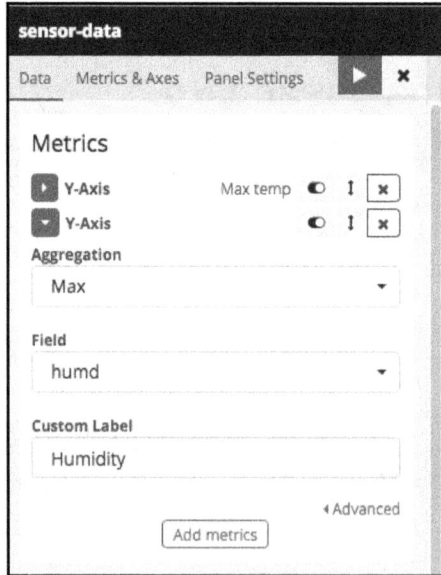

5. Now, under **Buckets**, select **X-Axis** and select the following:

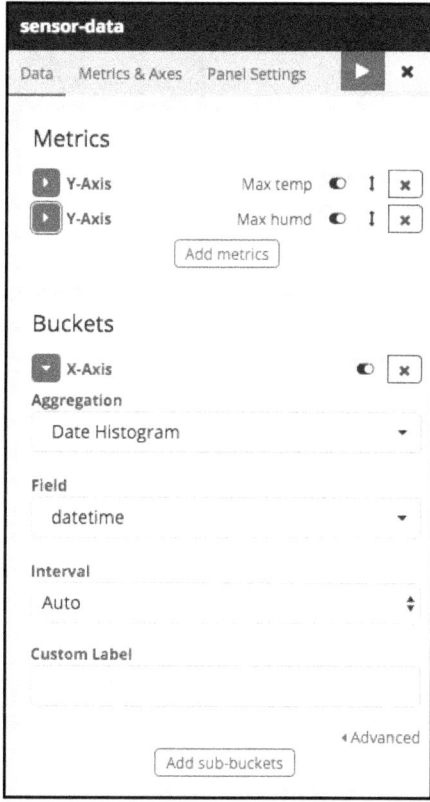

6. Click on the Play button above this panel and you should see a line chart as follows:

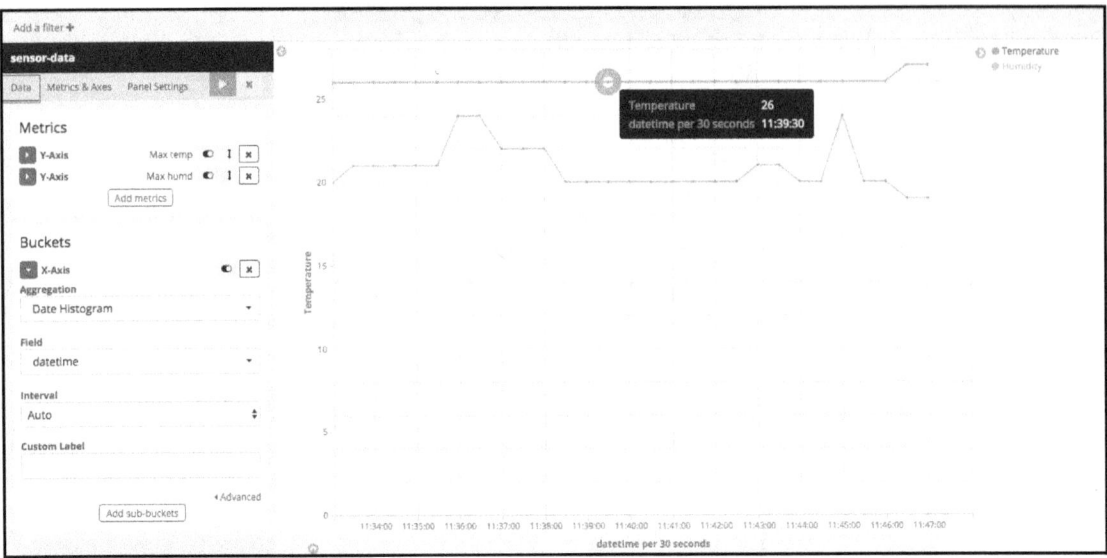

This is our temperature and humidity data over a period of time. As you can see, there are plenty of options to choose from regarding how you want to visualize the data:

1. Now, click on the **Save** option at the top of the menu on the page and name the visualization `Temperature & Humidity Visualization`.

2. Now, using the side menu, select **Dashboard** then **Create Dashboard**, click on **Add**, and select **Temperature & Humidity Visualization**.

3. Now, click on **Save** from the top-most menu on the page and name the dashboard **Pi3 DHT11 dashboard**.

Now we have our own dashboard, which show the temperature and humidity metrics:

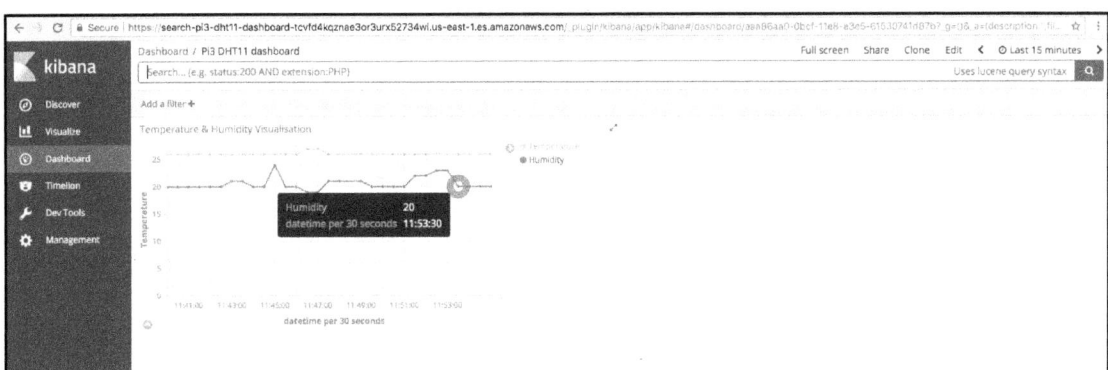

This wraps up our section on building a visualization using IoT Rule, Elasticsearch, and Kibana.

With this, we have seen the basic features and implementation process needed to work with the AWS IoT platform.

 Once you are done with your learning, DO NOT forget to delete the resources you have created. Otherwise you will be billed. You have been warned!

Summary

In this chapter, we have gone through the AWS IoT platform at a basic level. We have understood the basic components of this platform and then defined a use case that we wanted to implement with this platform.

Once we defined the use case, we went through the architecture and solution. Then, we set up our Thing, added the code needed in Raspberry Pi 3, and then subscribed to the data of the shadow topic to get data updates in real time.

Next, we set up an AWS IoT Rule that sent the incoming data to the Elasticsearch service and visualized it through Kibana. We finally set up the required infrastructure and configured our dashboard.

In the next chapter, we are going to build the same use case using the Microsoft Azure IoT platform.

Further reading

- **IoT Core:** https://aws.amazon.com/iot-core/
- **AWS IoT Device Management:**
  https://aws.amazon.com/iot-device-management/
- **AWS Greengrass:** https://aws.amazon.com/greengrass/
- **AWS IoT Analytics:** https://aws.amazon.com/iot-analytics/
- **Amazon FreeRTOS:** https://aws.amazon.com/freertos/

5
Azure IoT

In the last chapter, we saw how to work with the AWS IoT platform. We integrated an IoT Thing, which is our Raspberry Pi 3, along with a DHT11 temperature and humidity sensor. We have seen how to view the device shadow, and how to set rules and index data into the AWS Elasticsearch service. Then, using Kibana, we visualized the data in real time.

In this chapter, we are going to achieve all of these using the Azure IoT platform.

The topics covered in this chapter are as follows:

- Azure IoT architecture
- Setting up an end-to-end solution using Azure IoT
- Setting up a visualization dashboard for this solution

Azure IoT

Azure IoT offers an end-to-end suite for working with the Internet of Things. Azure IoT can help us build solutions such as remote monitoring, predictive maintenance, and connected factory, to name a few.

With Azure IoT, we can capture and analyze untapped data to improve business results.

The key IoT services are as follows:

- IoT hub
- Stream analytics
- Notification hubs
- Power BI

IoT hub

The IoT hub is analogous to the IoT middleware that we looked at in `Chapter 1,` *Introduction to IoT*. The IoT hub helps us to connect, monitor, and manage billions of IoT assets.

Some of the key features are as follows:

- Authentication per device
- Extended and comprehensive device management
- Communication with billions of IoT devices
- Device registration and provisioning
- Support of MQTT(S), AMQP, and HTTPS protocols for device-to-cloud communication

You can read more about the IoT hub here:
`https://azure.microsoft.com/en-in/services/iot-hub/.`

Stream analytics

Using simple SQL-like language, you can develop and run real-time analytics on multiple IoT or non-IoT streams of data. There is no infrastructure to manage and we can process data on demand using stream analytics.

Some of the key features are as follows:

- Analyzing data from all kinds of IoT devices
- Creating complex event processing (CEP) pipelines
- Scaling instantly
- Building real-time dashboards

You can read more about stream analytics here:
`https://azure.microsoft.com/en-in/services/stream-analytics/.`

Designing a sample application

In this section, we are going to build a sample application using the Azure IoT suite.

Solution

The solution we are going to build is going to be similar to the one from `Chapter 4`, *AWS IoT*. We are going to connect a DHT11 sensor to Raspberry Pi 3, transmit the data over to the Azure IoT hub using MQTTS, then take that data and pass it onto Power BI to build the visualization.

In the next section, we are going to look at the overall architecture of the solution.

Architecture

The following diagram explains the architecture of the IoT solution:

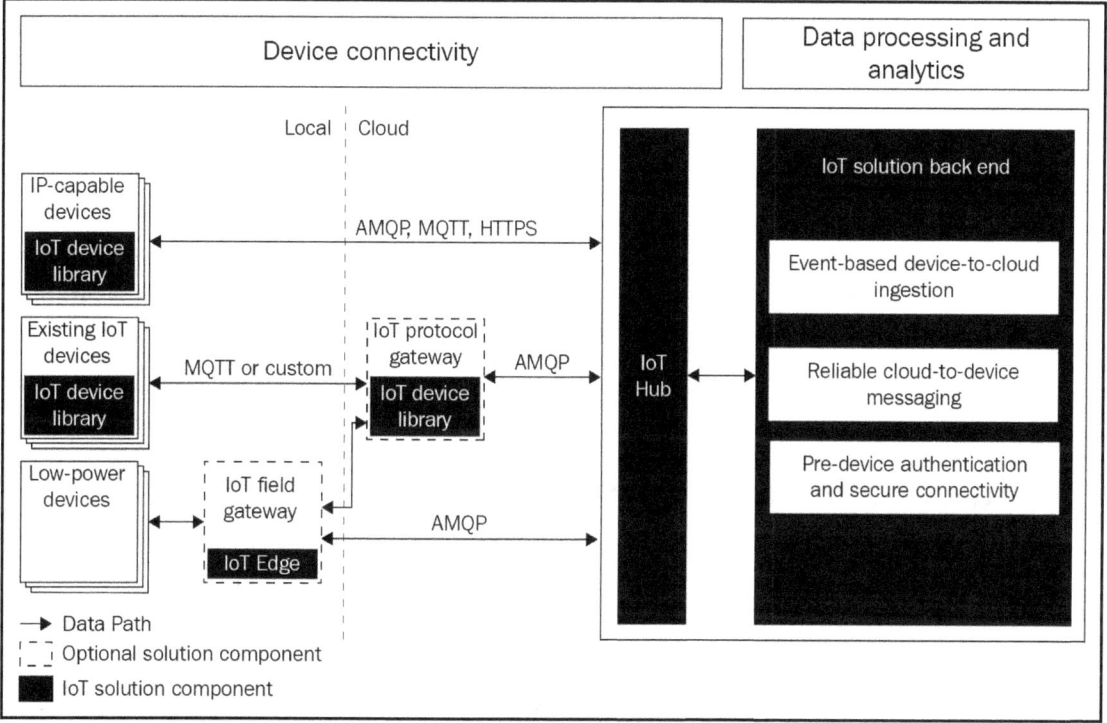

As illustrated in the previous diagram, a typical IoT solution consists of three main pieces:

- Device connectivity
- Data processing and analytics
- Presentation

In our implementation of the Azure IoT suite, we are going to work with all three. We are going to use existing IoT devices, such as a Raspberry Pi 3 with a DHT11 sensor, and then connect it to the IoT hub or, as illustrated in the previous diagram, the **IoT device gateway**.

Then, using the concept of **device twin**, we are going to persist the configuration and data. A device twin in Azure IoT is quite similar to a shadow device in AWS IoT. This block falls under the IoT solution backend.

The IoT solution backend consists of the following:

- Provisioning API
- App backend
- Storage
- Analytics and machine learning
- Solutions UX
- Business intelligence
- Presentation and business connectivity, which includes mobile apps, web apps, desktop apps, and business systems.

In our setup, we are going to follow the steps mentioned in the following sections.

End-to-end communication

Firstly, set up the device and publish the data to Azure IoT, as follows:

1. Create an Azure account, then create an Azure IoT hub
2. Set up the Raspberry Pi 3 and the DHT11 sensor
3. Set up the Azure IoT client on the Raspberry Pi 3
4. Start reading the sensor data, publish it to the device twin, and send the data event to the IoT hub
5. Subscribe to the data events from another client and visualize the data

Data visualization

We are going to use Power BI and stream analytics to build the dashboard. The steps we are going to follow are these:

1. Create a new Power BI account, then set up a new consumer group for events (built-in endpoint).
2. Create a stream analytics job. Set up input and outputs.
3. Build the query to stream data from the Azure IoT hub to Power BI.
4. Visualize the datasets in Power BI and build a dashboard.

Pricing

Do check out the pricing before you start experimenting with Azure IoT. You can find more information here: `https://azure.microsoft.com/en-in/pricing/details/iot-hub/`.

Building a sample application

We will start off by implementing the end-to-end solution, where we take the data from a DHT11 sensor and post it to the Azure IoT hub.

End-to-end communication

To get started with Azure IoT, we need to have an Azure account. If you do not have an Azure account, you can create one by navigating to this URL: `https://azure.microsoft.com/en-in/free/`.

Once you have created your account, you can log in and navigate to the Azure portal or you can visit `https://portal.azure.com` to reach the required page.

Setting up the IoT hub

The following are the steps required for the setup. Once we are on the portal dashboard, we will be presented with the dashboard home page as illustrated here:

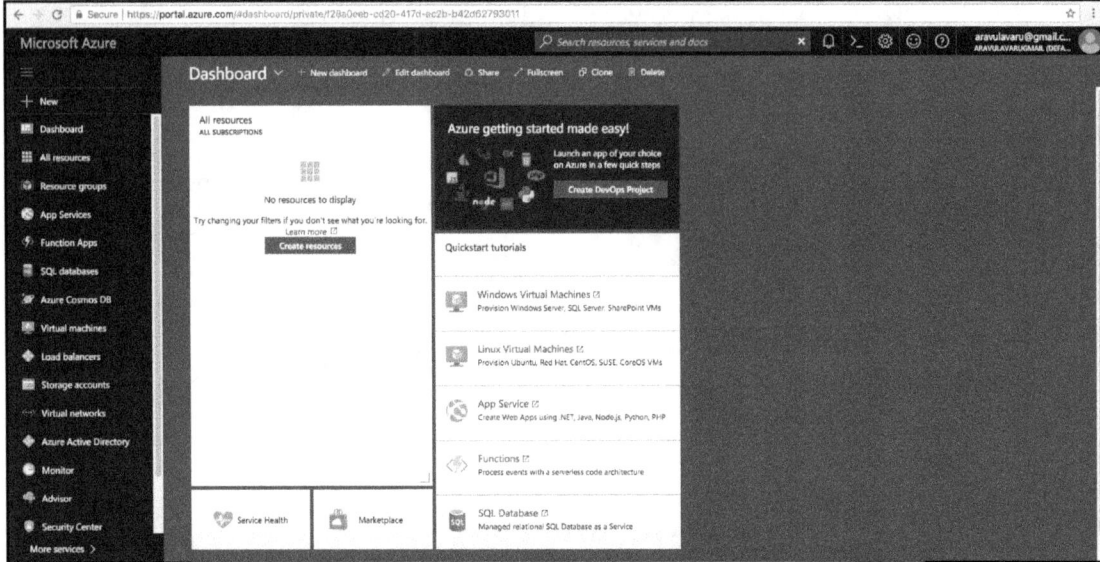

1. Click on **+New** from the top-left-hand-side menu, then, from the **Azure Marketplace**, select **Internet of Things | IoT Hub**, as depicted in the following screenshot:

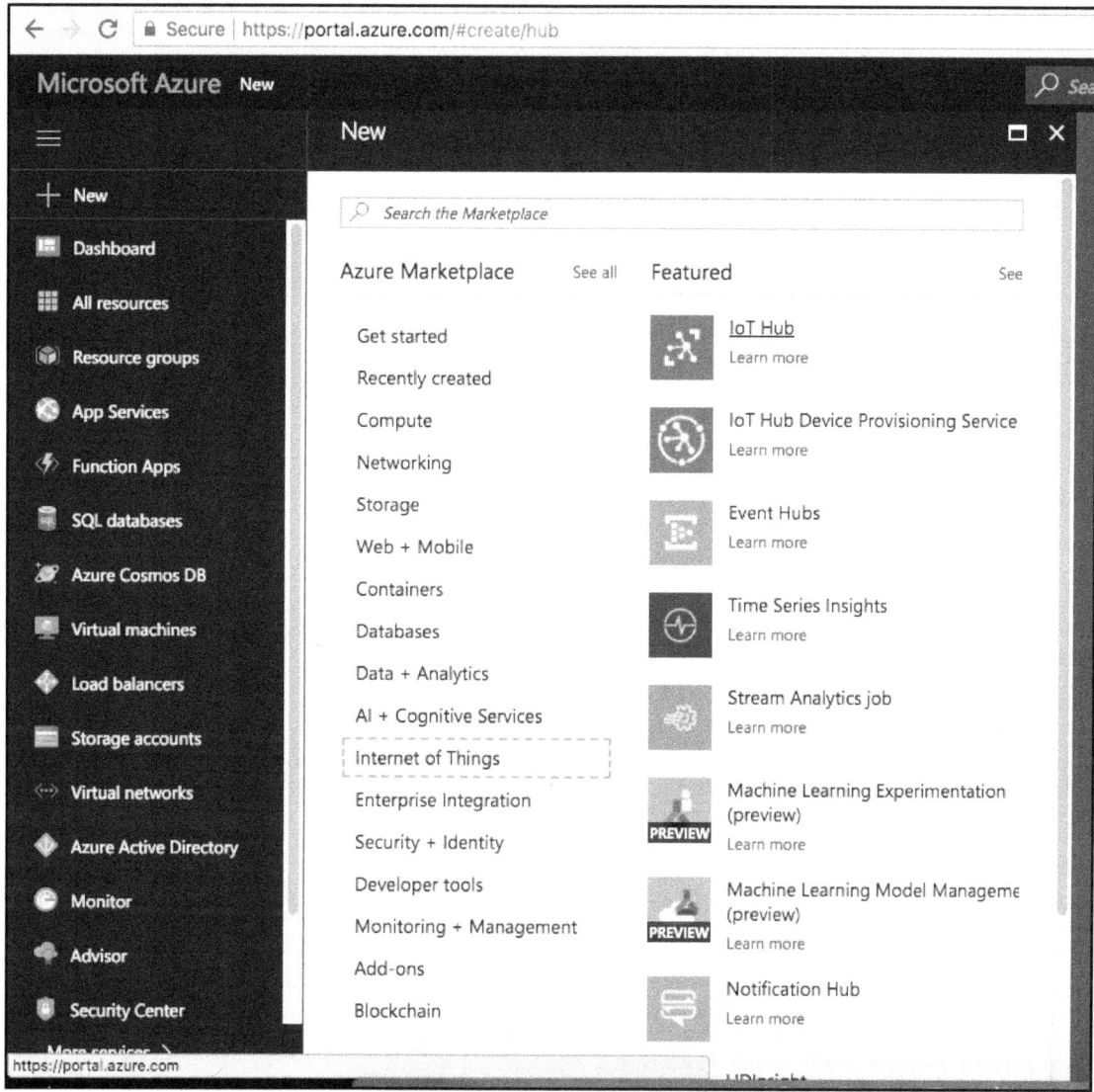

2. Fill in the **IoT hub** form to create a new IoT hub, as illustrated here:

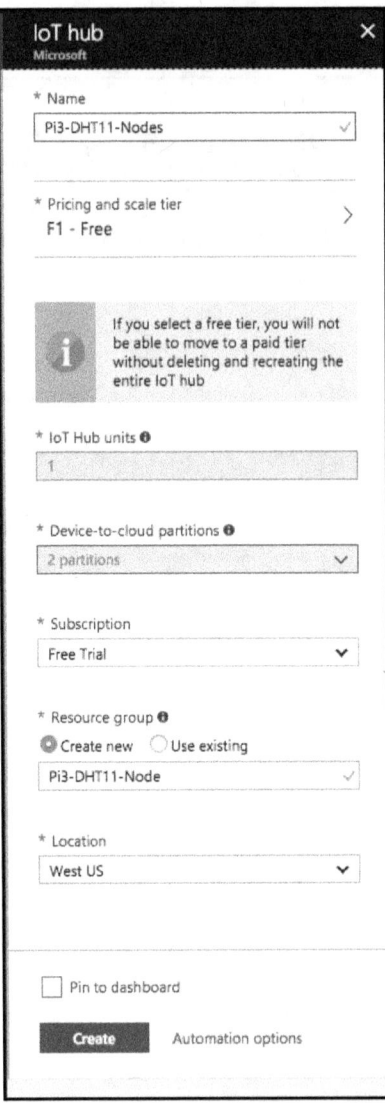

I have selected **F1-Free** for the pricing and selected **Free Trial** as a
Subscription, and, under **Resource group**, I have selected **Create new** and
named it Pi3-DHT11-Node.

3. Now, click on the **Create** button. It will take a few minutes for the IoT hub to be
   provisioned. You can keep an eye on the notifications to see the status.
4. If everything goes well, on your dashboard, under the **All resources** tile, you
   should see the newly created IoT hub. Click on it and you will be taken to your
   IoT hub page.
5. From the hub page, click on **IoT Devices** under the **EXPLORERS** section and you
   should see something similar to what is shown in the following screenshot:

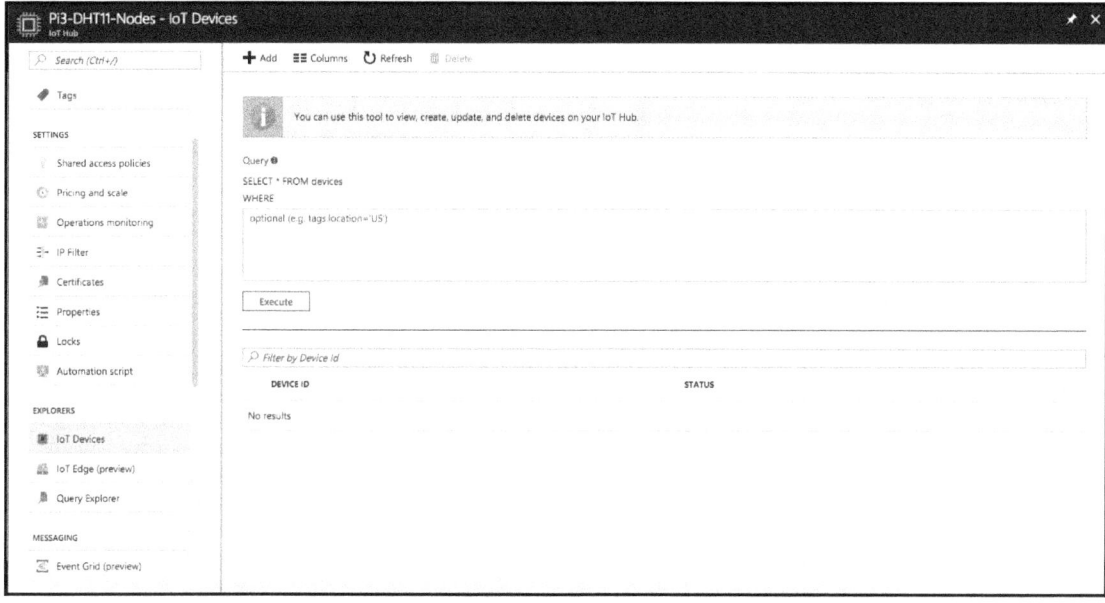

As you can see, there are no devices. Using the +Add button at the top, create a
new device.

6. Now, in the **Add Device** section, fill in the details as illustrated here:

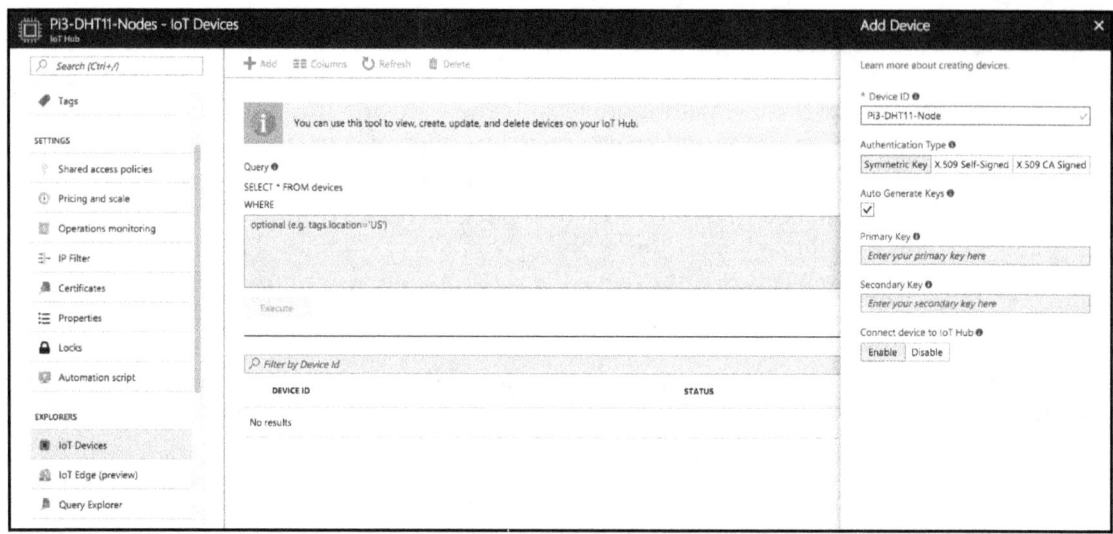

 Make sure the device is enabled; else you will not be able to connect using this device ID.

7. Once the device is created, you can click on it to see the information shown in the following screenshot:

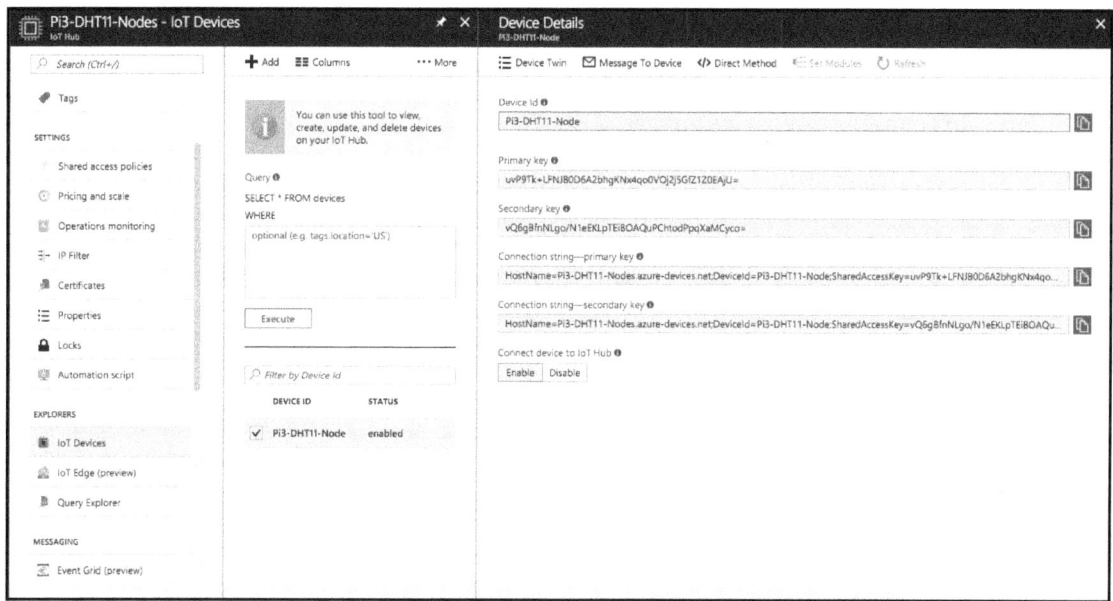

Do note the **Connection string-primary key** field. We will get back to this in our next section.

Setting up Raspberry Pi on the DHT11 node

Now that we have our device set up in Azure IoT, we are going to complete the remaining operations on the Raspberry Pi 3 to send data.

Things needed

The things required to set up the Raspberry Pi DHT11 node are as follows:

- **One Raspberry Pi 3**:
  https://www.amazon.com/Raspberry-Pi-Desktop-Starter-White/dp/B01CI5872
  2
- **One breadboard**:
  https://www.amazon.com/Solderless-Breadboard-Circuit-Circboard-Prototy
  ping/dp/B01DDI54II/

- **One DHT11 sensor**:
  `https://www.amazon.com/HiLetgo-Temperature-Humidity-Arduino-Raspberry/`
  `dp/B01DKC2GQ0`
- **Three male-to-female jumper cables**:
  `https://www.amazon.com/RGBZONE-120pcs-Multicolored-Dupont-Breadboard/d`
  `p/B01M1IEUAF/`

 If you are new to the world of Raspberry Pi GPIO's interfacing, take a look at *Raspberry Pi GPIO Tutorial: The Basics Explained* video tutorial on YouTube: `https://www.youtube.com/watch?v=6PuK9fh3aL8`.

The steps for setting up the smart device are as follows:

1. Connect the DHT11 sensor to the Raspberry Pi 3 as shown in the following schematic:

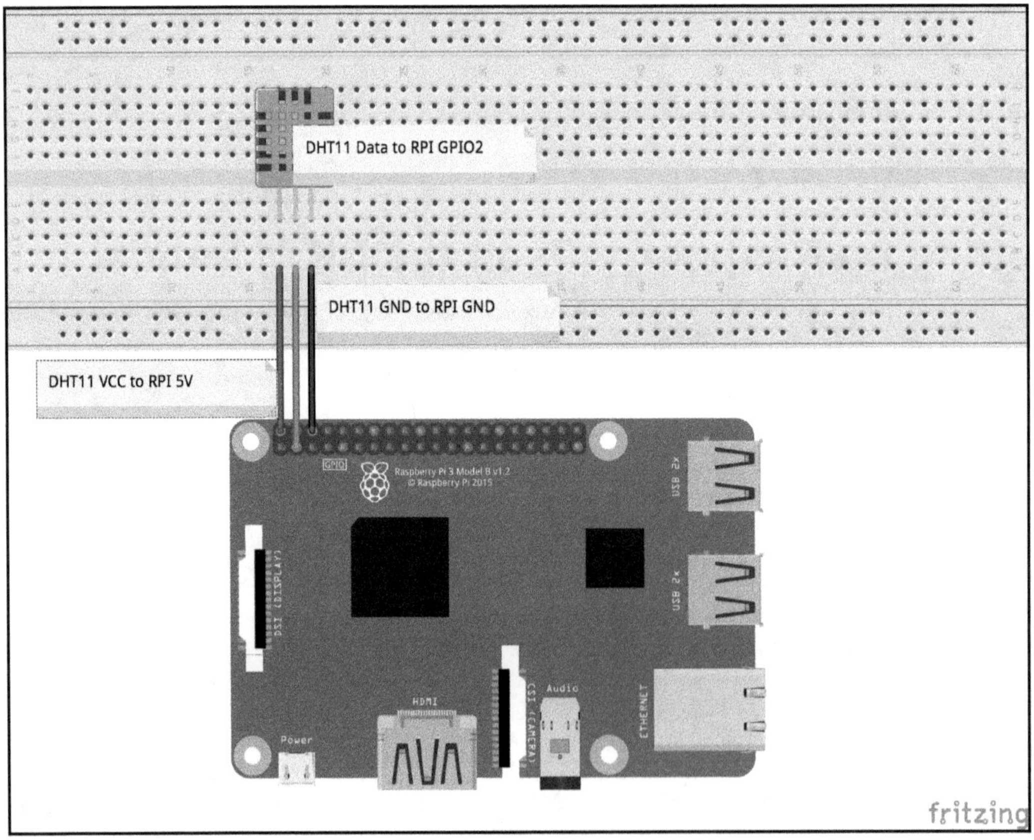

2. Next, power up the Raspberry Pi 3 and log into it.

3. On the desktop, create a new folder named `Azure-IoT-Device`. Open a new Terminal and `cd` into this newly created folder.

Setting up Node.js

Assuming that this is the same Raspberry Pi 3 board that was used in `Chapter 4`, *AWS IoT*, it should have Node.js installed. If Node.js is not installed, please refer to the following steps:

1. Open a new Terminal and run the following commands:

   ```
   $ sudo apt update
   $ sudo apt full-upgrade
   ```

2. This will upgrade all the packages that need upgrades. Next, we will install the latest version of Node.js. We will be using the Node 7.x version:

   ```
   $ curl -sL https://deb.nodesource.com/setup_7.x | sudo -Ebash-
   $ sudo apt install nodejs
   ```

3. This will take a moment to install, and, once your installation is done, you should be able to run the following commands to see the versions of Node.js and NPM:

   ```
   $ node -v
   $ npm -v
   ```

Developing the Node.js device app

Now we will set up the app and write the required code:

1. From the Terminal, once you are inside the `Azure-IoT-Device` folder, run the following command:

   ```
   $ npm init -y
   ```

2. Next, we will install `azure-iot-device-mqtt` from NPM (`https://www.npmjs.com/package/azure-iot-device-mqtt`). This module has the required client code to interface with Azure IoT.

Along with this, we are going to install the `azure-iot-device`
(`https://www.npmjs.com/package/azure-iot-device`) and `async` modules
(`https://www.npmjs.com/package/async`). Execute the following command:

```
$ npm install azure-iot-device-mqtt azure-iot-device async --save
```

3. Next, we will install `rpi-dht-sensor` from NPM
   (`https://www.npmjs.com/package/rpi-dht-sensor`). This module will help to
   read the DHT11 temperature and humidity values. Run the following command:

```
$ npm install rpi-dht-sensor --save
```

4. Your final `package.json` file should look like this:

```json
{
  "name":"Azure-IoT-Device",
  "version":"1.0.0",
  "description":"",
  "main":"index.js",
  "scripts":{
    "test":"echo"Error:notestspecified"&&exit1"
  },
  "keywords":[],
  "author":"",
  "license":"ISC",
  "dependencies":{
    "async":"^2.6.0",
    "azure-iot-device-mqtt":"^1.3.1",
    "rpi-dht-sensor":"^0.1.1"
  }
}
```

5. Now that we have the required dependencies installed, let's continue. Create a
   new file named `index.js` at the root of the `Azure-IoT-Device` folder. Your
   final folder structure should look similar to the following screenshot:

6. Open `index.js` in any text editor and update it as illustrated in the code snippet that can be found here: `https://github.com/PacktPublishing/Enterprise-Internet-of-Things-Handbook`.

7. In the previous code, we are creating a new MQTTS client from the `connectionString`. You can get the value of this connection string from **IoT Hub | IoT Devices | Pi3-DHT11-Node | Device Details | Connection string-primary key** as shown in the following screenshot:

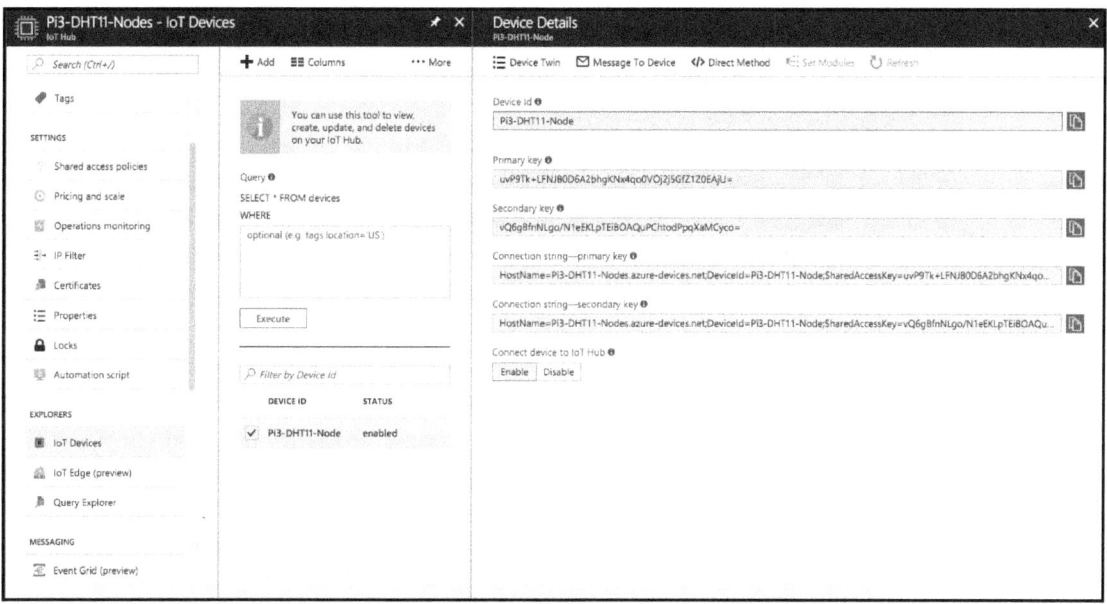

8. Update the `connectionString` in our code with the previous values. Going back to the code, we are using `client.open(connectCallback)` to connect to the Azure MQTT broker for our IoT hub, and, once the connection has been made successfully, we call the `connectCallback()`. In the `connectCallback()`, we get the device twin using `client.getTwin()`. Once we have gotten the device twin, we will start collecting the data, send this data to other clients listening to this device using `client.sendEvent()`, and then send the copy to the device twin using `twin.properties.reported.update`, so any new client that joins gets the latest saved data.

9. Now, save the file and run the `sudo node index.js` command. We should see the command output in the console of Raspberry Pi 3:

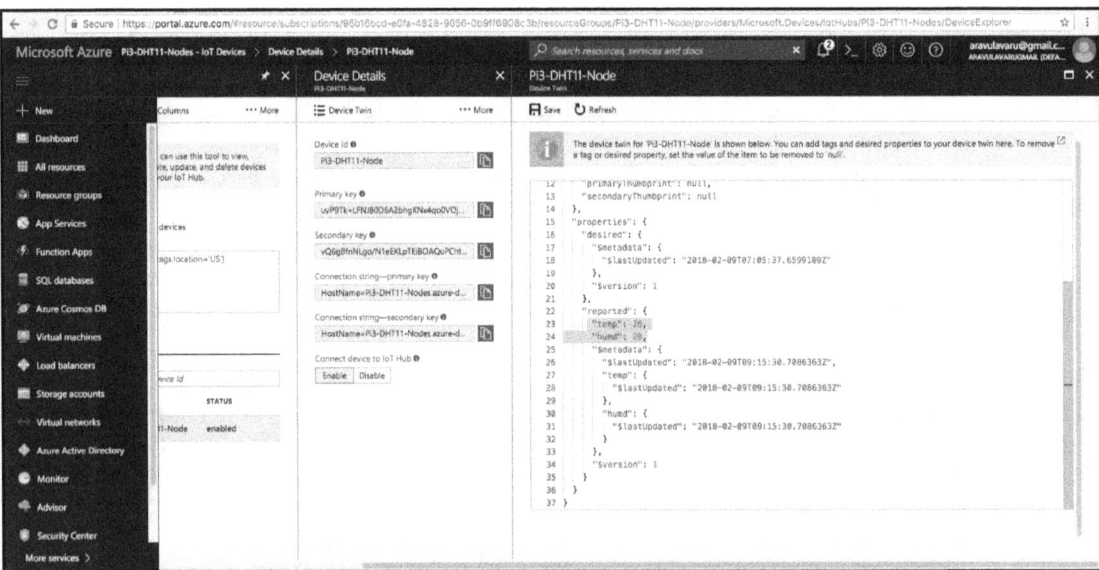

The device has successfully connected, and we are sending the data to both the device twin and the MQTT event.

Now, if we head back to the Azure IoT portal, navigate to **IoT Hub | IoT Device | Pi3-DHT11-Node | Device Details** and click on the device twin, we should see the last data record that was sent by the Raspberry Pi 3, as shown in the following image:

Now that we are able to send the data from the device, let's read this data from another MQTT client.

Reading the data from the IoT Thing

To read the data from the device, you can either use the same Raspberry Pi 3 or another computer. I am going to use my MacBook as a client that is interested in the data sent by the device:

1. Create a folder named `test_client`. Inside the `test_client` folder, run the following command:

   ```
   $ npm init --yes
   ```

2. Next, install the `azure-event-hubs` module (`https://www.npmjs.com/package/azure-event-hubs`) using the following command:

   ```
   $ npm install azure-event-hubs --save
   ```

3. Create a file named `index.js` inside the `test_client` folder and update it as detailed in the following code snippet:

   ```
   var EventHubClient = require('azure-event-hubs').Client;
   var connectionString = 'HostName=Pi3-DHT11-Nodes.azure-
   devices.net;SharedAccessKeyName=iothubowner;SharedAccessKey=J0MTJVy
   +RFkSaaenfegGMJY3XWKIpZp2HO4eTwmUNoU=';
   constTAG = '[TESTDEVICE]>>>>>>>>>';
   var printError = function(err) {
     console.log(TAG, err);
   };
   var printMessage = function(message) {
     console.log(TAG, 'Messagereceived:',
   JSON.stringify(message.body));
   };
   var client = EventHubClient.fromConnectionString(connectionString);
   client.open()
     .then(client.getPartitionIds.bind(client))
     .then(function(partitionIds) {
     returnpartitionIds.map(function(partitionId) {
       returnclient.createReceiver('$Default', partitionId, {
   'startAfterTime': Date.now() })
       .then(function(receiver) {
         //console.log(TAG, 'Createdpartitionreceiver:'|partitionId)
         console.log(TAG, 'Listening...');
   ```

```
        receiver.on('errorReceived', printError);
        receiver.on('message', printMessage);
      });
    });
  })
  .catch(printError);
```

4. In the previous code snippet, we have a `connectionString` variable. To get the value of this variable, head back to the Azure portal, via **IoT Hub | Shared access policies | iothubowner | Connection string-primary key** as illustrated in the following screenshot:

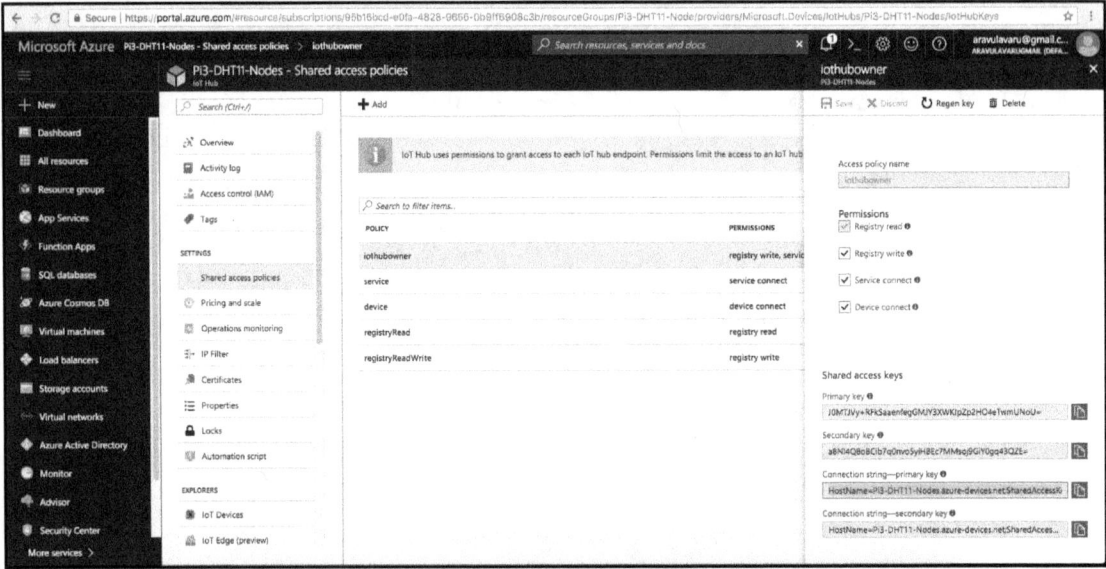

5. Copy the value from the **Connection string-primary key** field and update the code. Finally, run the following command:

```
$ node index.js
```

The following console screenshot shows the command's output:

```
● ● ●            test_client — node index.js — node index.js — 80×24
                              node                         node index.js    +
→  test_client node index.js                                             ]
[TEST DEVICE] >>>>>>>>>  Listening...
[TEST DEVICE] >>>>>>>>>  Listening...
[TEST DEVICE] >>>>>>>>>  Message received:  {"temp":26,"humd":20}
[TEST DEVICE] >>>>>>>>>  Message received:  {"temp":26,"humd":20}
[TEST DEVICE] >>>>>>>>>  Message received:  {"temp":26,"humd":20}
```

This way, any client that is interested in the data from this device can use this approach to get the latest data.

You can also use an MQTT library on the client side to do the same, but do keep in mind that this is not advisable as the connection string is exposed. Instead, you can have a backend micro service that can achieve the same for you and then expose the data via HTTPS.

With this, we conclude the section on posting data to Azure IoT and fetching that data. In the next section, we are going to work with building a dashboard for our data.

Building a dashboard

Now that we have seen how a client can read data from our device on demand, we will move to building a dashboard on which we will show data in real time.

For this, we are going to use an Azure stream analytics job and Power BI.

Azure stream analytics

Azure stream analytics is a managed event-processing engine set up with real-time analytic computations on streaming data. It can gather data coming from various sources, collate it, and stream it into a different source. Using stream analytics, we can examine high volumes of data streamed from devices, extract information from that data stream, and identify patterns, trends, and relationships.

You can read more about Azure stream analytics here:
`https://docs.microsoft.com/en-us/azure/stream-analytics/stream-analytics-introd`
`uction`.

Power BI

Power BI is a suite of business-analytics tools used to analyze data and share insights. A Power BI dashboard updates in real time and provides a single interface for exploring all the important metrics. With one click, users can explore the data behind their dashboard using intuitive tools that make finding answers easy.

Creating dashboards and accessing them across various sources is also quite easy.

You can read more about Power BI here:
`https://powerbi.microsoft.com/en-us/what-is-power-bi/`.

As we have seen in the architecture section, we are going to follow the steps given in the next section to create a dashboard in Power BI.

Execution steps

These are the steps that need to be followed:

1. Create a new Power BI account. Set up a new consumer group for events (built-in endpoint).
2. Create a stream analytics job. Set up input and outputs.
3. Build the query to stream data from the Azure IoT hub to Power BI.
4. Visualize the datasets in Power BI and build a dashboard.

So let's get started.

Signing up to Power BI

Navigate to the Power BI sign-in page (`https://powerbi.microsoft.com/en-us/landing/signin/`), and use the **Sign up free** option and get started today form on this page to create an account. Once an account has been created, validate the account.

Log in to Power BI with your credentials and you will land on your default workspace.

 At the time of writing, Power BI needs an official email to create an account.

Setting up events

Now that we have created a new Power BI, let's set up the remaining pieces:

1. Head back to `https://portal.azure.com` and navigate to the IoT hub we have created. From the side menu inside the IoT hub page, select **Endpoints** then **Events** under the **Built-in endpoints** section.

2. When the form opens, under the **Consumer groups** section, create a new consumer group with the name, `pi3-dht11-stream`, as illustrated, and then click on the **Save** button to save the changes:

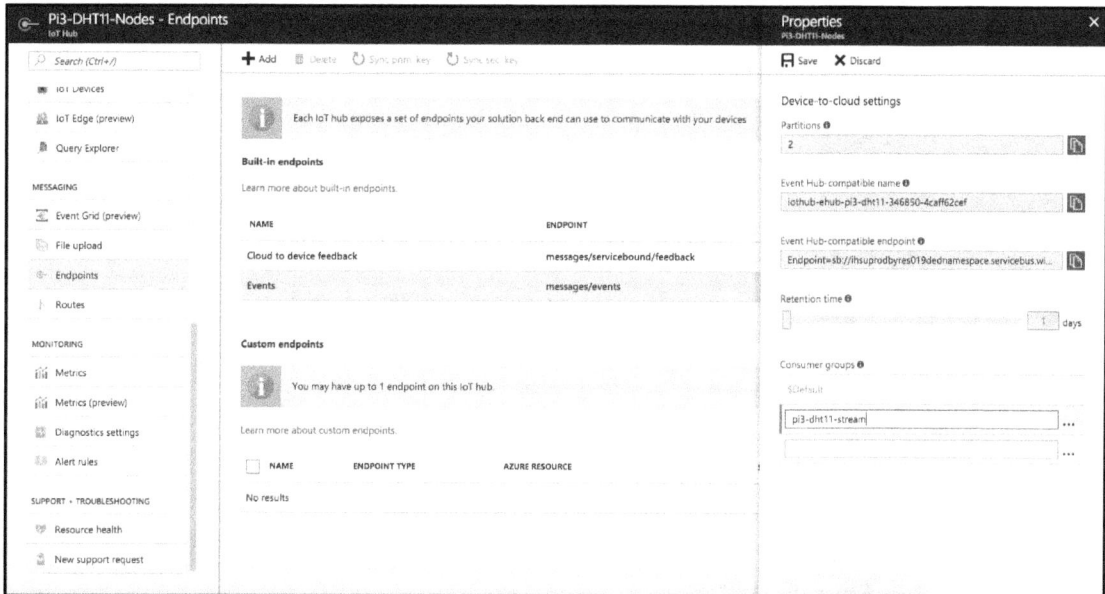

Next, we will create a new stream analytics job.

Creating a stream analytics job

Let's see how to create a stream analytics job by following these steps:

1. Now that the IoT hub setup is done, head back to the dashboard. From the top-left menu, click on **+New**, then **Internet of Things** and **Stream Analytics job**, as shown in the following screenshot:

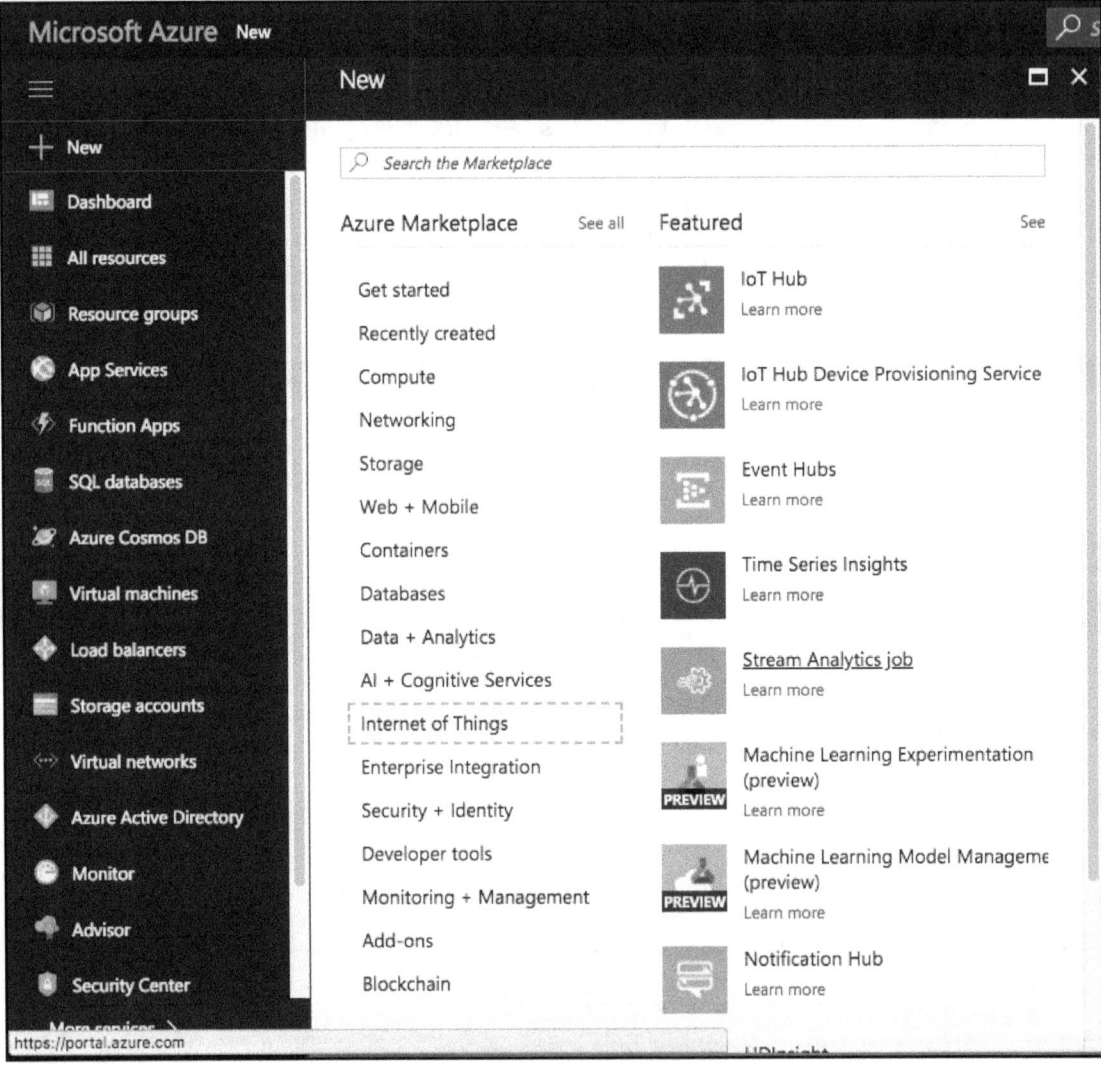

2. Fill in the **New Stream Analytics job** form, as illustrated here:

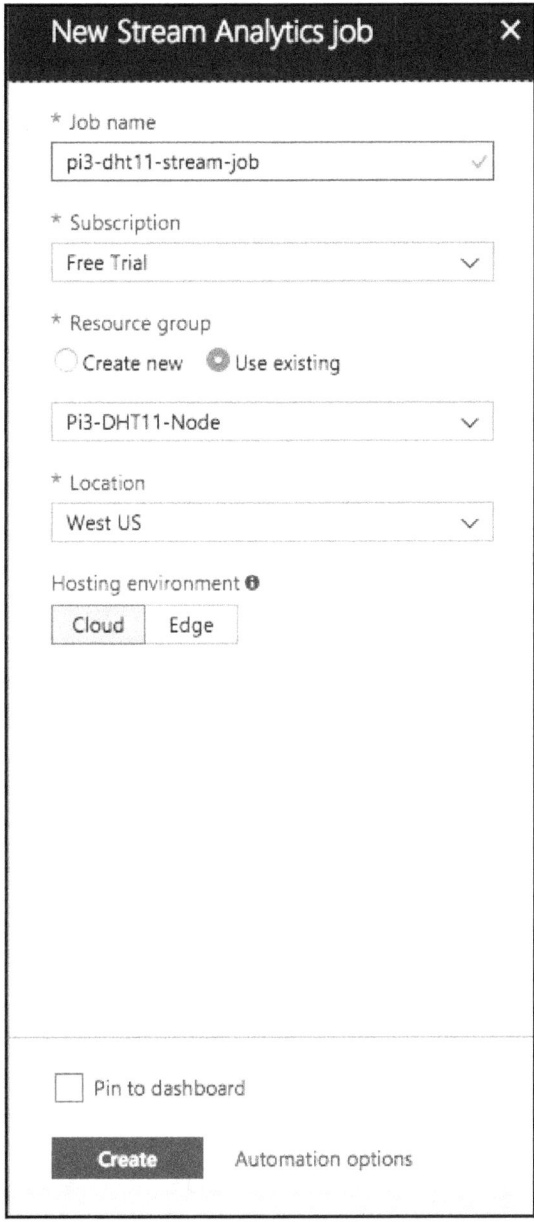

3. Then click on the **Create** button. It will take a couple of minutes to create a new job. Do keep an eye on the notification section for any updates.

4. Once the job has been created, it will appear on your dashboard. Select the job that was created and navigate to the **Inputs** section under **JOB TOPOLOGY**, as shown here:

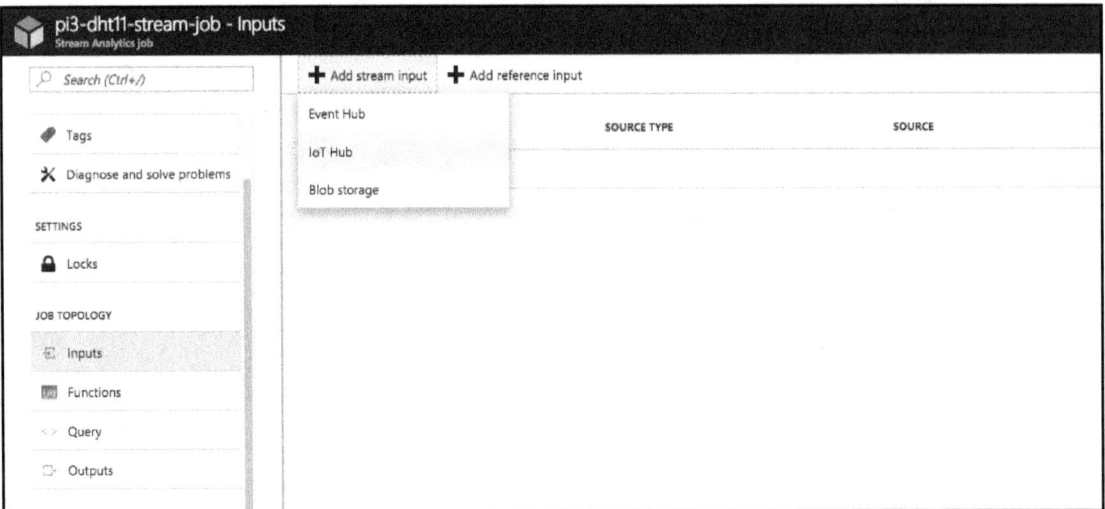

5. Click on **+Add stream input** and select **IoT Hub**, as shown in the previous screenshot.

6. Give the name `pi3dht11iothub` to the input alias, and click on **Save**.

7. Next, navigate to the **Outputs** section under **JOB TOPOLOGY**, as shown in the following screenshot:

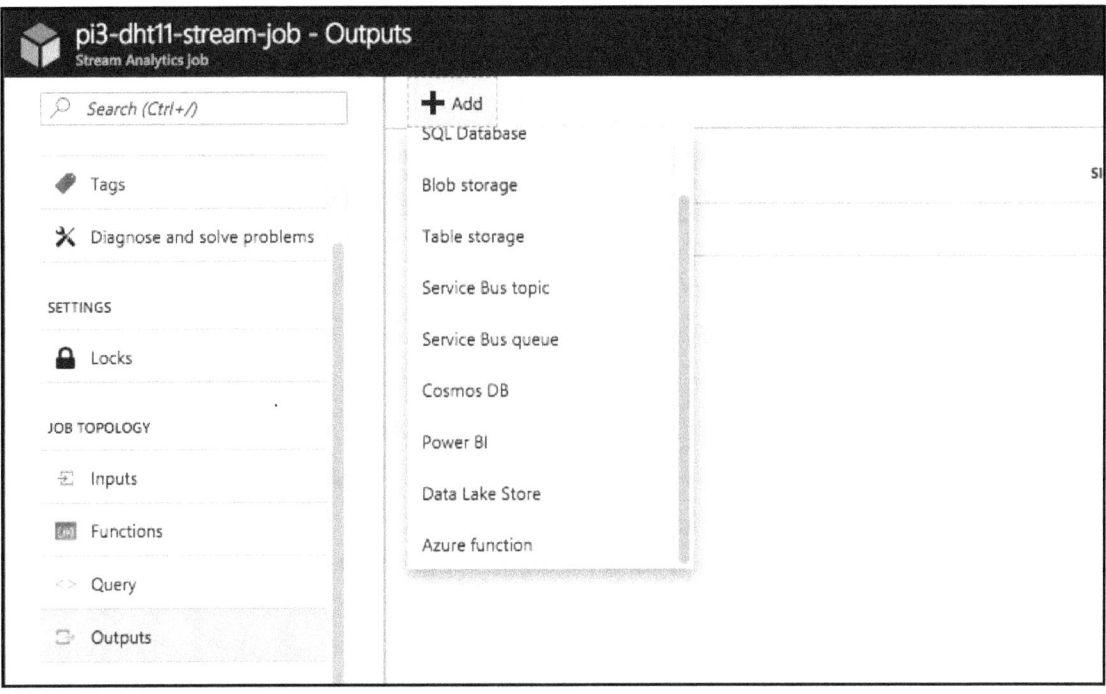

8. Click **+Add** and select **Power BI**, as shown in the previous screenshot. Fill in the details given in the following table:

Field	Value
Output alias	powerbi
Group workspace	**My workspace** (after completing the authorization step)
Dataset name	pi3dht11
Table name	dht11

9. Click the **Authorize** button to authorize the IoT hub to create the table and datasets, as well as to stream data. The final form before creation should look similar to this:

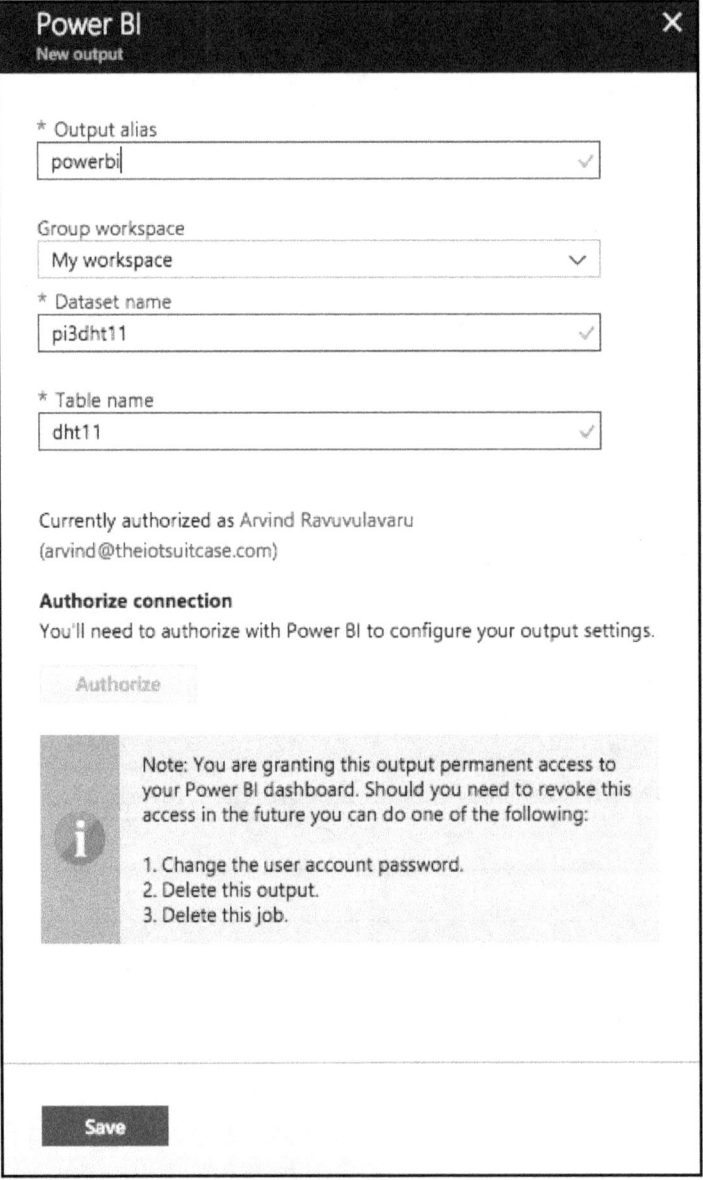

10. Click on **Save**. Next, click on **Query** under **JOB TOPOLOGY** and update it as depicted in the following screenshot:

11. Now, click on the **Save** button. Next, head over to the **Overview** section, click on **Start**, select **Now**, and then click on **Start**:

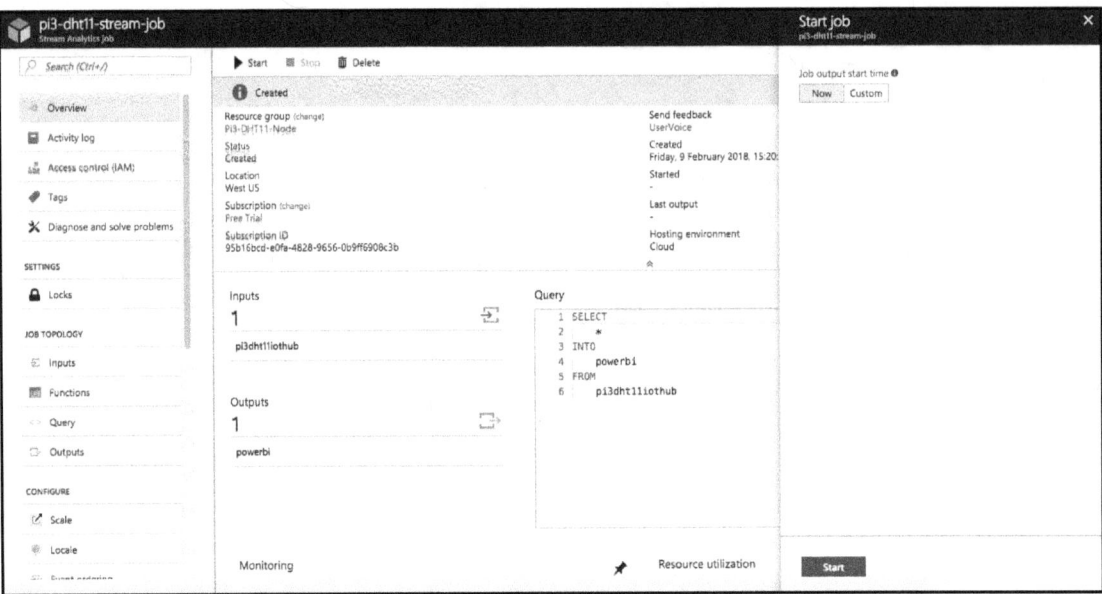

Once the job starts successfully, you should see the **Status** of **Running** instead of **Starting**.

Running the device

Now that the entire setup is done, we will start pumping data into the Power BI.

Head back to the Raspberry Pi 3 that was sending the DHT11 temperature and humidity data, and run our application.

We should see the data being published to the IoT hub as the `Data Sent` log gets printed:

```
pi@raspberrypi: ~/Desktop/Azure-IoT-Device                    _  □  ✕

File  Edit  Tabs  Help

pi@raspberrypi:~/Desktop/Azure-IoT-Device $ sudo node index.js
[Pi3-DHT11-Node] >>>>>>>>>  Client connected
[Pi3-DHT11-Node] >>>>>>>>>  Twin created
[Pi3-DHT11-Node] >>>>>>>>>  Twin Updated
[Pi3-DHT11-Node] >>>>>>>>>  Data Sent
[Pi3-DHT11-Node] >>>>>>>>>  Waiting for 30 seconds
[Pi3-DHT11-Node] >>>>>>>>>  Data Sent
[Pi3-DHT11-Node] >>>>>>>>>  Twin Updated
[Pi3-DHT11-Node] >>>>>>>>>  Waiting for 30 seconds
```

Building the visualization

Now that the data is being pumped to Power BI via the Azure IoT hub and stream analytics, we will start building the dashboard:

1. Log in to **Power BI**, navigate to the **My Workspace** that we selected when we created the **Output** in the **Stream Analytics job**, and select **Datasets**. We should see something similar to the screenshot illustrated here:

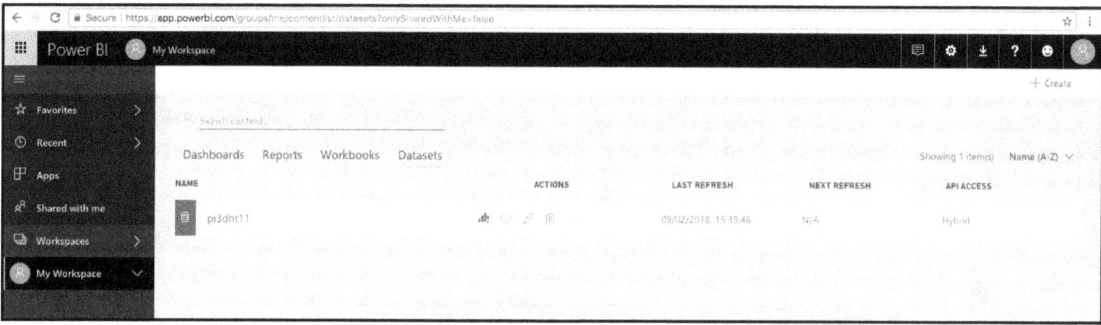

2. Using the first icon under the **ACTIONS** column, for the `pi3dht11` dataset, create a new report.

3. When you are in the report page, under **VISUALIZATIONS**, select line chart, drag **EventEnqueuedUtcTime** to the **Axis** field, and set the **temp** and **humd** fields to the values as shown in the following screenshot:

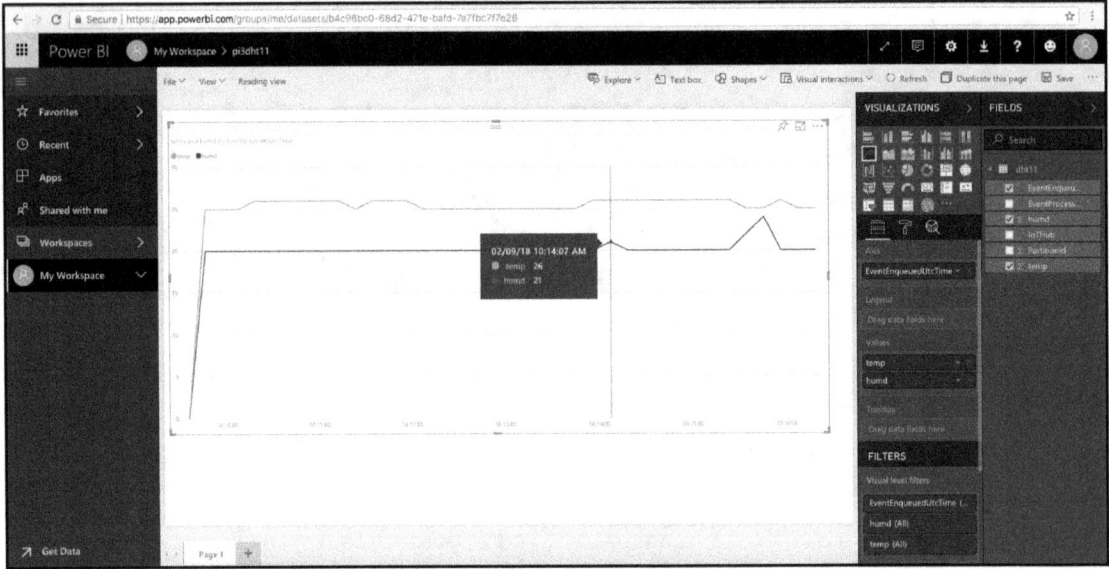

4. You can also see the graph data in real time. You can save this report for future reference.

This wraps up our section on building a visualization using Azure IoT hub, a stream analytics job, and Power BI.

With this, we have seen the basic features and implementation process for working with the Azure IoT platform.

Once you have completed your learning, DO NOT forget to delete the resources you have created. Otherwise you will be billed. You have been warned!

Summary

In this chapter, we have seen how to work with Azure IoT hub. We have created an IoT hub and set up a device. Also, we have written a Node.js client that runs on a Raspberry Pi 3, which sends the temperature and humidity data from a DHT11 sensor. We next set up a client that receives this data in real time.

After that, we set up Power BI and a stream analytics job to send data from the IoT hub to Power BI, and, in Power BI, we built a dashboard to visualize the data.

In the next chapter, we are going to work with the Google IoT platform.

6
Google Cloud IoT

In the previous chapter, we looked at how to build an end-to-end IoT solution using Raspberry Pi 3, a DHT11 temperature and humidity sensor, and the Azure IoT platform. In this chapter, we are going to implement this using Google IoT. Along with that, we are going to work on building a dashboard using Google Data Studio and BigQuery.

The topics covered in this chapter are:

- Google IoT architecture
- Setting up an end-to-end solution using Google IoT and Google Pub/Sub
- Setting up a visualization dashboard for the solution using Google Cloud Functions and Google Data Studio

Google Cloud IoT

Google Cloud Platform (**GCP**) is one of the most popular cloud platforms for building and hosting our own cloud applications. GCP provides services including computing, data storage, data analytics, and machine learning, among other things.

One of the new services of GCP is **Google Cloud IoT Core** (**GCIC**), which is still in beta at the time of writing.

GCIC is a fully managed service to easily and securely connect, manage, and ingest data from globally dispersed devices.

One of the key differentiators of GCIC compared to other platforms is how the IoT stack is completed decoupled. GCIC only consists of device management and publishing data to a topic. The Pub/Sub service takes over the remaining communication, unlike in AWS or Azure, where the IoT has everything baked into one service.

A quick overview of how the GCIC is structured is illustrated in the following diagram:

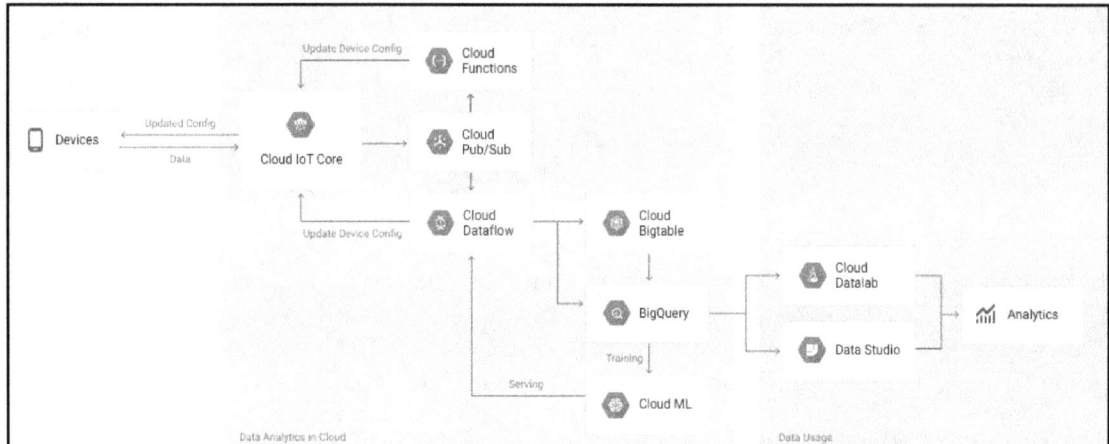

Source: https://cloud.google.com/iot-core/ and https://cloud.google.com/iot-core/images/benefits-diagram.png

On the left of the diagram, there are **Devices** that are out in the wilderness. These devices use the MQTTS protocol to connect and communicate with the GCIC. From there, the data can be sent to **Cloud Functions** or **Cloud Dataflow** and then this data can be indexed into any of Google's big data solutions services. Then, using a custom application or Google's own tools such as **Data Studio**, we can visualize the data.

We are going to follow a very similar approach for building our example as well.

For more information, navigate to this URL: `https://cloud.google.com/iot-core/`.

Designing a sample application

In this section, we are going to build a sample application using the Google Cloud IoT Core.

Solution

The solution we are going to build is going to be similar to the one from `Chapter 4`, *AWS IoT*. We are going to connect a DHT11 sensor to Raspberry Pi 3 and then transmit the data over GCIC using MQTTS. Once the data reaches the Pub/Sub topic, we will pass this data to a Google Cloud Function. The Google Cloud Function will then take this data and insert it into Google BigQuery. Finally, using a Google Data Studio BigQuery connector, we will connect the two services and build our visualizations and reports.

In the next section, we are going to look at the overall architecture of the solution.

Architecture

The following diagram explains the architecture of the solution:

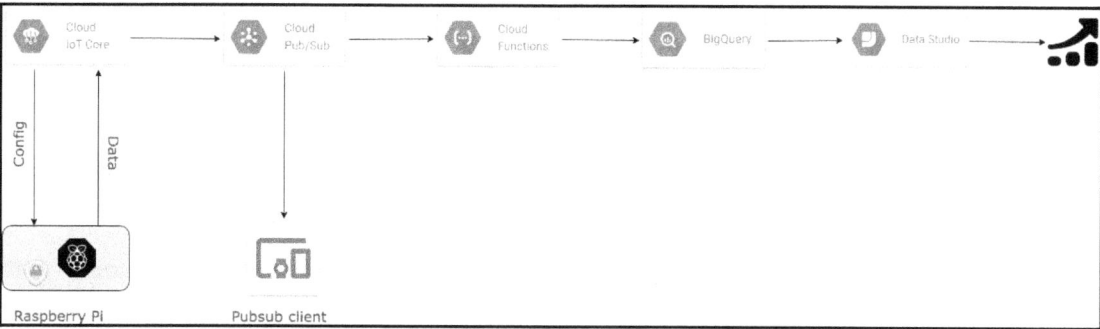

As we can see from the previous diagram, we are going to use Raspberry Pi 3 with a DHT11 sensor as our device, and Raspberry Pi 3 is going connect to Google IoT Core over MQTT with an SSL certificate. From here, we are going to publish data to the device state topic. The data we are going to send is the temperature and humidity sensor values.

Once that is done, we are going to create a client that can get the data from this device topic on demand. We are going to achieve this by creating a new subscriber on this topic.

To build our visualization, we are going to be using Google Data Studio. The data source for Google Data Studio is Google BigQuery, and to pump data into Google BigQuery, we are going to use Google Cloud Functions and listen to an event on the Pub/Sub state topic.

This concludes the overview of the solution that we are going to build.

End-to-end communication

The following are the steps we are going to follow to achieve the solution. First, we set up the IoT Thing and publish data to GCIC:

1. Create a Google account.
2. Create a new Google Cloud project.
3. Enable billing and APIs.
4. Create a new registry and a new device.
5. Define topics and attach certificates.
6. Set up Raspberry Pi 3 and the DHT11 sensor.
7. Start reading the sensor data and publish it to the state topic.
8. Create service account credentials. Set up a local machine.
9. Create a new Pub/Sub subscription. Create a Pub/Sub client and subscribe to the data.

Data visualization

Next, we set up the rules to send data to BigQuery to visualize the data:

1. Set up a BigQuery dataset, then set up a BigQuery table.
2. Set up a new Google Cloud Function. Now, set up Google Data Studio to read data from BigQuery.
3. Build some reports and visualizations.

So, now that we are clear as to what we want to do, let's get started.

Pricing

Do keep an eye on the pricing before you start experimenting with Google IoT Core. You can find more information at: `https://cloud.google.com/iot/pricing`.

As of February 2018, Google IoT Core is still in the beta stage, and the following screenshot shows the disclaimer from Google:

 Beta

This is a beta release of Cloud IoT Core. This product might be changed in backward-incompatible ways and is not subject to any SLA or deprecation policy.

So, things related to Google IoT Core that are represented in this chapter may or may not be the same when this book is published.

Building a sample application

We will start off by implementing the end-to-end solution, where we take the data from the DHT11 sensor and post it to the Google IoT Core state topic.

End-to-end communication

To get started with Google IoT Core, we need to have a Google account. If you do not have a Google account, you can create one by navigating to this URL: `https://accounts.google.com/SignUp?hl=en`.

Once you have created your account, you can login and navigate to Google Cloud Console: `https://console.cloud.google.com`.

Setting up a project

The first thing we are going to do is create a project. If you have already worked with Google Cloud Platform and have at least one project, you will be taken to the first project in the list or you will be taken to the **Getting started** page.

As of the time of writing this book, Google Cloud Platform has a free trial for 12 months with $300 if the offer is still available when you are reading this chapter, I would highly recommend signing up:

1. Once you have signed up, let's get started by creating a new project. From the top menu bar, select the **Select a Project** dropdown and click on the plus icon to create a new project. You can fill in the details as illustrated in the following screenshot:

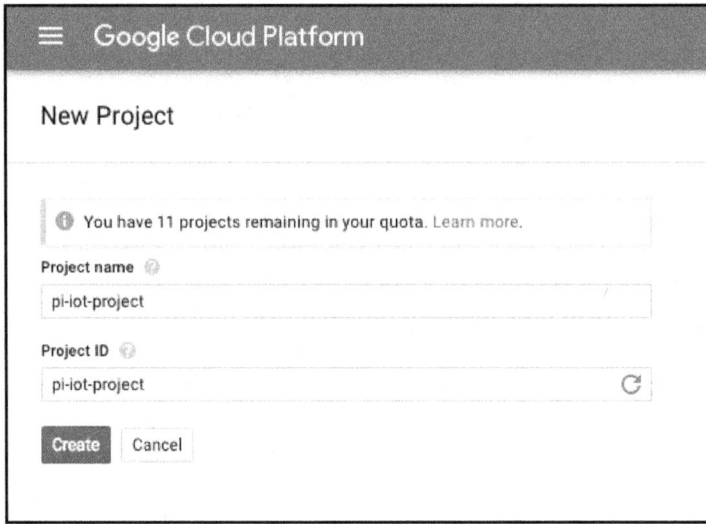

2. Click on the **Create** button. Once the project is created, navigate to the **Project** and you should land on the **Home** page.

Enabling APIs

Following are the steps to be followed for enabling APIs:

1. From the menu on the left-hand side, select **APIs & Services | Library** as shown in the following screenshot:

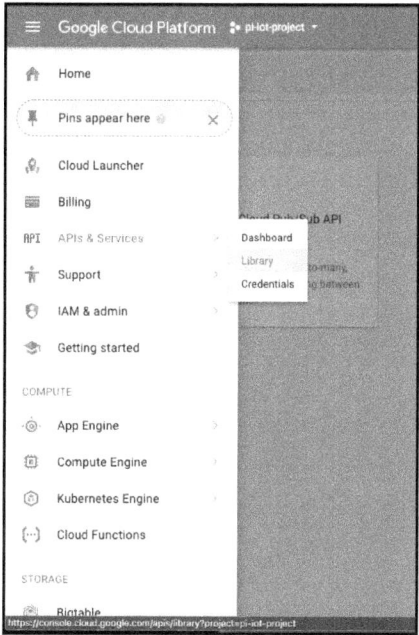

2. On the following screen, search for pubsub and select the **Pub/Sub API** from the results and we should land on a page similar to the following:

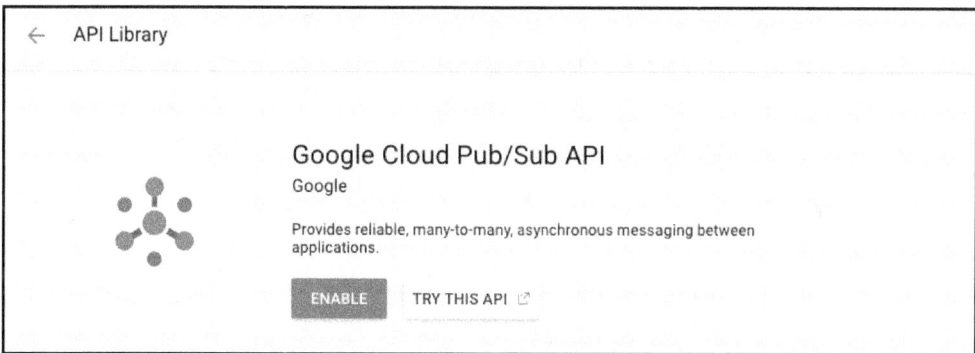

3. Click on the **ENABLE** button and we should now be able to use these APIs in our project.

4. Next, we need to enable the real-time API; search for `realtime` and we should find something similar to the following:

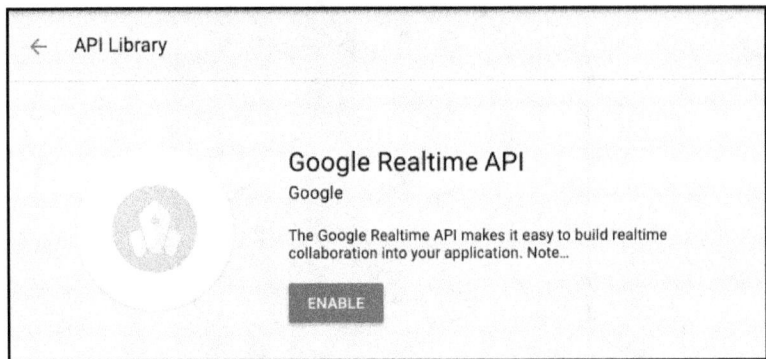

5. Click on the ENABLE & button.

Enabling device registry and devices

The following steps should be used for enabling device registry and devices:

1. From the left-hand side menu, select **IoT Core** and we should land on the **IoT Core** home page:

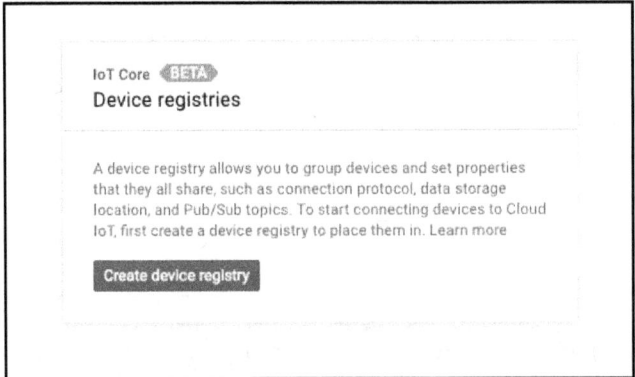

 Instead of the previous screen, if you see a screen to enable APIs, please enable the required APIs from here.

2. Click on the & **Create device registry** button. On the **Create device registry** screen, fill the details as shown in the following table:

Field	Value
Registry ID	`Pi3-DHT11-Nodes`
Cloud region	**us-central1**
Protocol	**MQTT** **HTTP**
Default telemetry topic	**device-events**
Default state topic	**dht11**

3. After completing all the details, our form should look like the following:

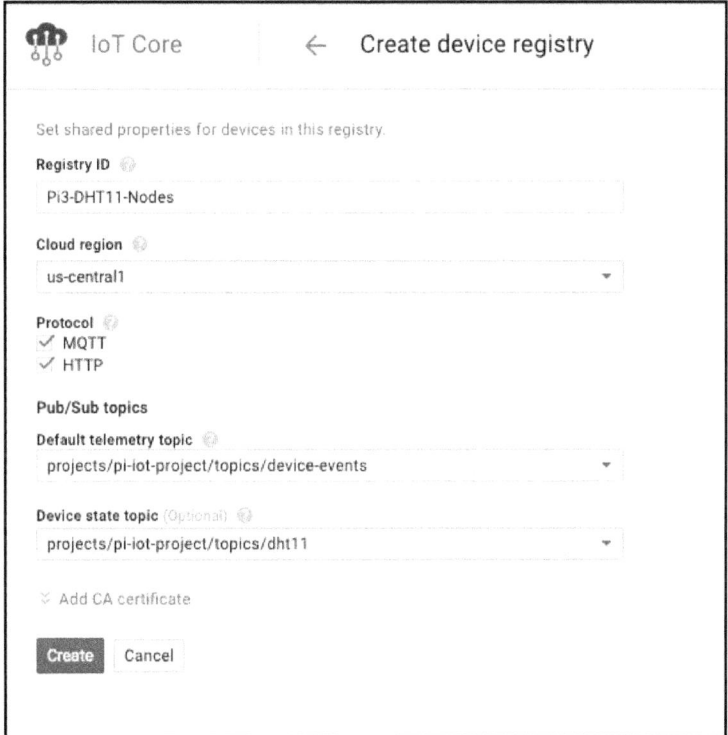

We will add the required certificates later on.

4. Click on the **Create** button and a new device registry will be created.
5. From the **Pi3-DHT11-Nodes** registry page, click on the **Add device** button and set the **Device ID** as `Pi3-DHT11-Node` or any other suitable name.
6. Leave everything as the defaults and make sure the **Device communication** is set to **Allowed** and create a new device.
7. On the device page, we should see a warning as highlighted in the following screenshot:

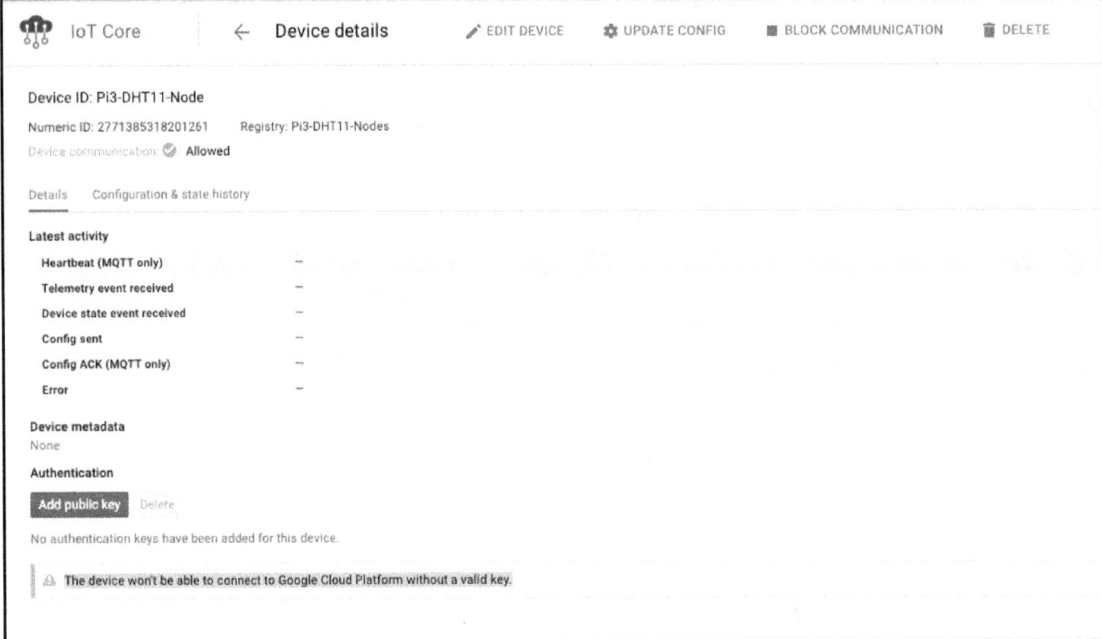

8. Now, we are going to add a new public key. To generate a public/private key pair, we need to have OpenSSL command line available. You can download and set up OpenSSL from here: `https://www.openssl.org/source/`.

9. Use the following command to generate a certificate pair at the default location on your machine:

```
openssl req -x509 -newkey rsa:2048 -keyout rsa_private.pem -nodes -
out rsa_cert.pem -subj "/CN=unused"
```

10. If everything goes well, you should see an output as shown here:

```
→ certs openssl req -x509 -newkey rsa:2048 -keyout rsa_private.pem -nodes -out rsa_cert.pem -sub
j "/CN=unused"
Generating a 2048 bit RSA private key
.....................................................................+++
............................................................+++
writing new private key to 'rsa_private.pem'
-----
→ certs tree
.
├── rsa_cert.pem
└── rsa_private.pem

0 directories, 2 files
```

 Do not share these certificates anywhere; anyone with these certificates can connect to Google IoT Core as a device and start publishing data.

11. Now, once the certificates are created, we will attach them to the device we have created in IoT Core.

12. Head back to the device page of the Google IoT Core service and under **Authentication** click on **Add public key**. On the following screen, fill it in as illustrated:

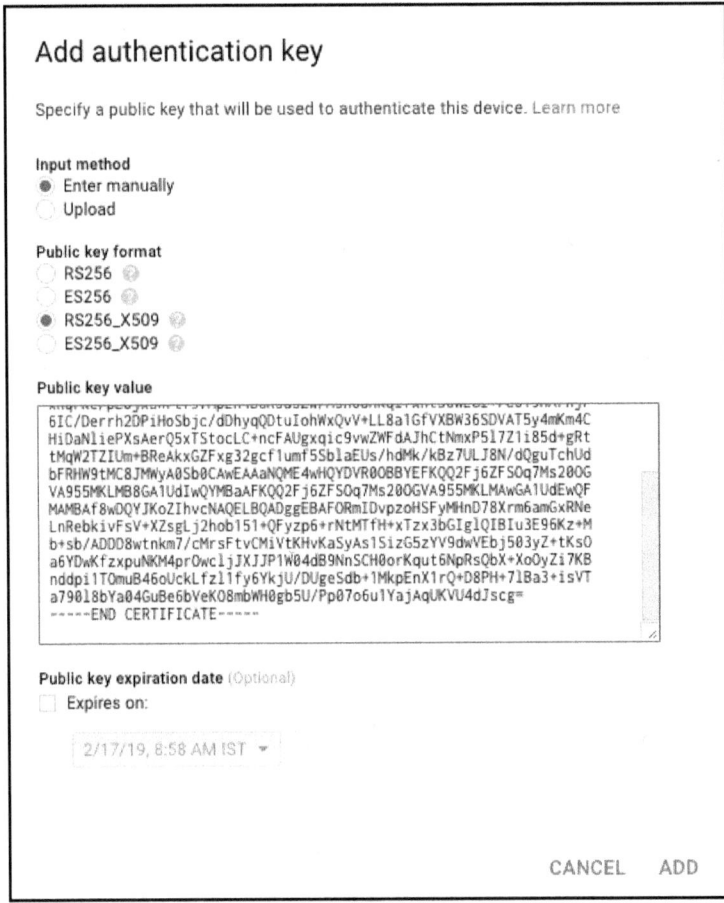

13. The public key value is the contents of `rsa_cert.pem` that we generated earlier. Click on the **ADD** button.

Now that the public key has been successfully added, we can connect to the cloud using the private key.

Setting up Raspberry Pi 3 with DHT11 node

Now that we have our device set up in Google IoT Core, we are going to complete the remaining operation on Raspberry Pi 3 to send data.

Things needed

The requirements for setting up Raspberry Pi 3 on a DHT11 node are:

- **One Raspberry Pi 3**:
  https://www.amazon.com/Raspberry-Pi-Desktop-Starter-White/dp/B01CI5872 2
- **One breadboard**:
  https://www.amazon.com/Solderless-Breadboard-Circuit-Circboard-Prototy ping/dp/B01DDI54II/
- **One DHT11 sensor**:
  https://www.amazon.com/HiLetgo-Temperature-Humidity-Arduino-Raspberry/ dp/B01DKC2GQ0
- **Three male-to-female jumper cables**:
  https://www.amazon.com/RGBZONE-120pcs-Multicolored-Dupont-Breadboard/d p/B01M1IEUAF/

 If you are new to the world of Raspberry Pi GPIO's interfacing, take a look at this *Raspberry Pi GPIO Tutorial: The Basics Explained* on YouTube:
https://www.youtube.com/watch?v=6PuK9fh3aL8.

The following steps are to be used for the setup process:

1. Connect the DHT11 sensor to Raspberry Pi 3 as shown in the following diagram:

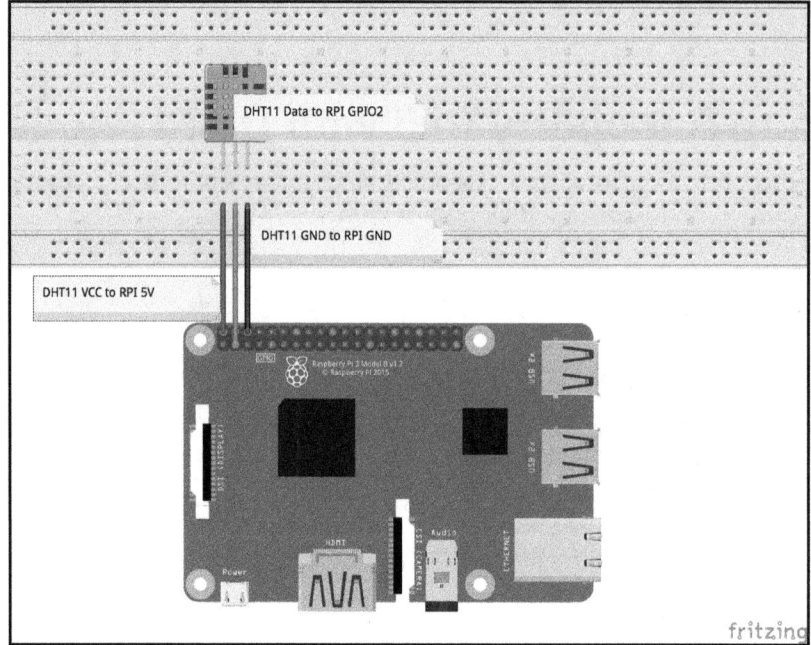

2. Next, power up Raspberry Pi 3 and log in to it. On the desktop, create a new folder named `Google-IoT-Device`. Open a new Terminal and `cd` into this folder.

Setting up Node.js

Assuming that this is the same Raspberry Pi 3 that was used in `Chapter 3`, *Getting Started With IoT Platforms*, it should have Node.js installed. If Node.js is not installed, please refer to the following steps:

1. Open a new Terminal and run the following commands:

```
$ sudo apt update
$ sudo apt full-upgrade
```

2. This will upgrade all the packages that need upgrades. Next, we will install the latest version of Node.js. We will be using the Node 7.x version:

```
$ curl -sL https://deb.nodesource.com/setup_7.x | sudo -E bash -
$ sudo apt install nodejs
```

3. This will take a moment to install, and once your installation is done, you should be able to run the following commands to see the version of Node.js and npm:

```
$ node -v
$ npm -v
```

Developing the Node.js device app

Now, we will set up the app and write the required code:

1. From the Terminal, once you are inside the `Google-IoT-Device` folder, run the following command:

```
$ npm init -y
```

2. Next, we will install `jsonwebtoken`
   (https://www.npmjs.com/package/jsonwebtoken) and `mqtt`
   (https://www.npmjs.com/package/mqtt) from npm. Execute the following command:

```
$ npm install jsonwebtoken mqtt--save
```

3. Next, we will install `rpi-dht-sensor`
   (https://www.npmjs.com/package/rpi-dht-sensor) from npm. This module will help in reading the DHT11 temperature and humidity values:

```
$ npm install rpi-dht-sensor --save
```

4. Your final `package.json` file should look similar to the following code snippet:

```
{
  "name": "Google-IoT-Device",
  "version": "1.0.0",
  "description": "",
  "main": "index.js",
  "scripts": {
    "test": "echo "Error: no test specified" && exit 1"
  },
  "keywords": [],
```

```
"author": "",
"license": "ISC",
"dependencies": {
  "jsonwebtoken": "^8.1.1",
  "mqtt": "^2.15.3",
  "rpi-dht-sensor": "^0.1.1"
}
}
```

5. Now that we have the required dependencies installed, let's continue. Create a new file named `index.js` at the `root` of the `Google-IoT-Device` folder. Next, create a folder named `certs` at the `root` of the `Google-IoT-Device` folder and move the two certificates we created using OpenSSL there.

6. Your final folder structure should look something like this:

7. Open `index.js` in any text editor and update it as shown here:

```
var fs = require('fs');
var jwt = require('jsonwebtoken');
var mqtt = require('mqtt');
var rpiDhtSensor = require('rpi-dht-sensor');

var dht = new rpiDhtSensor.DHT11(2); // `2` => GPIO2

var projectId = 'pi-iot-project';
var cloudRegion = 'us-central1';
var registryId = 'Pi3-DHT11-Nodes';
var deviceId = 'Pi3-DHT11-Node';

var mqttHost = 'mqtt.googleapis.com';
var mqttPort = 8883;
var privateKeyFile = '../certs/rsa_private.pem';
var algorithm = 'RS256';
var messageType = 'state'; // or event
```

```
var mqttClientId = 'projects/' + projectId + '/locations/' +
cloudRegion + '/registries/' + registryId + '/devices/' + deviceId;
var mqttTopic = '/devices/' + deviceId + '/' + messageType;

var connectionArgs = {
  host: mqttHost,
  port: mqttPort,
  clientId: mqttClientId,
  username: 'unused',
  password: createJwt(projectId, privateKeyFile, algorithm),
  protocol: 'mqtts',
  secureProtocol: 'TLSv1_2_method'
};

console.log('connecting...');
var client = mqtt.connect(connectionArgs);

// Subscribe to the /devices/{device-id}/config topic to receive
config updates.
client.subscribe('/devices/' + deviceId + '/config');

client.on('connect', function(success) {
  if (success) {
    console.log('Client connected...');
    sendData();
  } else {
    console.log('Client not connected...');
  }
});

client.on('close', function() {
  console.log('close');
});

client.on('error', function(err) {
  console.log('error', err);
});

client.on('message', function(topic, message, packet) {
  console.log(topic, 'message received: ', Buffer.from(message,
'base64').toString('ascii'));
});

function createJwt(projectId, privateKeyFile, algorithm) {
  var token = {
    'iat': parseInt(Date.now() / 1000),
    'exp': parseInt(Date.now() / 1000) + 86400 * 60, // 1 day
    'aud': projectId
```

```
  };
  var privateKey = fs.readFileSync(privateKeyFile);
  return jwt.sign(token, privateKey, {
    algorithm: algorithm
  });
}

function fetchData() {
  var readout = dht.read();
  var temp = readout.temperature.toFixed(2);
  var humd = readout.humidity.toFixed(2);

  return {
    'temp': temp,
    'humd': humd,
    'time': new Date().toISOString().slice(0, 19).replace('T', ' ')
// https://stackoverflow.com/a/11150727/1015046
  };
}

function sendData() {
  var payload = fetchData();

  payload = JSON.stringify(payload);
  console.log(mqttTopic, ': Publishing message:', payload);
  client.publish(mqttTopic, payload, { qos: 1 });

  console.log('Transmitting in 30 seconds');
  setTimeout(sendData, 30000);
}
```

In the previous code, we first define the `projectId`, `cloudRegion`, `registryId`, and `deviceId` based on what we have created. Next, we build the `connectionArgs` object, using which we are going to connect to Google IoT Core using MQTT-SN. Do note that the password property is a **JSON Web Token (JWT)**, based on the `projectId` and `privateKeyFile` algorithm.

 The token that is created by this function is valid only for one day. After one day, the cloud will refuse connection to this device if the same token is used.

The `username` value is the **Common Name (CN)** of the certificate we have created, which is *unused*.

Using `mqtt.connect()`, we are going to connect to the Google IoT Core. And we are subscribing to the device config topic, which can be used to send device configurations when connected.

Once the connection is successful, we `callsendData()` every 30 seconds to send data to the state topic.

Save the previous file and run the following command:

```
$ sudo node index.js
```

And we should see something like this:

```
pi@raspberrypi:~/Desktop/Google-IoT-Device

File   Edit   Tabs   Help

pi@raspberrypi:~/Desktop/Google-IoT-Device $ sudo node index.js
connecting...
Client connected...
/devices/Pi3-DHT11-Node/config message received:
/devices/Pi3-DHT11-Node/state : Publishing message: {"temp":"0.00","humd":"0.00","time":"2018-02-17 03:57:08"}
Transmitting in 30 seconds
/devices/Pi3-DHT11-Node/state : Publishing message: {"temp":"26.00","humd":"20.00","time":"2018-02-17 03:57:14"}
Transmitting in 30 seconds
/devices/Pi3-DHT11-Node/state : Publishing message: {"temp":"26.00","humd":"20.00","time":"2018-02-17 03:57:19"}
Transmitting in 30 seconds
/devices/Pi3-DHT11-Node/state : Publishing message: {"temp":"26.00","humd":"22.00","time":"2018-02-17 03:57:25"}
Transmitting in 30 seconds
/devices/Pi3-DHT11-Node/state : Publishing message: {"temp":"26.00","humd":"20.00","time":"2018-02-17 03:57:30"}
Transmitting in 30 seconds
```

As you can see from the previous Terminal logs, the device first gets connected then starts transmitting the temperature and humidity along with time. We are sending time as well, so we can save it in the BigQuery table and then build a time series chart quite easily.

Now, if we head back to the **Device** page of Google IoT Core and navigate to the **Configuration & state history** tab, we should see the data that we are sending to the state topic here:

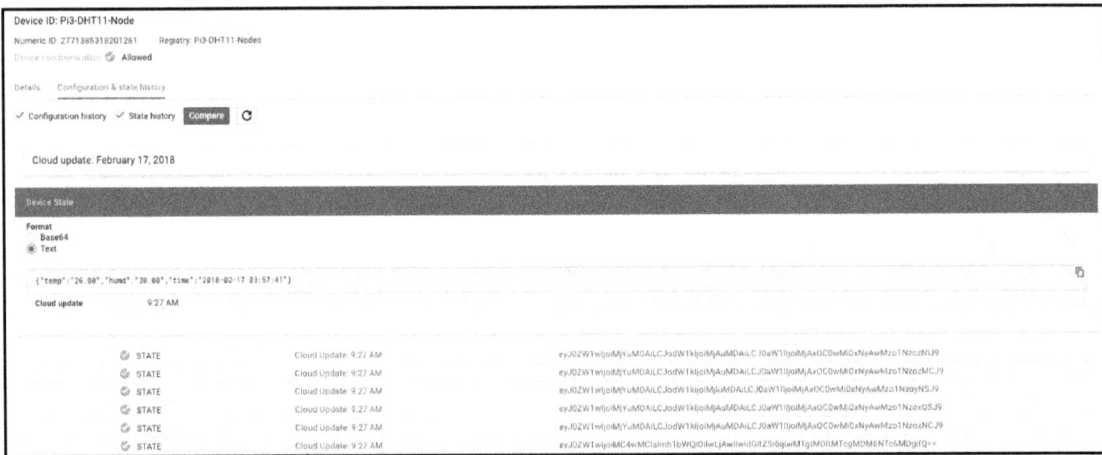

Now that the device is sending data, let's actually read the data from another client.

Reading the data from the device

For this, you can either use the same Raspberry Pi 3 or another computer. I am going to use MacBook as a client that is interested in the data sent by the Thing.

Setting up credentials

Before we start reading data from Google IoT Core, we have to set up our computer (for example, MacBook) as a trusted device, so our computer can request data. Let's perform the following steps to set the credentials:

1. To do this, we need to create a new **Service account key**. From the left-hand-side menu of the Google Cloud Console, select **APIs & Services | Credentials**. Then click on the **Create credentials** dropdown and select **Service account key** as shown in the following screenshot:

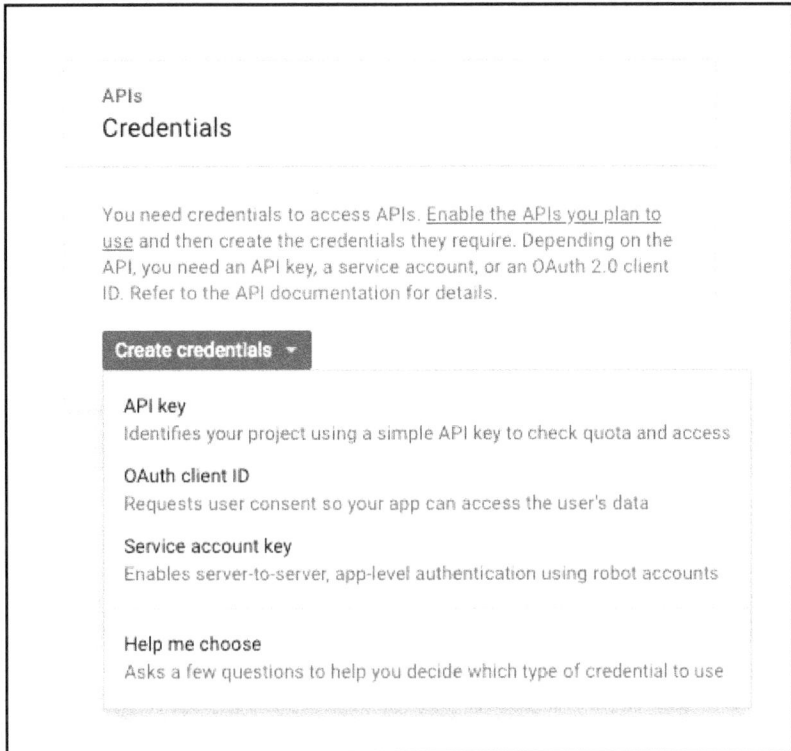

2. Now, fill in the details as shown in the following screenshot:

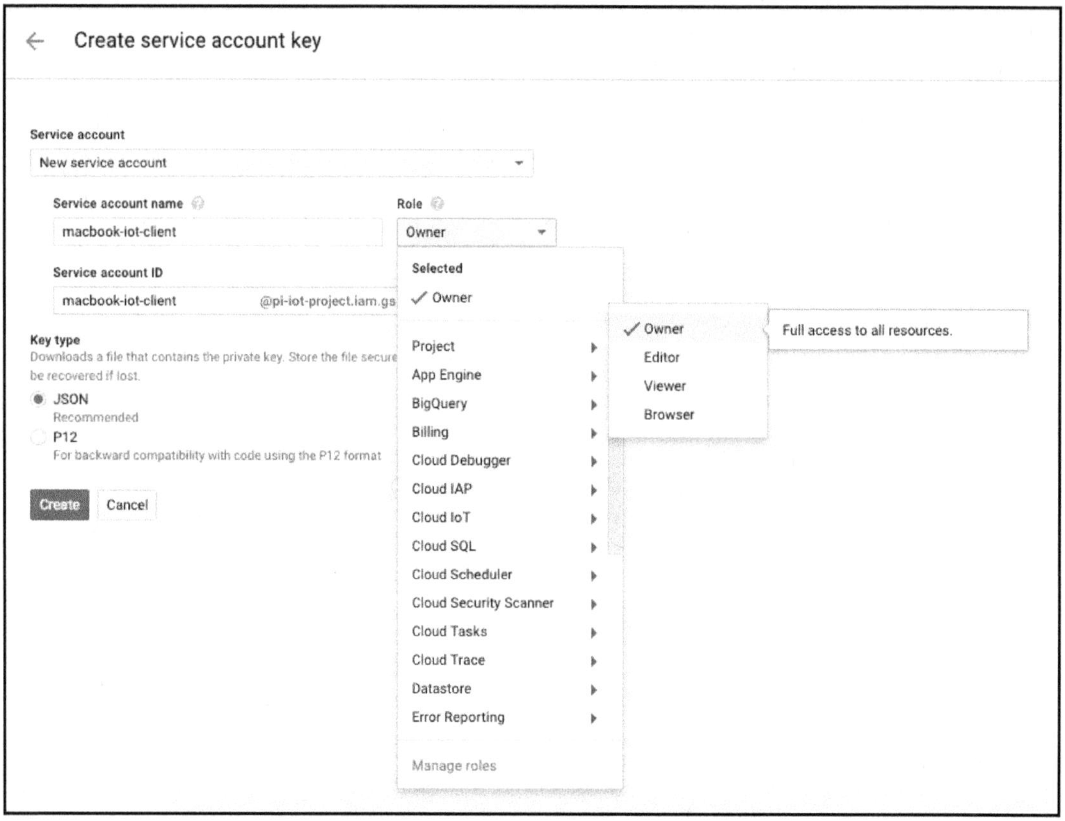

←   Create service account key

Service account

New service account ▾

Service account name ⓘ   Role ⓘ

macbook-iot-client   Owner ▾

Service account ID   **Selected**

macbook-iot-client   @pi-iot-project.iam.gs   ✓ Owner

Key type
Downloads a file that contains the private key. Store the file secure
be recovered if lost.

Project	▸	✓ Owner Full access to all resources.
App Engine	▸	Editor
BigQuery	▸	Viewer
Billing	▸	Browser

◉ JSON
   Recommended
○ P12
   For backward compatibility with code using the P12 format

Cloud Debugger	▸
Cloud IAP	▸
Cloud IoT	▸
Cloud SQL	▸
Cloud Scheduler	▸
Cloud Security Scanner	▸
Cloud Tasks	▸
Cloud Trace	▸
Datastore	▸
Error Reporting	▸

[Create]   [Cancel]

Manage roles

We have given access to the entire project for this client and as an **Owner**.
Do not select these settings if this is a production application.

3. Click on **Create** and you will be asked to download and save the file.

Do not share this file; this file is as good as giving someone owner-level
permissions to all assets of this project.

4. Once the file is downloaded somewhere safe, create an environment variable with the name `GOOGLE_APPLICATION_CREDENTIALS` and point it to the path of the downloaded file.

 You can refer to *Getting Started with Authentication* at `https://cloud.google.com/docs/authentication/getting-started` if you are facing any difficulties.

Setting up subscriptions

The data from the device is being sent to Google IoT Core using the state topic. If you recall, we have named that topic `dht11`. Now, we are going to create a subscription for this topic:

1. From the menu on the left side, select **Pub/Sub** | **Topics**. Now, click on **New subscription** for the `dht11` topic, as shown in the following screenshot:

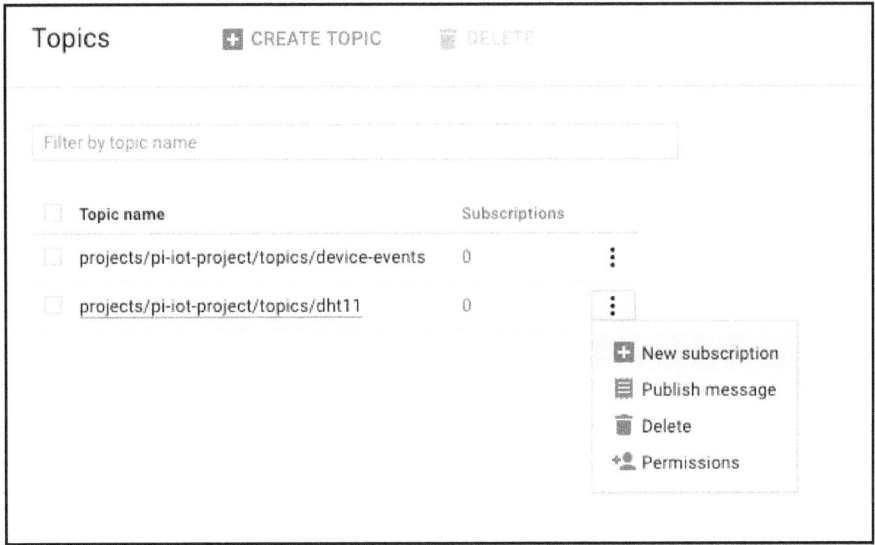

2. Create a new subscription by setting up the options selected in this screenshot:

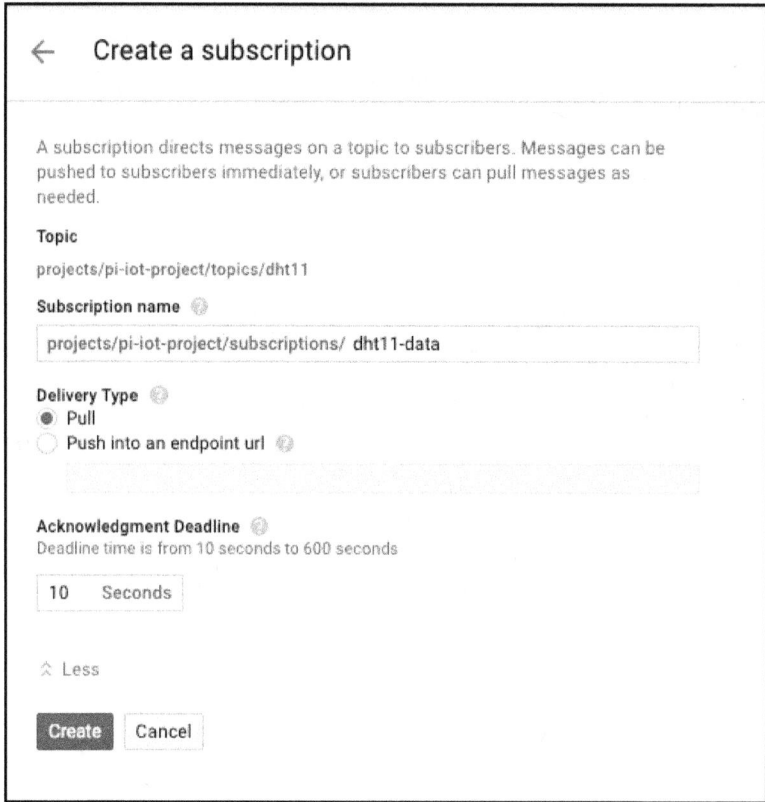

3. We are going to use the subscription named `dht11-data` to get the data from the state topic.

Setting up the client

Now that we have provided the required credentials as well as subscribed to a Pub/Sub topic, we will set up the Pub/Sub client. Follow these steps:

1. Create a folder named `test_client` inside the `test_client` directory. Now, run the following command:

```
$ npm init -y
```

2. Next, install the `@google-cloud/pubsub` (https://www.npmjs.com/package/@google-cloud/pubsub) module with the help of the following command:

```
$ npm install @google-cloud/pubsub --save
```

3. Create a file inside the `test_client` folder named `index.js` and update it as shown in this code snippet:

```
var PubSub = require('@google-cloud/pubsub');
var projectId = 'pi-iot-project';
var stateSubscriber = 'dht11-data'

// Instantiates a client
var pubsub = new PubSub({
  projectId: projectId,
});

var subscription = pubsub.subscription('projects/' + projectId +
'/subscriptions/' + stateSubscriber);
var messageHandler = function(message) {
  console.log('Message Begin >>>>>>>>');
  console.log('message.connectionId', message.connectionId);
  console.log('message.attributes', message.attributes);
  console.log('message.data', Buffer.from(message.data,
'base64').toString('ascii'));
  console.log('Message End >>>>>>>>>>');

  // "Ack" (acknowledge receipt of) the message
  message.ack();
};

// Listen for new messages
subscription.on('message', messageHandler);
```

4. Update the `projectId` and `stateSubscriber` in the previous code. Now, save the file and run the following command:

```
$ node index.js
```

5. We should see the following output in the console:

```
test_client — node index.js — node index.js — 117×27
                                    node                                    node index.js
→ test_client node index.js
Message Begin >>>>>>>>
message.connectionId 76c1da76-8ee1-49be-9fcf-f37a8e6b42c4
message.attributes { projectId: 'pi-iot-project',
  deviceId: 'Pi3-DHT11-Node',
  deviceNumId: '2771385318201261',
  deviceRegistryId: 'Pi3-DHT11-Nodes',
  deviceRegistryLocation: 'us-central1' }
message.data {"temp":"29.00","humd":"18.00","time":"2018-02-17 06:25:34"}
Message End >>>>>>>>>>
```

This way, any client that is interested in the data of this device can use this approach to get the latest data.

With this, we conclude the section on posting data to Google IoT Core and fetching the data. In the next section, we are going to work on building a dashboard.

Building a dashboard

Now that we have seen how a client can read the data from our device on demand, we will move on to building a dashboard, where we display data in real time.

For this, we are going to use Google Cloud Functions, Google BigQuery, and Google Data Studio.

Google Cloud Functions

Cloud Functions are solution for serverless services. Cloud Functions is a lightweight solution for creating standalone and single-purpose functions that respond to cloud events.

You can read more about Google Cloud Functions at `https://cloud.google.com/functions/`.

Google BigQuery

Google BigQuery is an enterprise data warehouse that solves this problem by enabling super-fast SQL queries using the processing power of Google's infrastructure.

You can read more about Google BigQuery at `https://cloud.google.com/bigquery/`.

Google Data Studio

Google Data Studio helps to build dashboards and reports using various data connectors, such as BigQuery or Google Analytics.

You can read more about Google Data Studio at `https://cloud.google.com/data-studio/`.

 As of April 2018, these three services are still in beta.

As we have already seen in the *Architecture* section, once the data is published on the state topic, we are going to create a cloud function that will get triggered by the data event on the Pub/Sub client. And inside our cloud function, we are going to get a copy of the published data and then insert it into the BigQuery dataset.

Once the data is inserted, we are going to use Google Data Studio to create a new report by linking the BigQuery dataset to the input.

So, let's get started.

Setting up BigQuery

The first thing we are going to do is set up BigQuery:

1. From the side menu of the Google Cloud Platform Console, our project page, click on the BigQuery URL and we should be taken to the **Google BigQuery** home page. Select **Create new dataset**, as shown in the following screenshot:

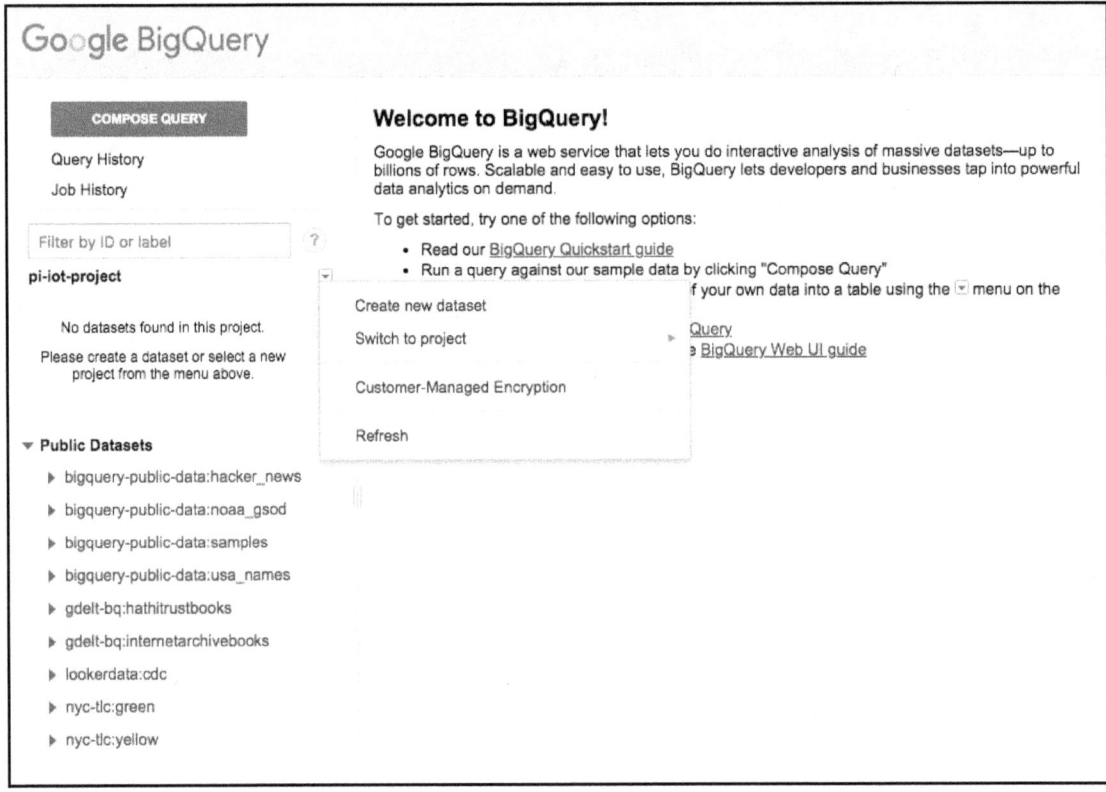

2. Create a new dataset with the values illustrated in the following screenshot:

3. Once the dataset is created, click on the plus sign next to the dataset and create an empty table. We are going to name the table `dht11_data` and we are going have three fields in it, as shown here:

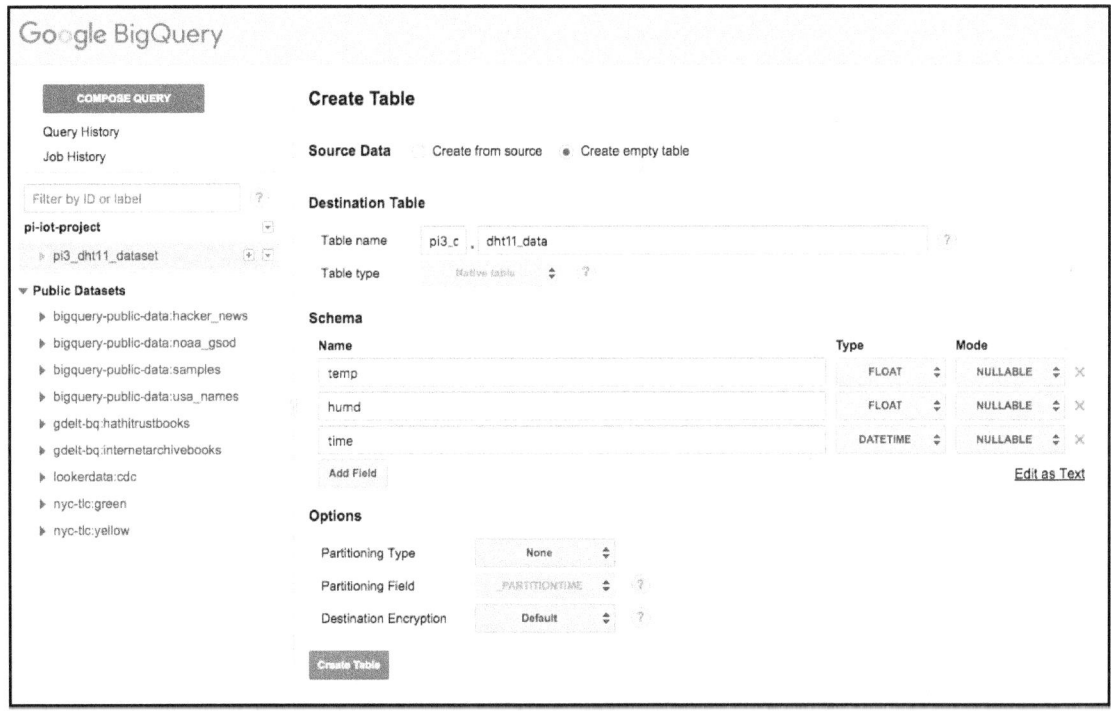

4. Click on the **Create Table** button to create the table.

Now that we have our table ready, we will write a cloud function to insert the incoming data from Pub/Sub into this table.

Setting up Google Cloud Function

Now, we are going to set up a cloud function that will be triggered by the incoming data:

1. From the Google Cloud Console's left-hand-side menu, select **Cloud Functions** under **Compute**. Once you land on the **Google Cloud Functions** homepage, you will be asked to enable the cloud functions API. Click on **Enable API**:

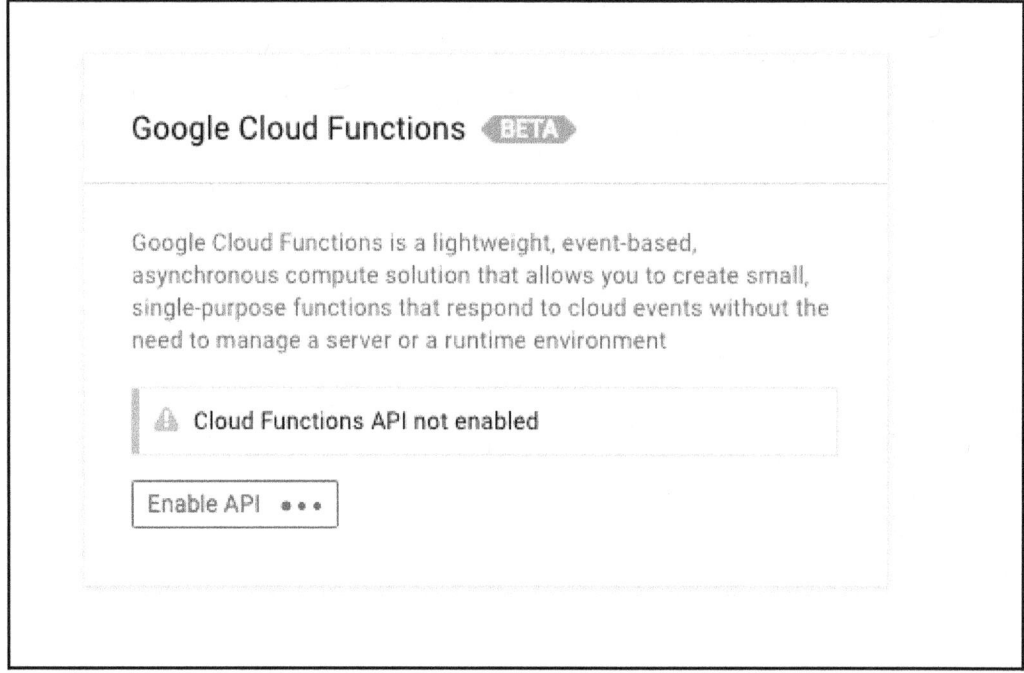

2. Once the API is enabled, we will be on the **Create function** page. Fill in the form as shown here:

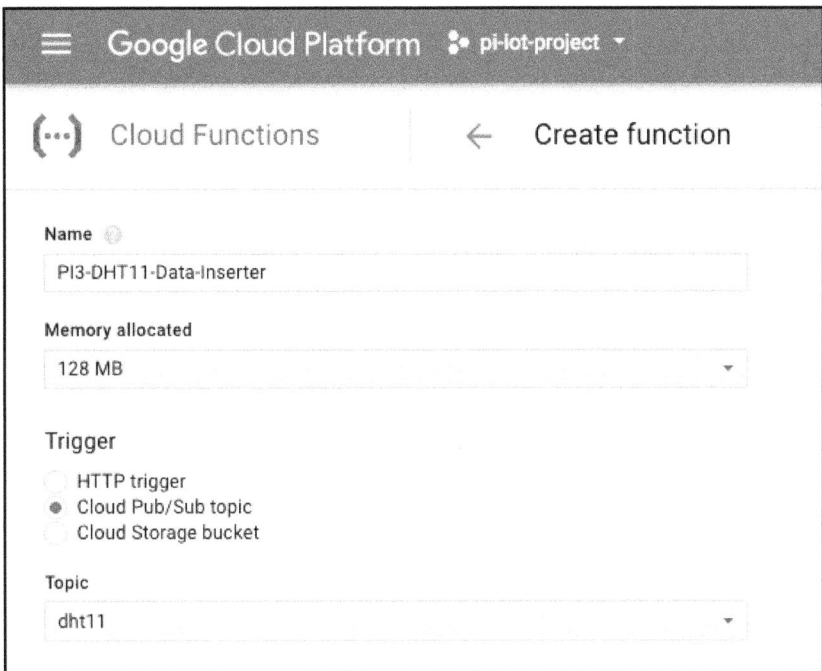

The **Trigger** is set to **Cloud Pub/Sub topic** and we have selected **dht11** as the **Topic**.

3. Under the **Source code** section; make sure you are in the **index.js** tab and update it as shown here:

```
var BigQuery = require('@google-cloud/bigquery');
var projectId = 'pi-iot-project';

var bigquery = new BigQuery({
  projectId: projectId,
});

var datasetName = 'pi3_dht11_dataset';
var tableName = 'dht11_data';

exports.pubsubToBQ = function(event, callback) {
```

```
   var msg = event.data;
   var data = JSON.parse(Buffer.from(msg.data,
'base64').toString());
   // console.log(data);
   bigquery
     .dataset(datasetName)
     .table(tableName)
     .insert(data)
     .then(function() {
       console.log('Inserted rows');
       callback(); // task done
     })
     .catch(function(err) {
       if (err && err.name === 'PartialFailureError') {
         if (err.errors && err.errors.length > 0) {
           console.log('Insert errors:');
           err.errors.forEach(function(err) {
             console.error(err);
           });
         }
       } else {
         console.error('ERROR:', err);
       }

       callback(); // task done
     });
};
```

4. In the previous code, we were using the BigQuery Node.js module to insert data into our BigQuery table. Update `projectId`, `datasetName`, and `tableName` as applicable in the code.

5. Next, click on the **package.json** tab and update it as shown:

```
{
 "name": "cloud_function",
 "version": "0.0.1",
 "dependencies": {
  "@google-cloud/bigquery": "^1.0.0"
 }
}
```

Finally, for the **Function to execute** field, enter `pubsubToBQ`. `pubsubToBQ` is the name of the function that has our logic and this function will be called when the data event occurs.

Click on the **Create** button and our function should be deployed in a minute.

Running the device

Now that the entire setup is done, we will start pumping data into BigQuery:

1. Head back to Raspberry Pi 3 which was sending the DHT11 temperature and humidity data, and run the application. We should see the data being published to the state topic:

2. Now, if we head back to the **Cloud Functions** page, we should see the requests coming into the cloud function:

3. You can click on **VIEW LOGS** to view the logs of each function execution:

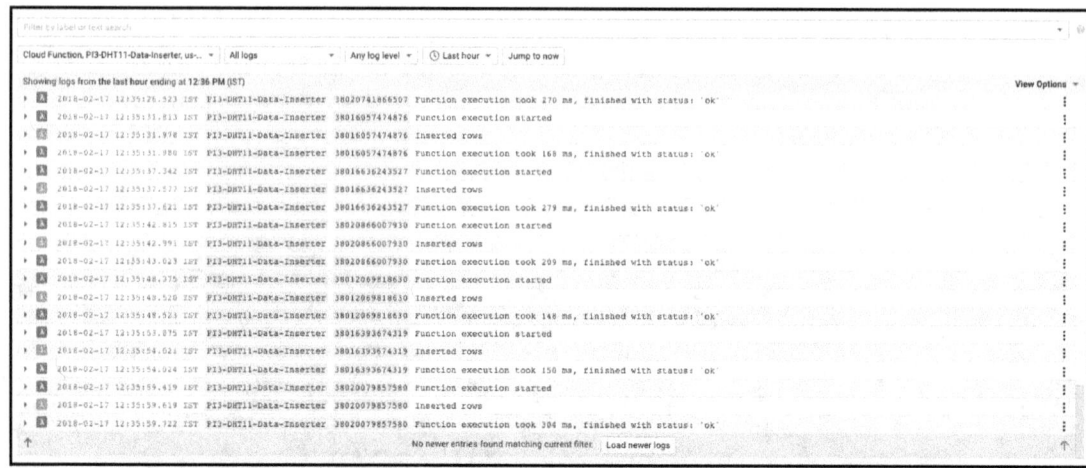

4. Now, head over to our table in BigQuery and click on the **RUN QUERY** button; run the query as shown in the following screenshot:

5. Now, all the data that was generated by the DHT11 sensor is timestamped and stored in BigQuery.

6. You can use the **Save to Google Sheets** button to save this data to Google Sheets and analyze the data there or plot graphs, as shown here:

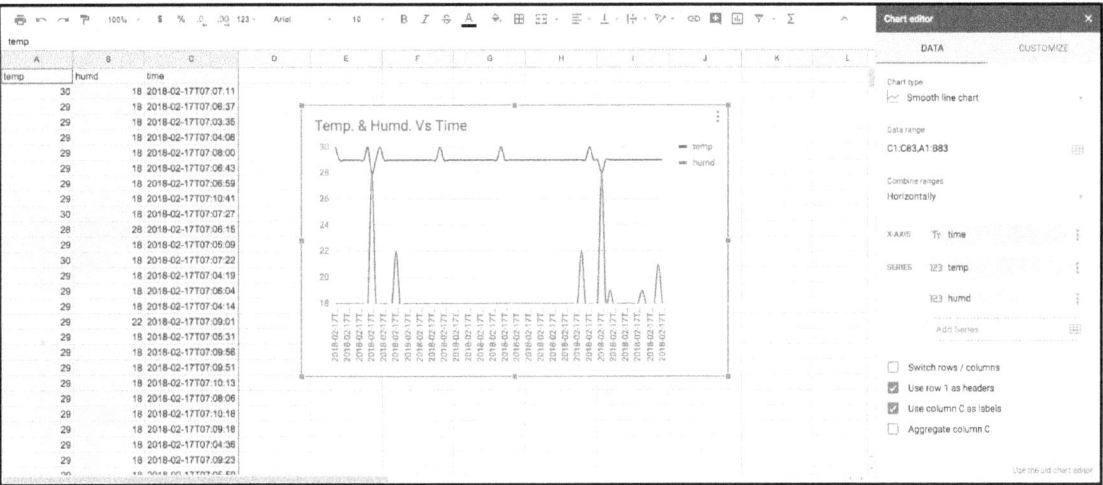

Or we can go one step ahead and use the Google Data Studio to do the same.

Google Data Studio reports

Now that the data is ready in BigQuery, we are going to set up Google Data Studio and then connect both of them, so we can access the data from BigQuery in Google Data Studio:

1. Navigate to `https://datastudio.google.com` and log in with your Google account.

2. Once you are on the **Home** page of Google Data Studio, click on the **Blank** report template. Make sure you read and agree to the terms and conditions before proceeding.

3. Name the report `PI3 DHT11 Sensor Data`. Using the **Create new data source** button, we will create a new data source.

4. Click on **Create new data source** and we should land on a page where we need to create a new **Data Source**. From the list of **Connectors**, select **BigQuery**; you will be asked to authorize Data Studio to interface with BigQuery, as shown in the following screenshot:

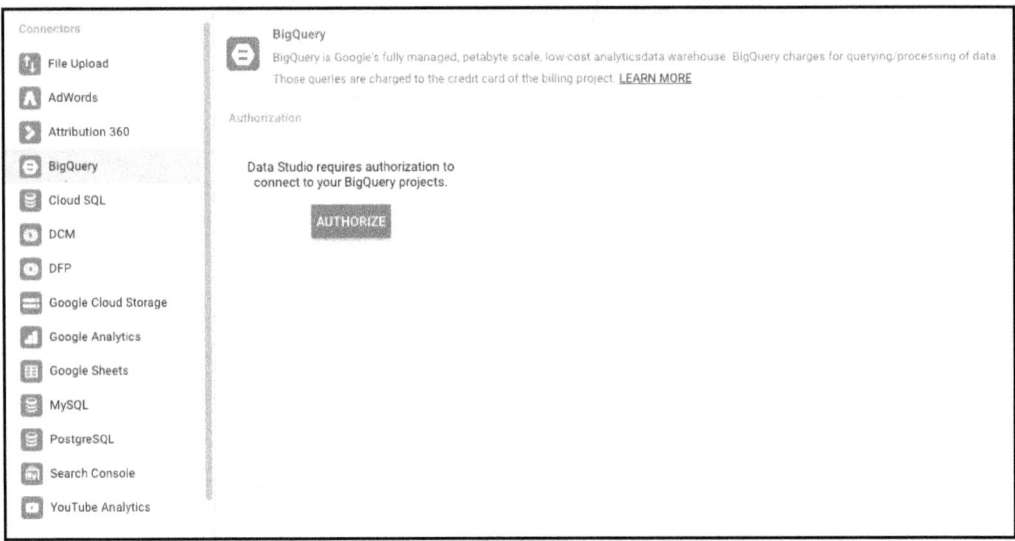

5. Once we authorized, we will be shown our projects and related datasets and tables:

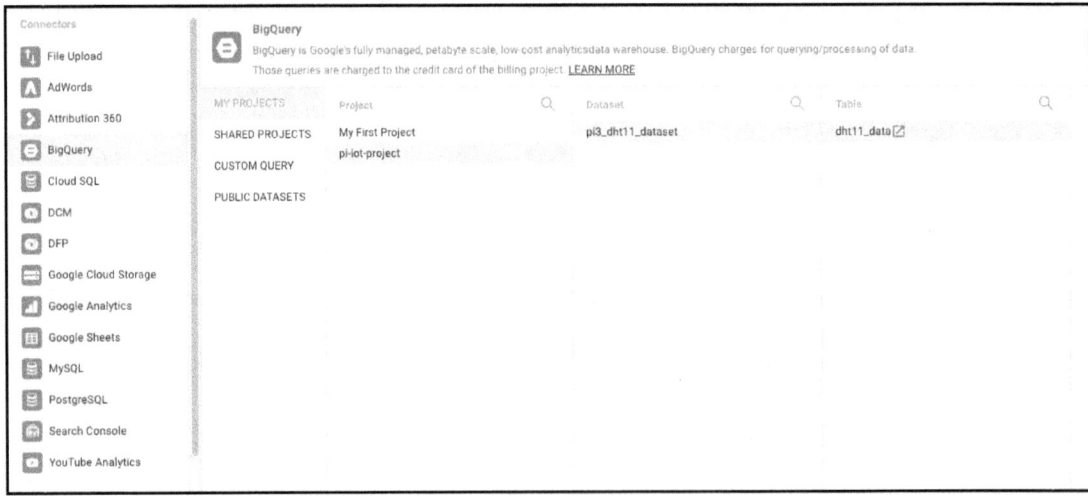

6. Select the **dht11_data** table and click on **Connect**. This fetches the metadata of the table as shown here:

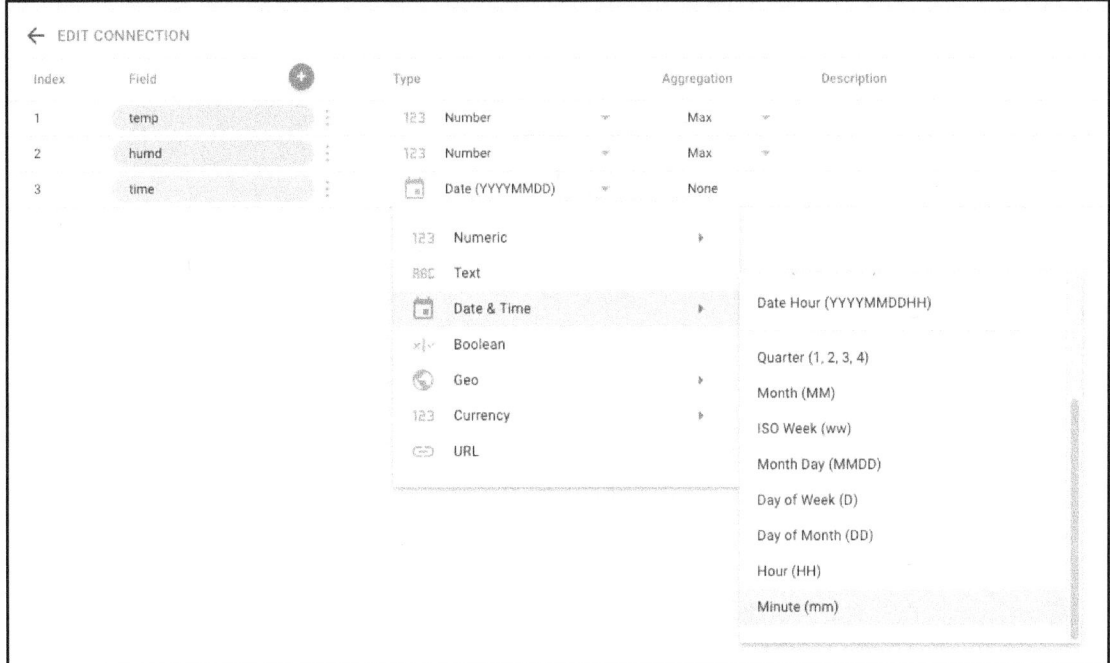

7. Set the **Aggregation** for the **temp** and **humd** fields to **Max** and set the **Type** for time as **Date & Time**. Pick **Minute (mm)** from the sub-list.

8. Click on **Add to report** and you will be asked to authorize Google Data Studio to read data from the table.

9. Once the data source has been successfully linked, we will create a new time series chart.

10. From the menu, select **Insert** | **Time Series** link. Update the data configuration of the chart as shown in the following screenshot:

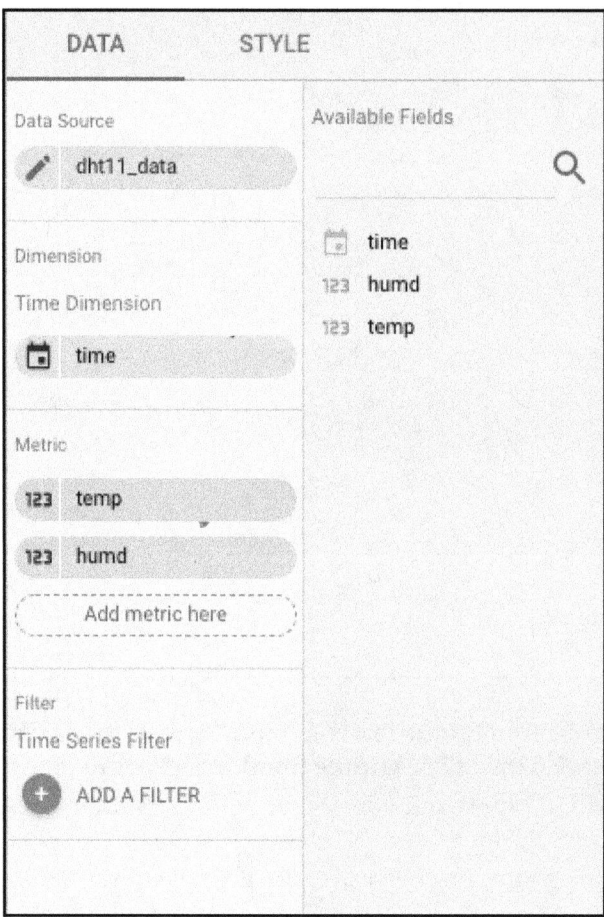

You can play with the styles as per your preference and we should see something similar to the following screenshot:

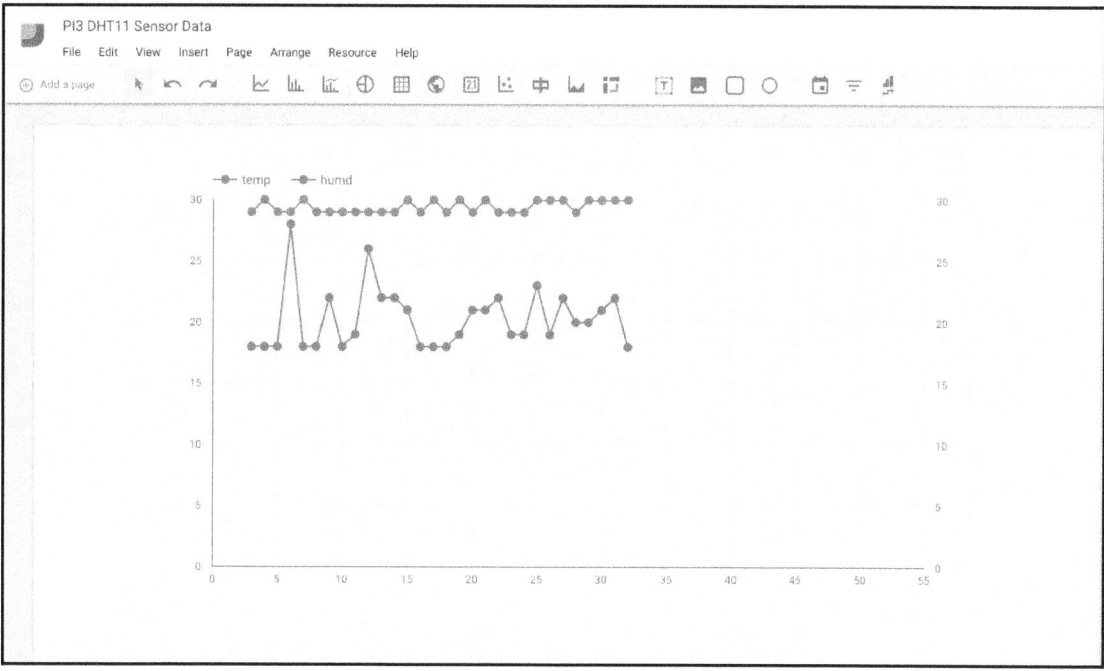

This report can then be shared with any user.

 We have selected the granularity of time as minutes. You can change it to hours, days, or months based on the volume of data.

With this, we have seen the basic features and implementation process needed to work with Google Cloud IoT Core as well other features of the platform.

 Once you are done with your learning, do not forget to delete the resources you have created. Otherwise you will be billed. You have been warned!

Summary

In this chapter, we have seen how to work with Google IoT Core as well as how to set up a device and subscribe to the state topic. We have seen how a client can subscribe to this topic and receive the data in real time.

Next, we used Google Cloud Functions to index the data from the state topic into BigQuery and from there we used Google Data Studio to visualize the data.

This concludes our exploration of Google IoT Core and how we can use Google Cloud Platform for IoT.

In the next chapter, we are going to look at the IBM Watson IoT platform.

7
IBM Watson IoT

In the previous chapter, we looked at how to build an end-to-end IoT solution using Raspberry Pi 3, a DHT11 temperature and humidity sensor, and the Google IoT Core platform. In this chapter, we are going to implement it using the IBM Watson IoT platform. Along with that, we are going to work on building a visualization dashboard.

Topics covered in this chapter are as follows:

- IBM Watson IoT architecture
- Setting up an end-to-end solution using IBM Watson IoT
- Setting up a visualization dashboard for the solution

IBM Watson IoT

The IBM Watson IoT platform, like the other platforms we have looked at, provides an end-to-end platform for building IoT solutions. It is a fully-managed, cloud-hosted service that can process data from millions of devices and generate some value from it.

IBM Watson IoT primarily uses the MQTT messaging protocol for communication.

The following are the features offered by IBM Watson IoT:

- **Device management**: Using the device management service, we can perform device actions such as rebooting or updating firmware, receiving device diagnostics and metadata, or performing bulk device addition and removal.
- **Responsive, scalable connectivity**: Uses the industry-standard MQTT protocol (OASIS ratified) to connect devices and applications. MQTT is designed for the efficient exchange of data to and from devices in real time.
- **Secure communication**: Securely receive data from and send commands to your devices. Do this using MQTT with TLS to secure all communication between your devices and the IBM Watson service.

As well as having access to real-time data coming from your devices, we can opt to store data for a period of our choice, allowing us to have access to historical and real-time data for our devices.

You can read more about IBM Watson IoT here: `https://internetofthings.ibmcloud.com`.

You can also check out this video on how IBM Watson plays the popular US TV game Jeopardy named, *Miles vs. Watson: The Complete Man Against Machine Showdown* at: `https://www.youtube.com/watch?v=YgYSv2KSyWg`.

Designing the sample application

In this section, we are going to build a sample application using the IBM Watson IoT.

Solution

The solution we are going to build is going to be similar to the one from `Chapter 3`, *Getting Started with IoT Platforms*. We are going to connect a DHT11 sensor to Raspberry Pi 3 and then transmit the data over to the IBM Watson IoT platform using MQTTS. Then we will take that data and build a visualization.

In the next section, we are going to look at the overall architecture of the solution.

Architecture

The following diagram explains the architecture of the solution:

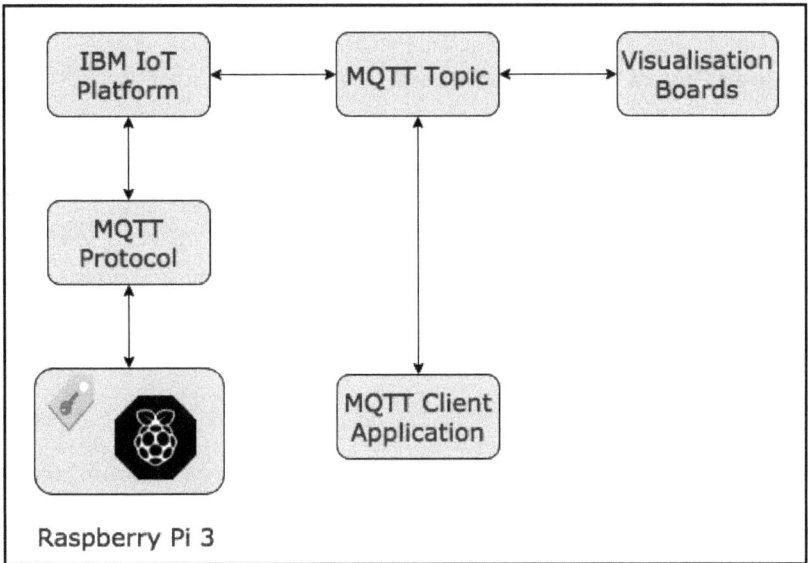

As we can see from the previous diagram, we are using a Raspberry Pi running MQTT client software over TLS with token-based authentication, connecting to the IBM IoT platform. The Raspberry Pi is connected to the DHT11 temperature and humidity sensor.

Using the MQTTS connection between the IoT platform and the Raspberry Pi 3, we will publish the temperature and humidity data on a custom topic of our choice.

Once the platform receives the data, it will resend it to all other MQTT clients connected to the platform that are authorized and subscribed to the custom topic.

Apart from this, using the Boards component in the IBM Watson IoT platform, we can visualize the data in real time, without much effort.

Following is an overview of the solution that we are going to build.

End-to-end communication

The following are the steps we are going to perform to achieve the solution.

First, set up the thing and publish data to IBM Watson IoT:

1. Create an IBM Bluemix cloud account.
2. Create a new IoT platform.
3. Create a new device type.
4. Create a new device. Set up Raspberry Pi and DHT11.
5. Set up the `ibmiotf` module on the Raspberry Pi.
6. Start reading the sensor data and publish it to the custom topic.
7. Subscribe to the custom topic from another client to visualize the data.

Data visualization

Next, using the Boards component of the IBM IoT platform, we are going to create a real-time visualization:

1. Create a new schema that defines our data
2. Create a new board
3. Set up a real-time line chart

So, now that we are clear as to what we want to do, let's get started.

Pricing

Do keep an eye on the pricing before you start experimenting with IBM Watson IoT. You can find more information here: `https://www.ibm.com/internet-of-things/spotlight/watson-iot-platform/pricing`.

For this book, we are going to use the **Lite** plan.

Building the sample application

We will start off by implementing the end-to-end solution, where we take the data from the DHT11 sensor and post it to a custom topic.

End-to-end communication

To get started with IBM IoT, we need to have a Bluemix account. If you do not have a Bluemix account, you can create one by navigating to this URL: `https://console.bluemix.net/registration`.

Once you have created your account, you can login and navigate to the Bluemix console. Or you can follow this link: `https://console.bluemix.net/dashboard/apps/` to reach the page.

Creating a platform

The first step we are going to take is to create a platform:

1. From the console dashboard page, click on the **Create Resource** button.
2. From the following screen, select **Internet of Things Platform**:

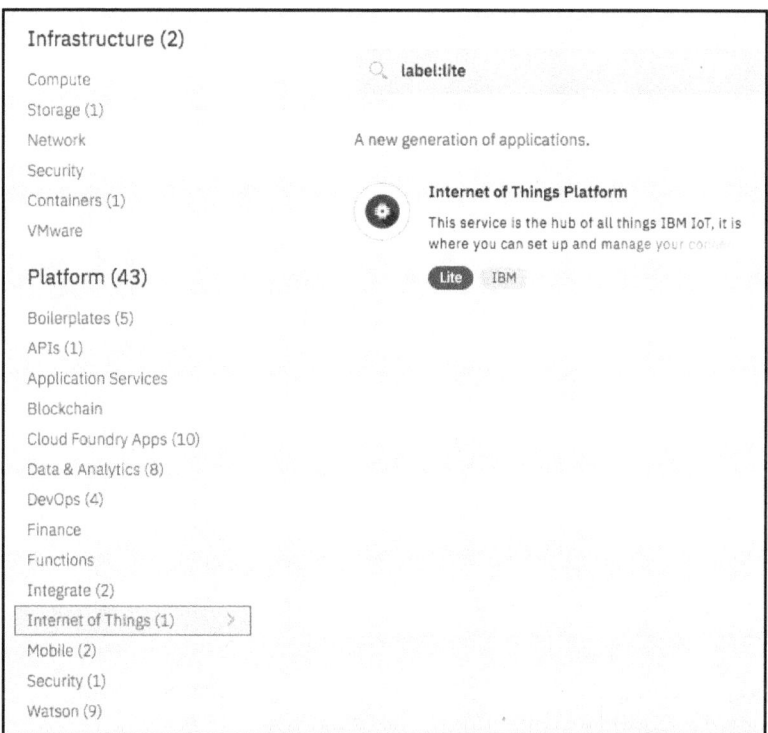

3. Provide a **Service name** and set the fields as applicable:

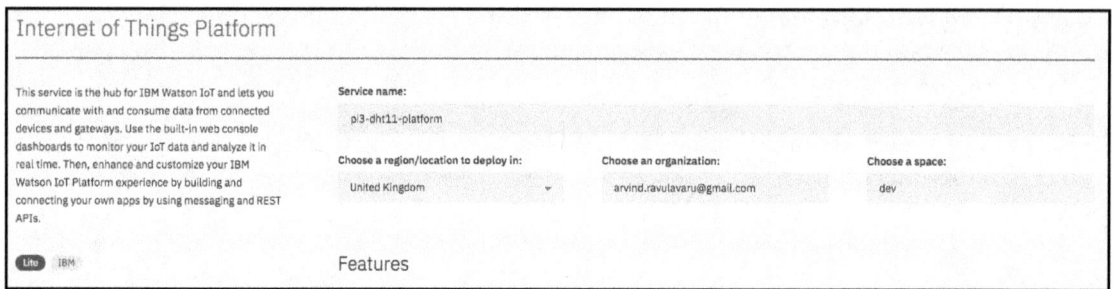

4. Click on the **Create** button. Once the platform has been created, you should be redirected to a page similar to the one illustrated here:

5. Click on the **Launch** button to navigate to your dashboard and you should see something like this:

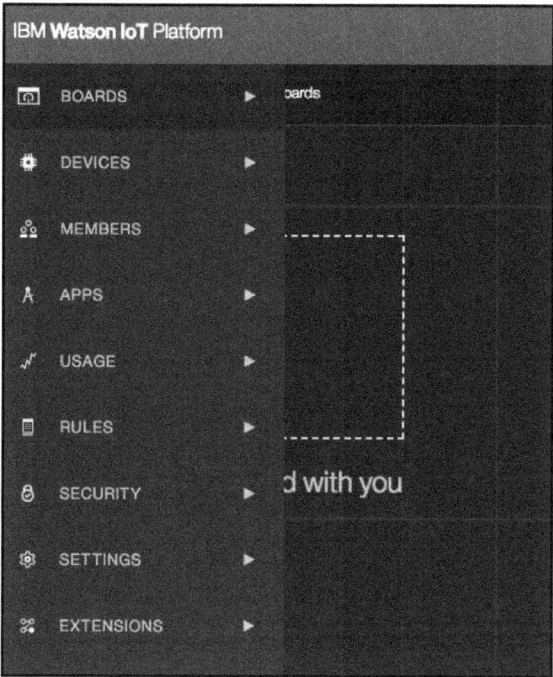

6. Click on **DEVICES** in the left-hand side menu and select **Device Types**. Using the **Add Device Type** button, create a new device type, as shown:

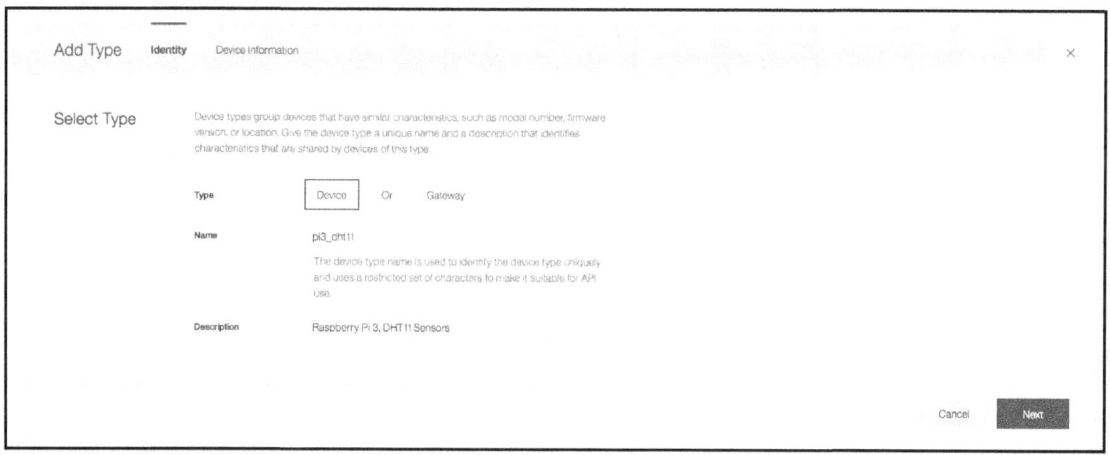

7. Click on the **Next** button and fill in the device metadata as applicable. Once the device type has been created we will then create the device.

8. Click on **Browse** in the top menu and you will be taken to the **Browse Devices** screen. Click on **Add Device** and fill in the form as follows:

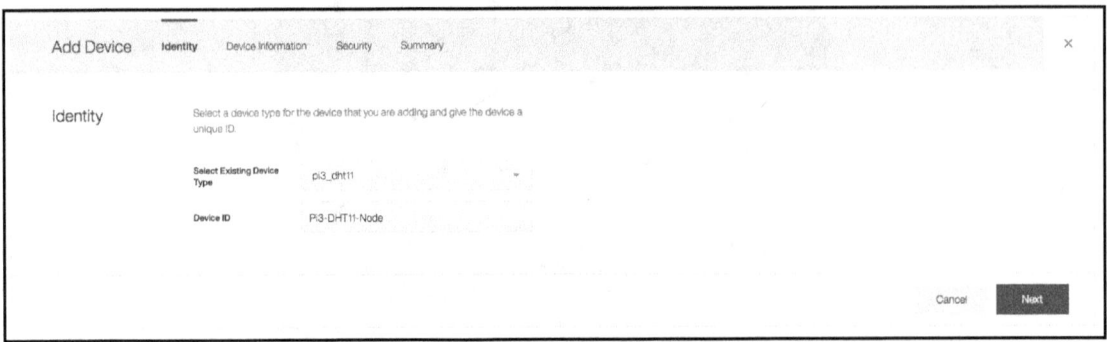

9. Click **Next** and fill in the metadata as applicable. Click **Next**. On the **Device Security** page, leave the token field blank.
10. Let the platform generate a token for us. If you would like, you can also provide a token of your own:

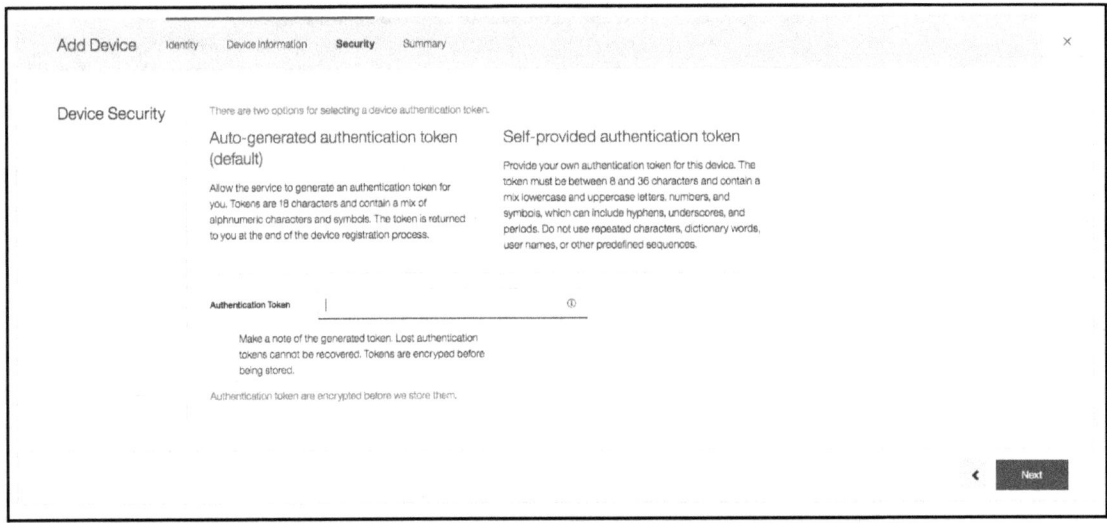

11. Click **Next**, review the summary, and click **Done**. Once the device has been successfully created, we should see the following information:

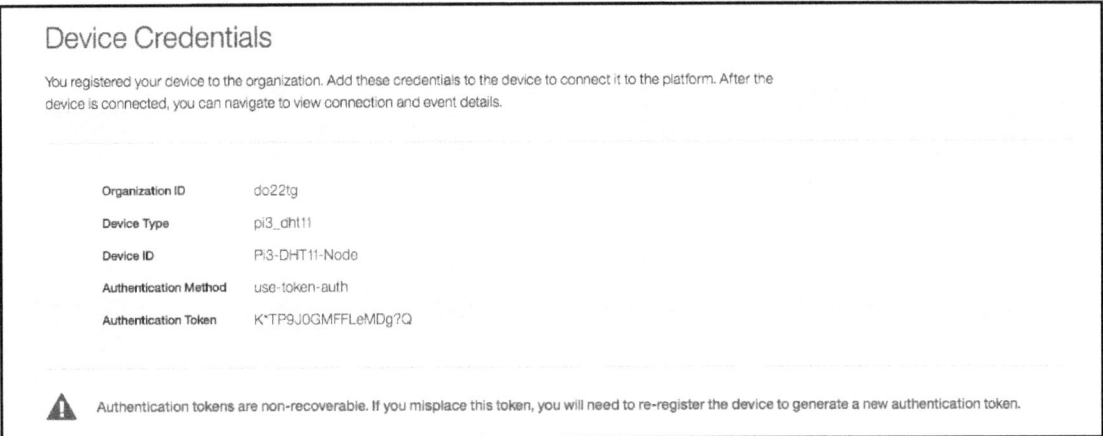

Do not share this information with anyone. That would be like sharing the password for a device that connects to the IBM IoT platform.

Also, make a note of the authentication token. Once we navigate away from this page, it will not appear again.

On the same page, using the menu on the left-hand side, select **Recent Events** and you should navigate down the same page as follows:

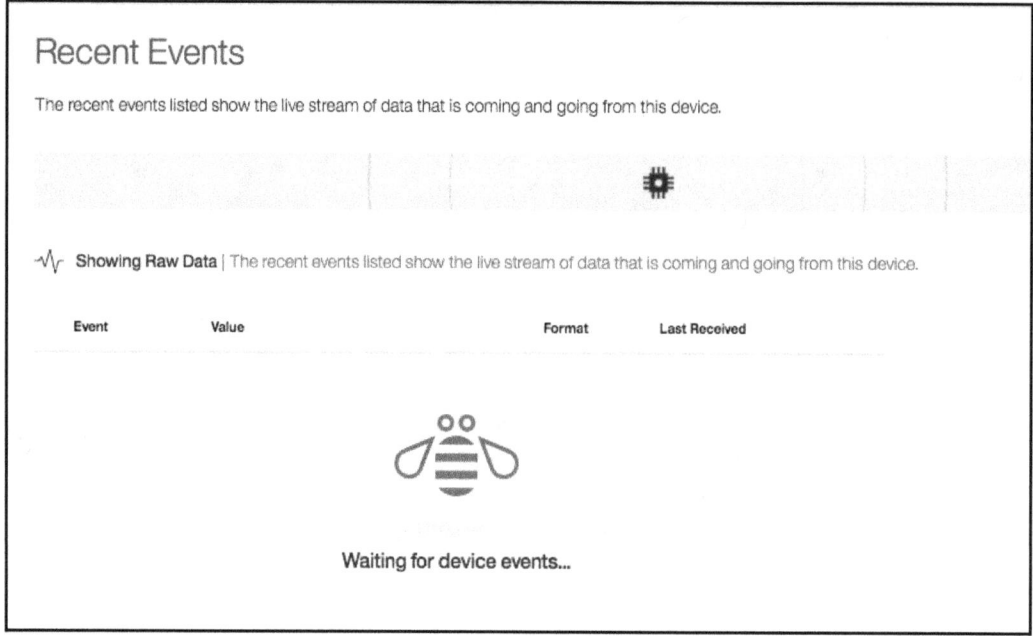

Once the Raspberry Pi starts publishing data, we should see it here. Let's leave this page as is and move on to the Raspberry Pi.

Setting up a Raspberry Pi 3 with DHT11 node

Now that we have our device set up in the IBM IoT platform, we are going to complete the remaining operation on the Raspberry Pi to publish data.

Things needed

The following are required to set up a Raspberry Pi DHT11 node:

- **One Raspberry Pi 3**: https://www.amazon.com/Raspberry-Pi-Desktop-Starter-White/dp/B01CI58722
- **One breadboard**: https://www.amazon.com/Solderless-Breadboard-Circuit-Circboard-Prototyping/dp/B01DDI54II/

- **One DHT11 sensor**: https://www.amazon.com/HiLetgo-Temperature-Humidity-Arduino-Raspberry/dp/B01DKC2GQ0
- **Three male-to-female jumper cables**: https://www.amazon.com/RGBZONE-120pcs-Multicolored-Dupont-Breadboard/dp/B01M1IEUAF/

If you are new to the world of Raspberry Pi GPIO's interfacing, take a look at, *Raspberry Pi GPIO Tutorial: The Basics Explained* at: https://www.youtube.com/watch?v=6PuK9fh3aL8.

Perform the following steps:

1. Connect the DHT11 sensor to the Raspberry Pi as shown in the following diagram:

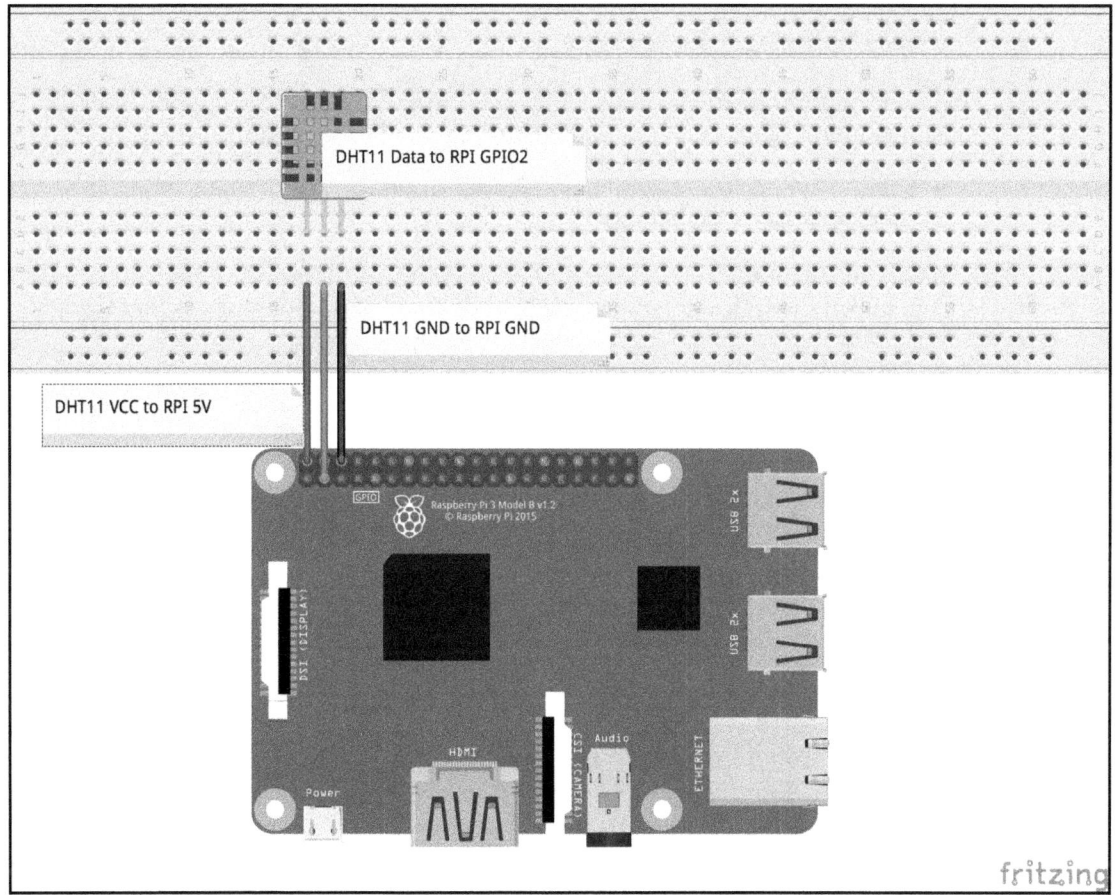

2. Next, power up the Raspberry Pi and log into it. On the desktop, create a new folder named `IBM-IoT-Device`.

3. Open a new Terminal and `cd` into the `IBM-IoT-Device` directory.

Setting up Node.js

Assuming that this is the same Raspberry Pi that was used in `Chapter 3`, *Getting Started with IoT Platforms*, it should have Node.js installed. If Node.js is not installed, please refer to the following steps:

1. Open a new Terminal and run the following commands:

   ```
   $ sudo apt update
   $ sudo apt full-upgrade
   ```

2. This will upgrade all the packages that need upgrades. Next, we will install the latest version of Node.js. We will be using the Node 7.x version:

   ```
   $ curl -sL https://deb.nodesource.com/setup_7.x | sudo -E bash -
   $ sudo apt install nodejs
   ```

3. This will take a moment to install and once your installation is done, you should be able to run the following commands to see the version of Node.js and npm:

   ```
   $ node -v
   $ npm -v
   ```

Developing the Node.js thing app

Now, we will set up the app and write the required code:

1. From the Terminal, once you are inside the `IBM-IoT-Device` folder, run the following:

   ```
   $ npm init -y
   ```

2. Next, we will install the `ibmiotf` module (https://www.npmjs.com/package/ibmiotf) from npm. Run the following:

   ```
   $ npm install ibmiotf --save
   ```

3. Next, we will install `rpi-dht-sensor` (https://www.npmjs.com/package/rpi-dht-sensor) from npm. This module will help in reading the DHT11 temperature and humidity values:

```
$ npm install rpi-dht-sensor --save
```

4. Your final `package.json` file should look like this:

```
{
  "name": "IBM-IoT-Device",
  "version": "1.0.0",
  "description": "",
  "main": "index.js",
  "scripts": {
    "test": "echo "Error: no test specified" && exit 1"
  },
  "keywords": [],
  "author": "",
  "license": "ISC",
  "dependencies": {
    "ibmiotf": "^0.2.41",
    "rpi-dht-sensor": "^0.1.1"
  }
}
```

5. Now that we have the required dependencies installed, let's continue. Create a new file named `index.js` at the root of the `IBM-IoT-Device` folder. Open `index.js` in any text editor and update it as shown:

```
var Client = require('ibmiotf');
var rpiDhtSensor = require('rpi-dht-sensor');
var dht = new rpiDhtSensor.DHT11(2); // `2` => GPIO2
var config = {
  'org': 'do22tg',
  'domain': 'internetofthings.ibmcloud.com',
  'type': 'pi3_dht11',
  'id': 'Pi3-DHT11-Node',
  'auth-method': 'token',
  'auth-token': 'K*TP9J0GMFFLeMDg?Q'
};
var deviceClient = new Client.IotfDevice(config);
//setting the log level to trace. By default it's 'warn'
deviceClient.log.setLevel('debug');
deviceClient.connect();
deviceClient.on('connect', function() {
  var QOS = 2;
  console.log("connected");
```

```
setInterval(function function_name() {
  var data = fetchData();
  deviceClient.publish('dht11', 'json', JSON.stringify(data),
QOS);
  }, 30000);
});
deviceClient.on('reconnect', function() {
  console.log('Reconnected!!!');
});
deviceClient.on('disconnect', function() {
  console.log('Disconnected from IoTF');
});
deviceClient.on('error', function(argument) {
  console.log(argument);
});
function fetchData() {
  var readout = dht.read();
  var temp = readout.temperature.toFixed(2);
  var humd = readout.humidity.toFixed(2);
  return {
    "temp": temp,
    "humd": humd
  };
}
```

In the previous code, we are creating a new `deviceClient` using `Client.IotfDevice()` with the config we have defined. Next, we have initiated a new connection and once connected, we are fetching the temperature and humidity data and then publishing it on to a custom topic named `dht11` as JSON:

In the configuration:

- `org` is the organization ID
- `type` is the device type for this device
- `id` is the device ID that we have used to create this device
- `auth-method` is the token we are using for token-based authentication
- `auth-token` is the value that was auto generated

Update the previous values as applicable from the created device screen. Save the previous file and run the following command:

```
$ sudo node index.js
```

And we should see something like this:

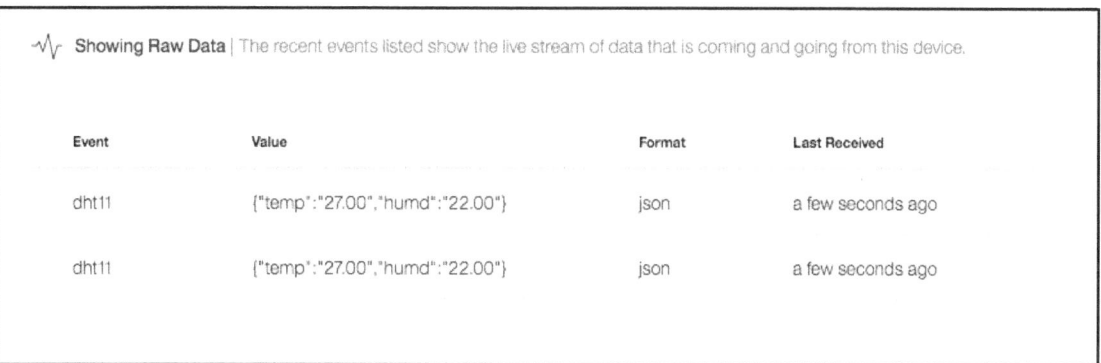

As we can see from the preceding logs, the device uses our credentials to connect to the platform over SSL, and once successfully connected we are going to send data every 30 seconds.

Now, if we head back to the device screen, **Recent events**, we should see the data appear in real time as shown:

-\/\- **Showing Raw Data**	The recent events listed show the live stream of data that is coming and going from this device.		
Event	**Value**	**Format**	**Last Received**
dht11	{"temp":"27.00","humd":"22.00"}	json	a few seconds ago
dht11	{"temp":"27.00","humd":"22.00"}	json	a few seconds ago

Now that the device is publishing data, let us actually read the data coming from this device.

Reading the data from the device

For us to read data from another client, we need to first create a new client. Once the new application client is created, we use its API key to connect to the platform and request data from this device.

Click on **Apps** in the side menu and under **API Keys** click the **Generate API Key** button. This will create a new **API Key** and **Authentication Token** as shown:

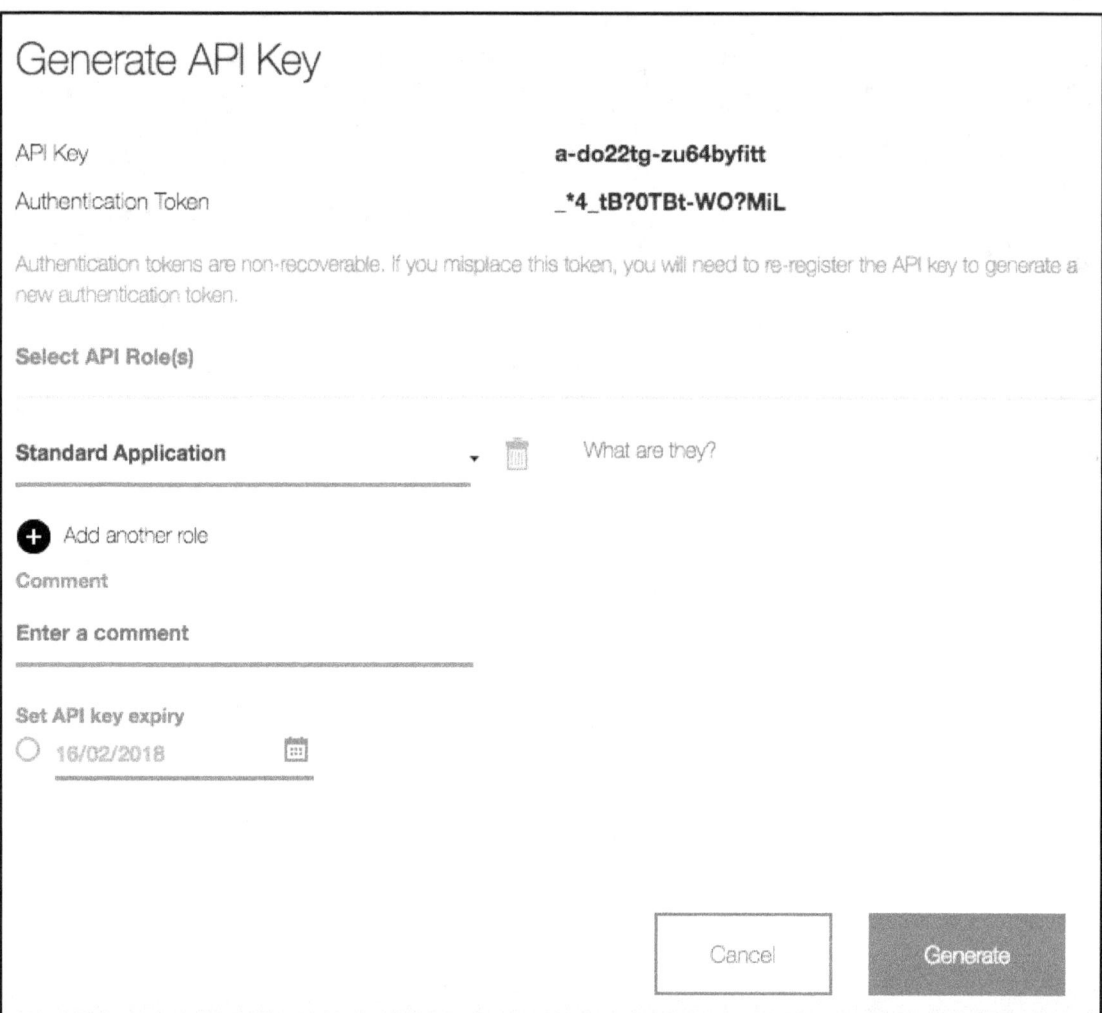

Make sure to make a copy of the **API Key** and **Authentication Token** before clicking on the **Generate** button.

Now that we have created a new application client, we will set up the code for it.

For this, you can either use the same Raspberry Pi or another computer. I am going to use MacBook as a client that is interested in the data sent by the device.

On my local computer I am going to create the following setup, which is very similar to what we have done on the Raspberry Pi:

1. Create a folder named `test_client`. Inside the `test_client` folder, run the following command:

   ```
   $ npm init -y
   ```

2. Next, install `ibmiotf` as follows:

   ```
   $ npm install ibmiotf --save
   ```

3. Create a file inside the `test_client` folder named `index.js` and update it as shown in the following snippet:

   ```
   var iotf = require('ibmiotf');
   var appClientConfig = {
       org: 'do22tg',
       id: 'Pi3-DHT11-Node',
       "auth-key": 'a-do22tg-zu64byfitt',
       "auth-token": '_*4_tB?0TBt-WO?MiL'
   };

   var appClient = new iotf.IotfApplication(appClientConfig);

   //setting the log level to trace. By default its 'warn'
   appClient.log.setLevel('debug');

   appClient.connect();

   appClient.on('connect', function() {
       console.log("connected");
       appClient.subscribeToDeviceEvents();
       appClient.subscribeToDeviceEvents('myevt');
   });

   appClient.on('deviceEvent', function(deviceType, deviceId,
   eventType, format, payload) {
       console.log("Device Event from :: " + deviceType + " : " +
   deviceId + " of event " + eventType + " with payload : " +
   payload);
   });

   appClient.on('reconnect', function() {
       console.log("Reconnected!!!");
   });
   ```

```
appClient.on('disconnect', function() {
    console.log('Disconnected from IoTF');
});

appClient.on('error', function(argument) {
    console.log(argument);
});
```

4. Update the `appClientConfig` as per your authentication key and token. The ID in `appClientConfig` is the ID of the device we want to listen to. Save the file and run the following command:

   $ node index.js

We should see the following output:

```
● ● ●                    test_client — node index.js — node index.js — 113×36
                                         node                                        node index.js  +
→  test_client
→  test_client node index.js
[BaseClient:connect] Connecting to IoTF with host : ssl://do22tg.messaging.internetofthings.ibmcloud.com:8883 and
 with client id : a:do22tg:Pi3-DHT11-Node
[ApplicationClient:connnect] ApplicationClient Connected
connected
[ApplicationClient:subscribeToDeviceEvents] Calling subscribe with QoS 0
[ApplicationClient:subscribe] Subscribing to topic iot-2/type/+/id/+/evt/+/fmt/+ with QoS 0
[ApplicationClient:subscribe] Subscribed to topic iot-2/type/+/id/+/evt/+/fmt/+ with QoS 0
[ApplicationClient:subscribeToDeviceEvents] Calling subscribe with QoS 0
[ApplicationClient:subscribe] Subscribing to topic iot-2/type/myevt/id/+/evt/+/fmt/+ with QoS 0
[ApplicationClient:subscribe] Subscribed to topic iot-2/type/myevt/id/+/evt/+/fmt/+ with QoS 0
Device Event from :: pi3_dht11 : Pi3-DHT11-Node of event dht11 with payload : {"temp":"28.00","humd":"19.00"}
Device Event from :: pi3_dht11 : Pi3-DHT11-Node of event dht11 with payload : {"temp":"28.00","humd":"19.00"}
```

This way, any client that is interested in the data of this device can use this approach to get the latest data.

With this we conclude the section on posting data to the IBM IoT platform and fetching it. In the next section, we are going to work on building visualization for this data.

Building the dashboard

Now that we have seen how a client can read the data from our device on demand, we will move on to building a dashboard, where we show data in real time.

For this we are going to make use of the Boards concept. Before we get started with this, we need to create a schema to define how our data looks.

Creating a schema

Let's look at how to create a schema:

1. Click on **Devices**, then **Manage Schemas**, and then **Create New Schema**. On the following screen, select the **Device Type** as shown:

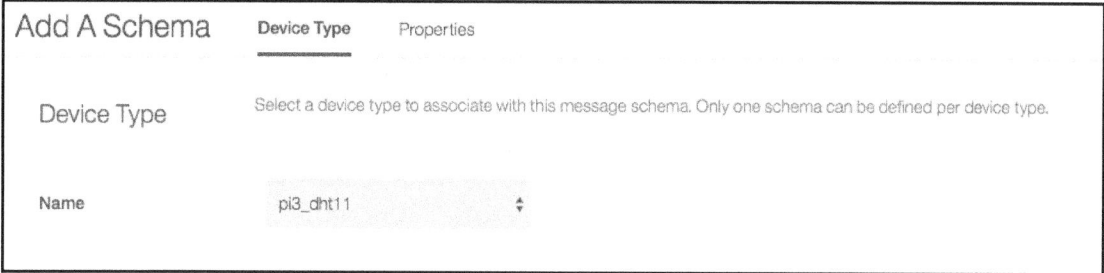

2. Click **Next** and add two properties as shown:
   - **Property 1**: temperature

Field	Value
Property	temp
Name	**Temperature**
Type	**float**

   - **Property 2**: humidity

Field	Value
Property	humd
Name	**Humidity**
Type	**float**

3. And click on **Finish**. This will create our schema that we are going to use in the next step.

Creating a board

Follow these steps to create a board:

1. From the left-hand side menu, click on **BOARDS** and you should see something like this:

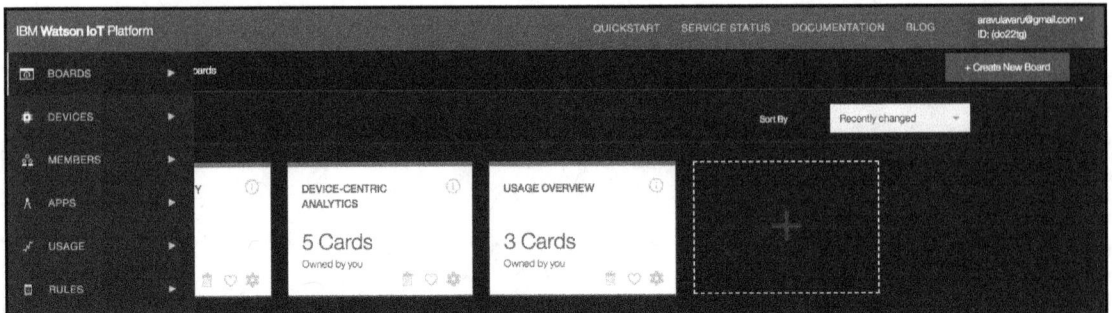

2. Now, click on the **+ Create New Board** button and fill in the screen as shown:

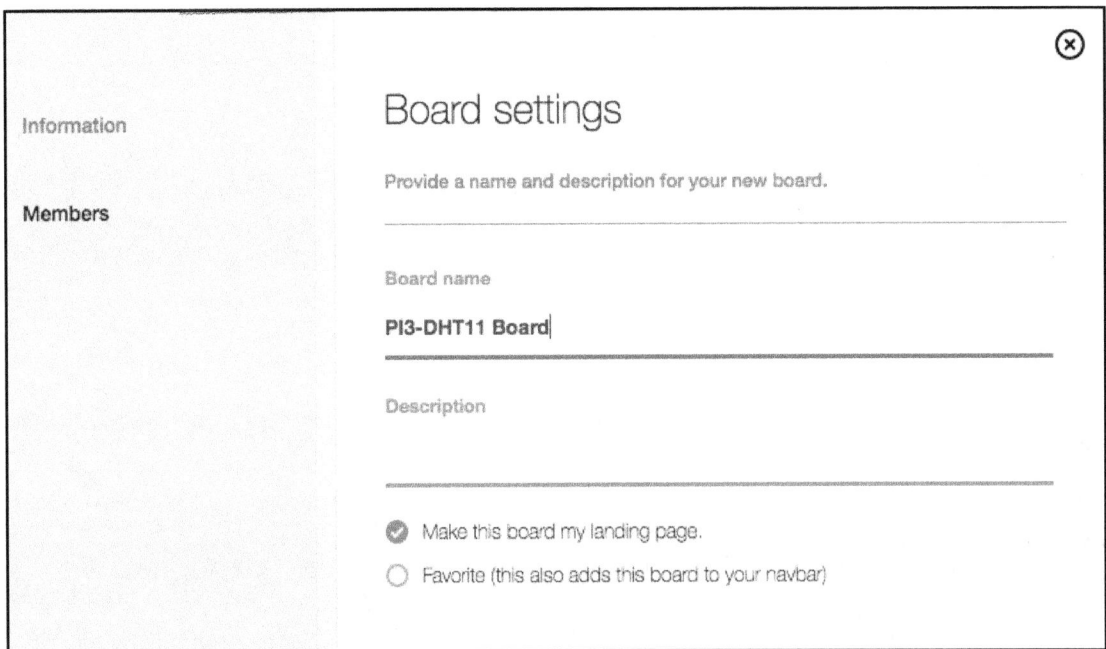

3. Click on the **Next** button and finally click on **Create** to create the board. Once the board has been successfully created, it will appear next to the list of existing Boards.

4. Click on **PI3-DHT11 Board** and we will land on an empty board. Click on **Add New Card** and select **Line Chart** from the following screen:

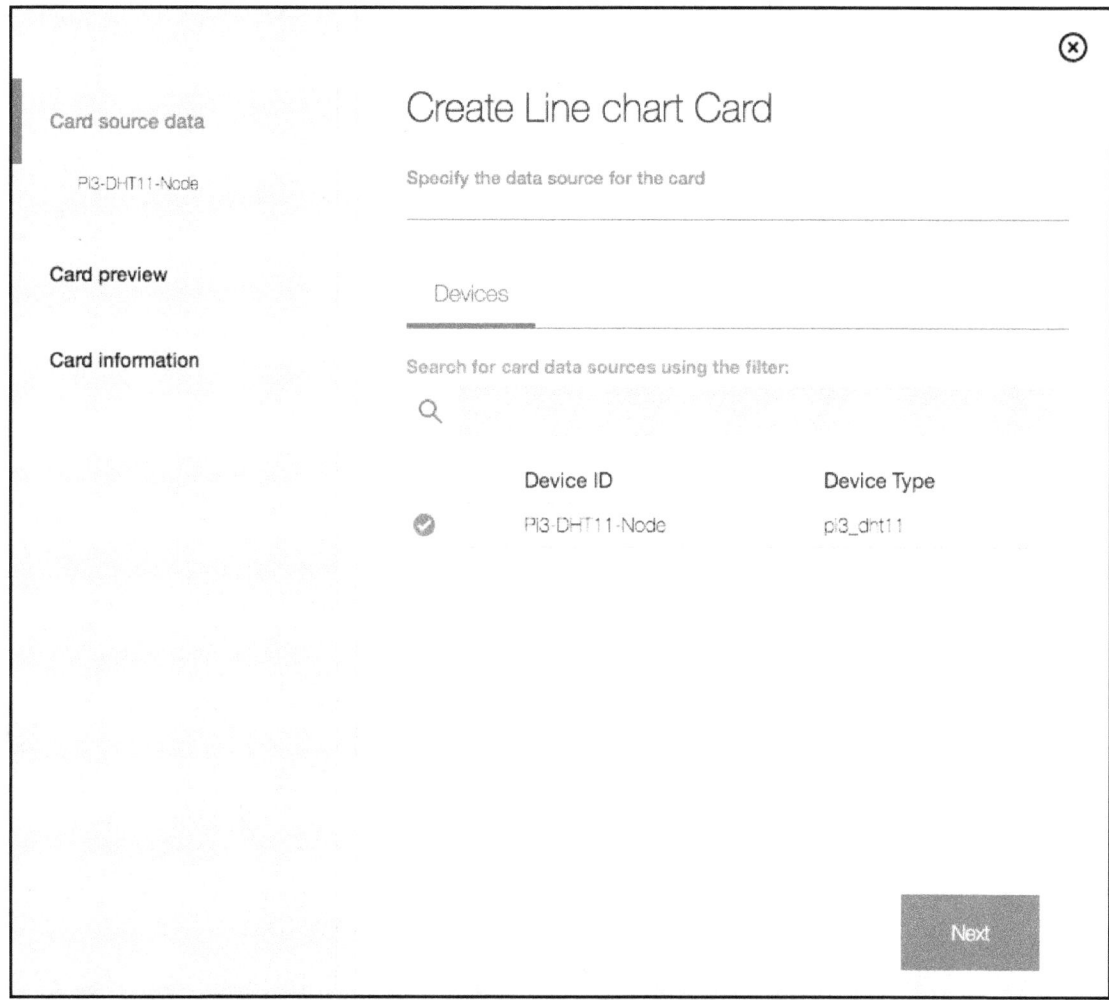

5. Click on **Next**, and now we will add datasets. Update the source data using the auto-populated dropdown as shown:

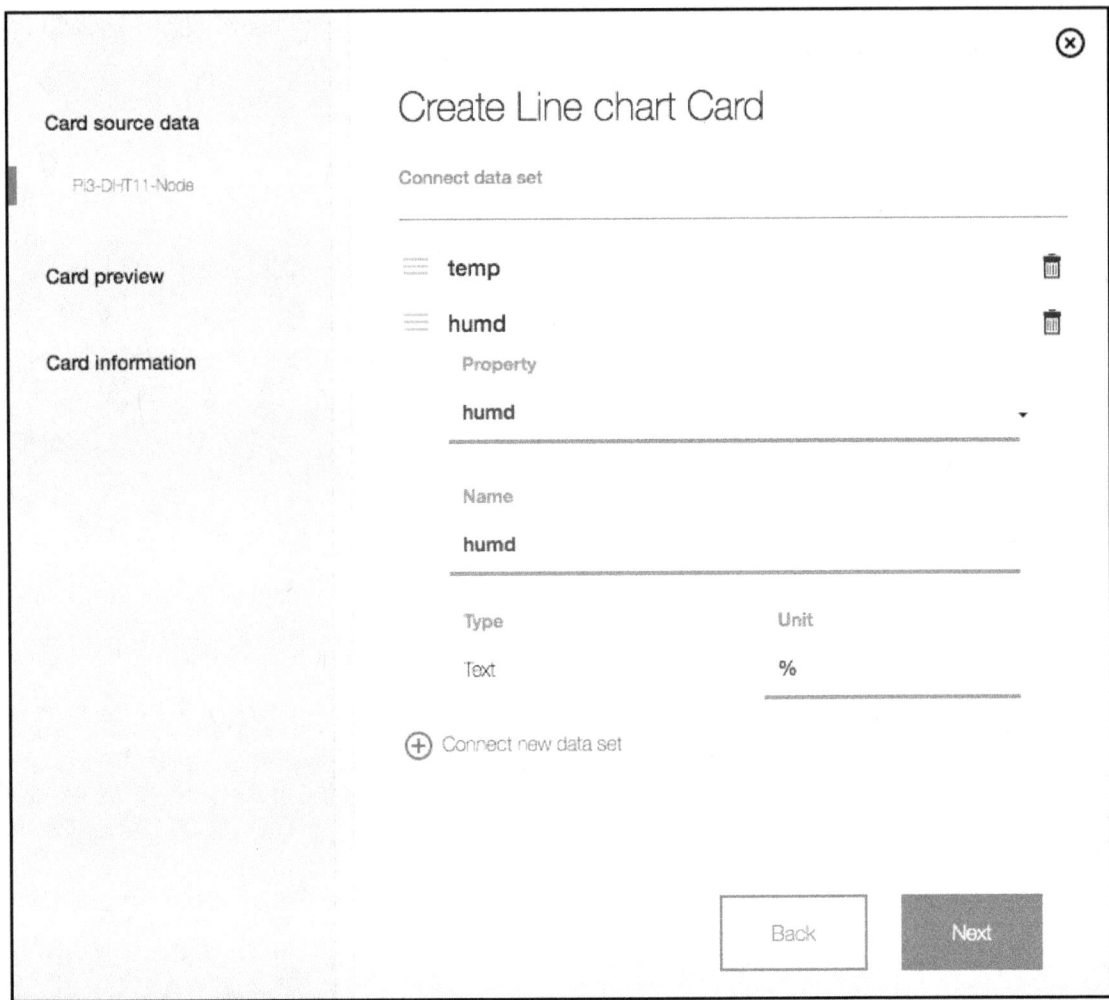

The preceding values come from the schema we have created:

1. Click on **Next** and select **XL** as the size of the card. Click on **Next** again and pick a color.
2. Once done, click on **Submit** and we should see a new real-time graph as shown:

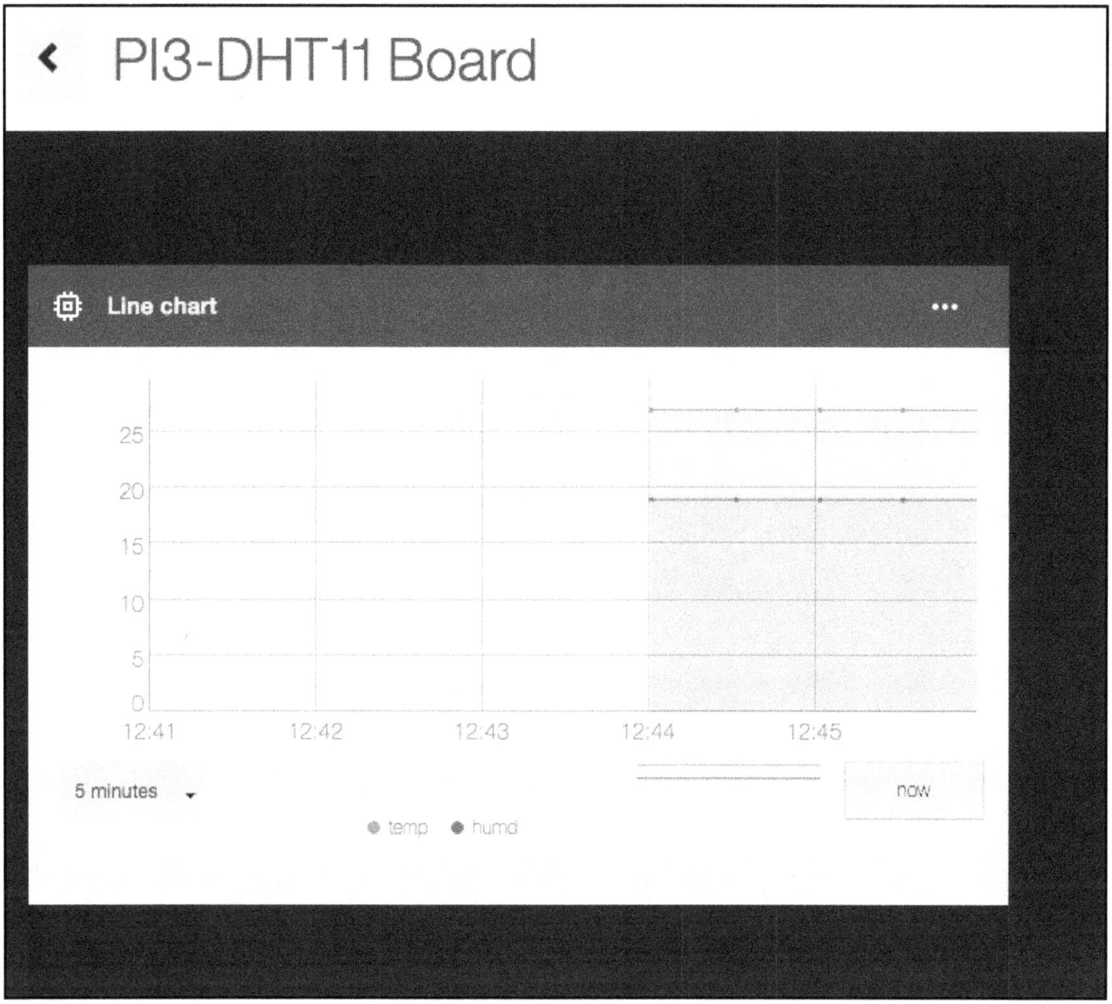

‹ PI3-DHT11 Board

⊡ **Line chart**   •••

25
20
15
10
5
0
12:41   12:42   12:43   12:44   12:45

5 minutes ▾   now

● temp   ● humd

With this we have seen the basic features and implementation processes for working with the AWS IoT platform.

> Once you are done with your learning, do not forget to delete the
> resources you have created. Otherwise you will be billed. You have been
> warned!

Summary

In this chapter, we have seen how to work with the IBM Watson IoT platform. We have created a new IoT platform, then we created new device types, and then finally devices. Using token-based authentication, we have connected the device to the IoT platform and have published the temperature and humidity data on a custom topic.

We have created another application client and subscribed to the data from this device and we were able to view that data in real time.

We have used Boards to create a new card, which displayed the temperature and humidity data in real time.

In the next chapter, we are going to work with the Kaa IoT Platform.

8
Kaa IoT

In the last chapter, we have seen how to build an end-to-end IoT solution using the Raspberry Pi 3, a DHT11 temperature and humidity sensor, and IBM Watson IoT. In this chapter, we are going to implement it using an open source IoT platform named Kaa. Along with this, we are going to work on building a visualization dashboard using ThingsBoard.

Topics covered in this chapter are:

- Kaa IoT architecture
- Setting up an end-to-end solution using Kaa IoT
- Setting up a visualization dashboard for the solution using ThingsBoard

Kaa IoT

Kaa is open source IoT middleware that provides the core IoT stack needed to build IoT solutions. The Kaa middleware provides a rich toolset for IoT product development and thus dramatically reduces associated cost, risks, and time-to-market.

For a quick start, Kaa offers a set of out-of-the-box, enterprise-grade IoT features that can be easily plugged in and used to implement most IoT use cases.

Some key features of Kaa are as follows:

- Active load balancing
- Configuration management
- Data collection
- Endpoint provisioning and registration
- Events
- Notifications

You can read more about Kaa and its platform features at:
`https://kaaproject.github.io/kaa/docs/v0.10.0/Programming-guide/Key-platform-fe atures/`. For this chapter, we are going to use the latest Kaa version-v0.10.0.

How does Kaa work?

The following diagram is taken from `https://www.kaaproject.org/overview/` and explains how Kaa works:

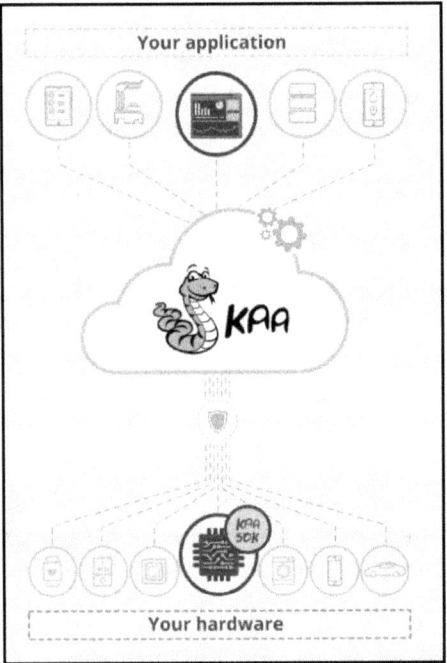

Kaa provides middleware for connecting hardware with enterprise applications. With Kaa's SDK, we can deploy it to most popular hardware and this SDK acts like a bidirectional secure bridge between the hardware and the application.

Not only does the middleware provide the connectivity tools, but it also provides various ways of exporting data. Now that we are aware of how Kaa works, we are going to make use of this to build our sample application.

Designing a sample application

In this section, we are going to build a sample application using the Kaa IoT stack.

Solution

The solution we are going to build will be similar to the one from `Chapter 3`, *Getting Started with IoT Platforms*. We are going to connect a DHT11 sensor to the Raspberry Pi 3 and then transmit the data over to the Kaa IoT platform. Then we'll take that data and pass it on to ThingsBoard to build a visualization. In the next section, we are going to look at the overall architecture of the solution.

Architecture

The following diagram explains the architecture of the solution:

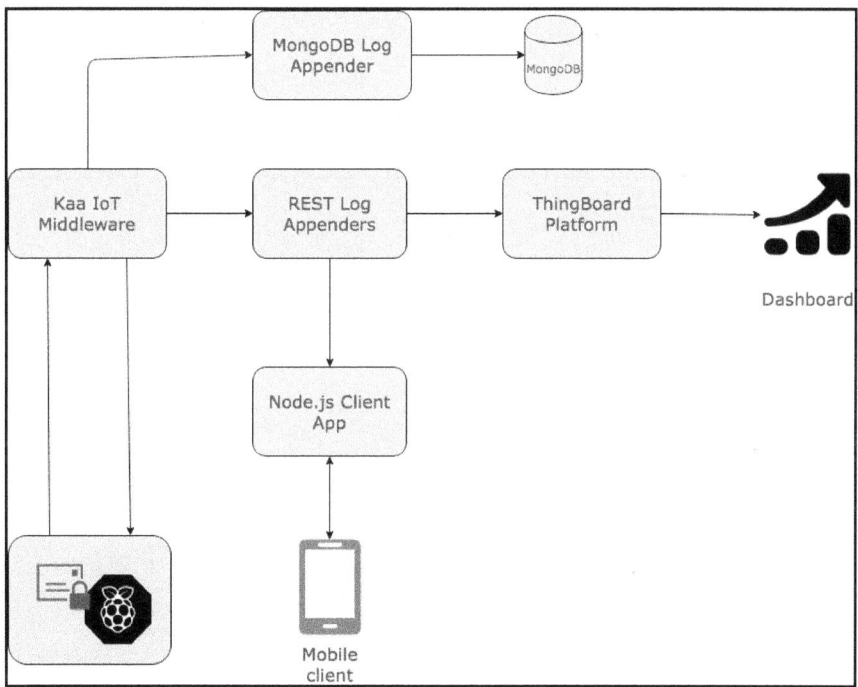

As we can see from the preceding diagram, we are using two open source stacks to build our end-to-end solution.

We are setting up the Kaa SDK on our Raspberry Pi 3 and then sending the DHT11 temperature and humidity data to the Kaa IoT middleware. Next, we are going to set up two REST log appenders that will take care of cascading the data from the IoT middleware to our end clients.

We are going to set up one REST appender to send data to a Node.js application that can be further built to send data to an app. We are also going to create another log appender to send our data to the ThingsBoard IoT platform. And from there, we are going to build a dashboard to view the data.

End-to-end communication

The following are the steps we are going to follow to achieve the preceding solution. First, set up the Thing and publish data to Kaa IoT:

1. Download VirtualBox
2. Download the Kaa image
3. Set up Kaa
4. Create an application
5. Set up data and a configuration schema
6. Set up REST appenders
7. Download SDK
8. Set up the Raspberry Pi and DHT11
9. Set up the client app and publish the data
10. Set up a Node.js server
11. View incoming data from the device

Data visualization

Next, we set up another log appender to send data to the ThingsBoard platform:

1. Create a ThingsBoard demo account
2. Create a new device
3. Set up the REST log appender to post data to ThingsBoard
4. Build the required dashboard

So, now that we are clear as to what we want to do, let's get started.

Pricing

Kaa is an open source platform with an Apache 2.0 license; read more here: `https://github.com/kaaproject/kaa/blob/master/LICENSE`. ThingsBoard supports two editions; one is the community, which is what we are going to use, and the one is professional edition, for more serious users.

You can read more about this here: `https://thingsboard.io/installations/`. The only charges that a user will incur are from the hosting services of the Kaa platform.

Building a sample application

We will start off by implementing an end-to-end solution, where we take the data from the DHT11 sensor and post it to the Kaa IoT.

Downloading Kaa

The first step we are going to do is set up Kaa. There are two approaches that we can follow:

- Local Sandbox running on VirtualBox
- Deployment to the AWS platform

In this chapter, we are going to follow the first option: setting up VirtualBox and then running a Kaa Sandbox image in it. If you do not have VirtualBox already installed, you can download it from here: `https://www.virtualbox.org/wiki/Downloads`.

Once you have downloaded and installed VirtualBox, we need to download a Kaa Sandbox image. We are going to use Kaa version 0.10.0 in this chapter:

1. Head over to `https://www.kaaproject.org/download-kaa/` and download Kaa Sandbox. This file is around 2 GB.

2. Once you have downloaded both VirtualBox and Kaa Sandbox, double-click on the Kaa Sandbox image and it should launch in VirtualBox with pre-filled values, as shown in the following screenshot:

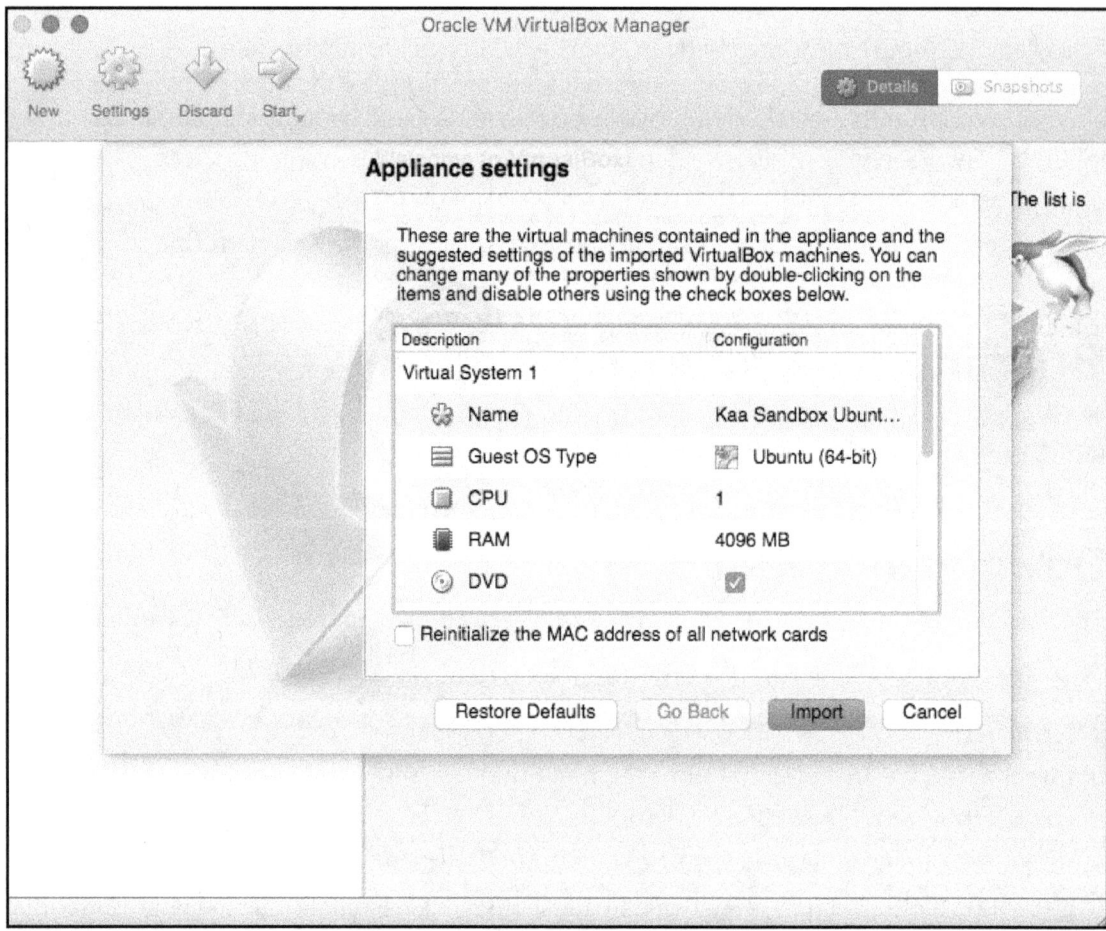

3. Click on the **Import** button. It will take VirtualBox a couple of minutes to set up the image based on your system configuration.
4. Once the image has been set up, single click the image and click on **Settings**. Next, select the **System** tab and **Processor** tab. You need to have at least two CPUs for everything to work fine, as shown:

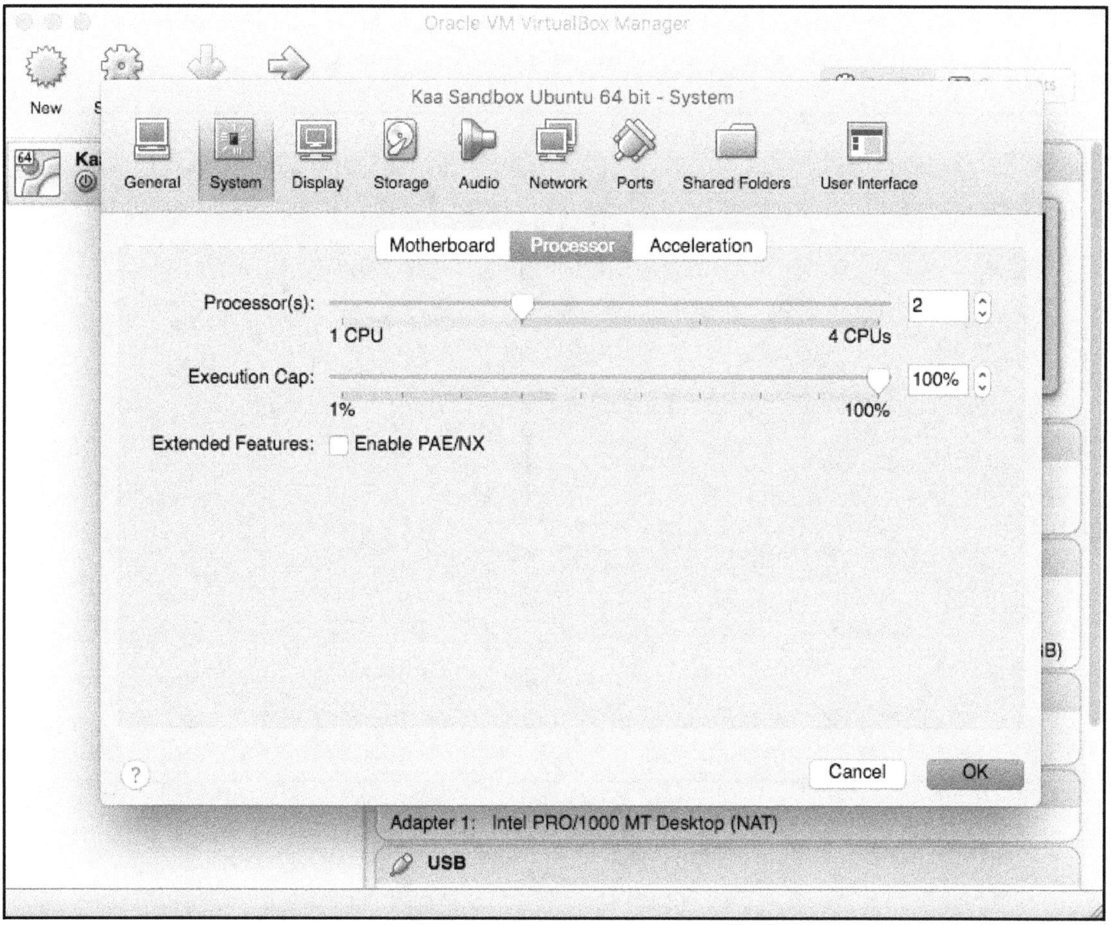

If you are using a low-end machine, you can use the alternative setup approach of deploying to AWS.

5. Click **OK** and start the virtual machine. You will see some logs rolling and if everything goes fine, you should land on the following screen:

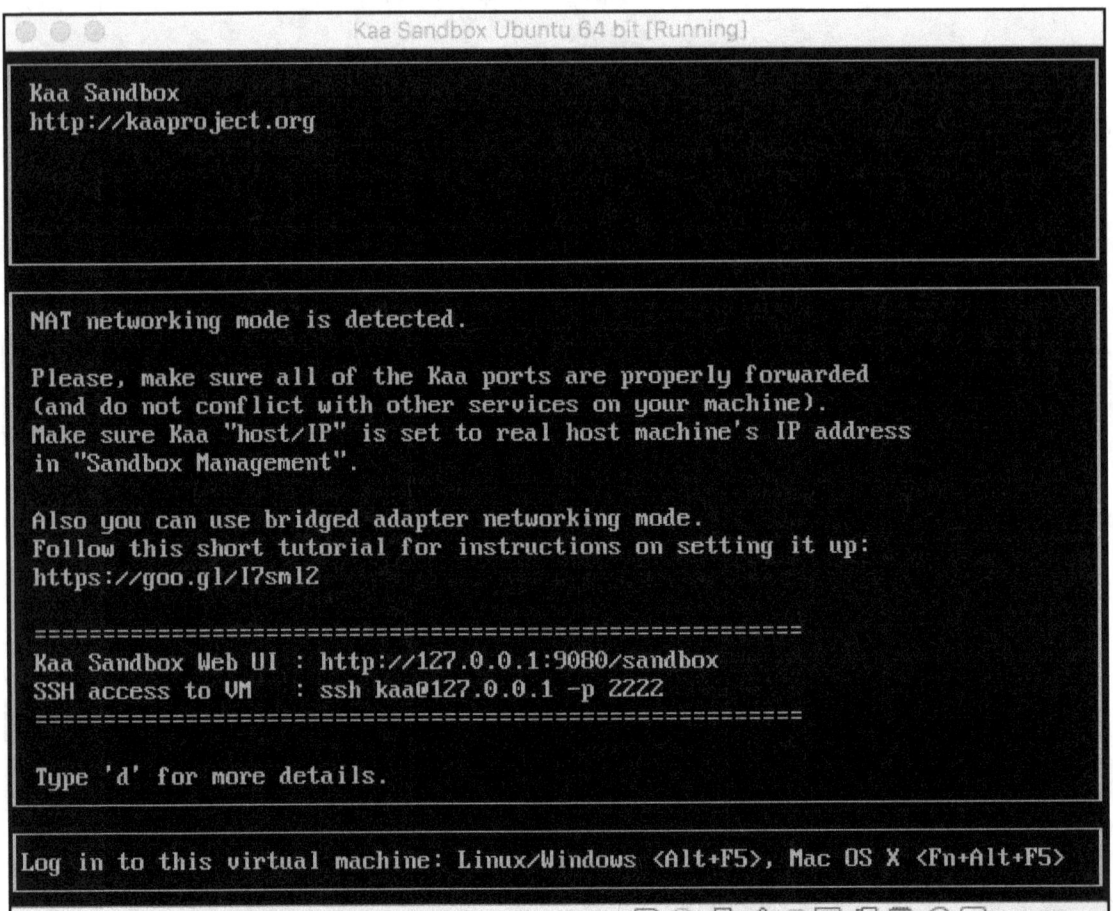

6. Type d on your keyboard and you should see the credentials screen as shown:

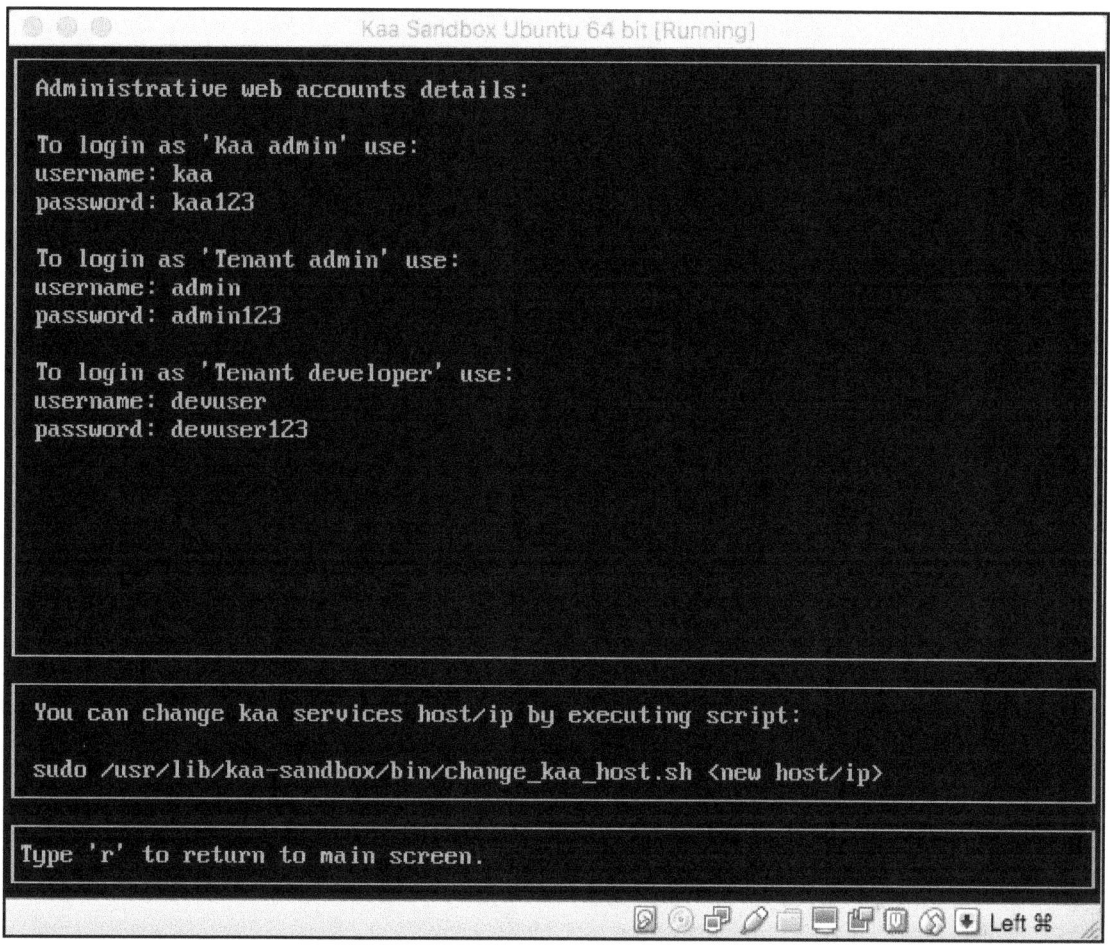

```
Administrative web accounts details:

To login as 'Kaa admin' use:
username: kaa
password: kaa123

To login as 'Tenant admin' use:
username: admin
password: admin123

To login as 'Tenant developer' use:
username: devuser
password: devuser123




You can change kaa services host/ip by executing script:

sudo /usr/lib/kaa-sandbox/bin/change_kaa_host.sh <new host/ip>

Type 'r' to return to main screen.
```

7. For this chapter, we are going to go with the defaults.

8. After the launch of the virtual machine, wait for a minute and head over to `http://localhost:9080/sandbox/`. If everything works well, we should see the Sandbox home page. There should be a popup asking us to change the Kaa host/IP, as follows:

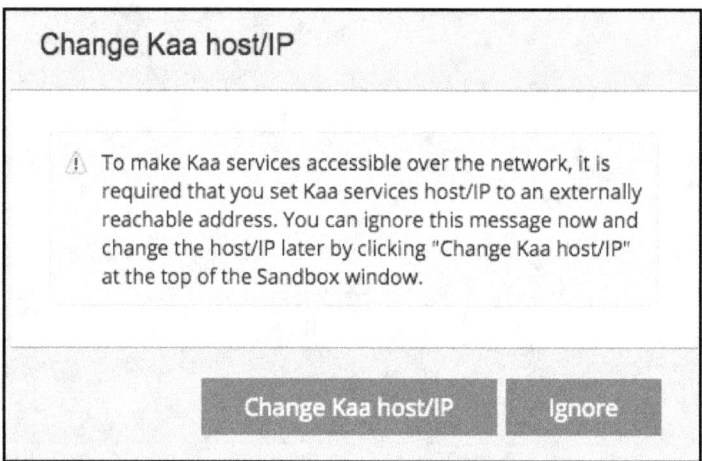

9. We need to change the IP here because I am assuming the Raspberry Pi and the computer on which Kaa Sandbox is running are connected to the same Wi-Fi or wired network.

10. Earlier, the Raspberry Pi posted data to the internet or cloud-hosted servers. This time, the middleware is running on our computer, so we need to route the traffic from the Raspberry Pi to here.

11. If you have hosted the Kaa Sandbox on AWS, you can use the EC2 server's public IP, and update it in the next step.

12. To get the IP address of the machine where Kaa is running, you can use the following:

- In Windows, you can use:

```
> ipconfig
```

- For *nix systems, you can use:

```
$ ifcong
```

13. And then copy the IP address and paste it into the **Sandbox Management** screen as shown here:

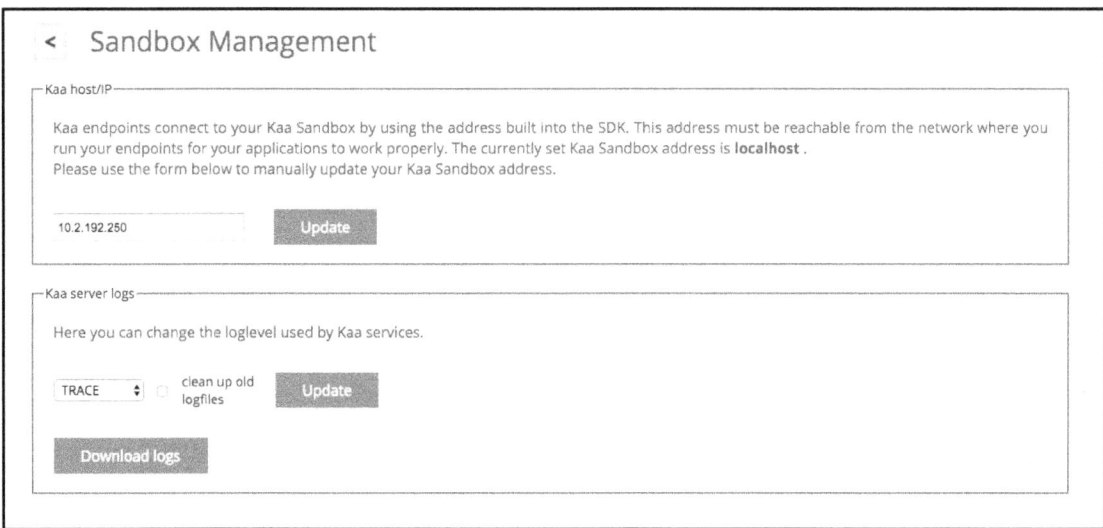

14. Click on **Update** and we should see that the Kaa node is redeployed. Wait for the deployment to be completed and head over to `http://IPADDRESS:9080/sandbox/` (in my case, it would be `http://10.2.192.250:9080/sandbox/`) and you should see the Sandbox home screen we saw seen earlier.

With this, we are done with the setup of the Kaa middleware. In the next setup, we are going to create a new application and continue.

Setting up a project

Now that the Kaa middleware is up and running, we are going to set up a new application:

1. From the Kaa Sandbox home screen, click on **Administration UI** or navigate to `http://10.2.192.250:8080/kaaAdmin/` where `10.2.192.250` is your IP address that has been set up in the last step.

2. As we saw in the last section, we have three sets of credentials. Use `admin` and `admin123` to log in to the administration UI and create an application.

3. Once we log in, we should see a few applications are already present. For our example, we are going to create our own application.

4. Click on the **Add** button and fill in the form as shown here:

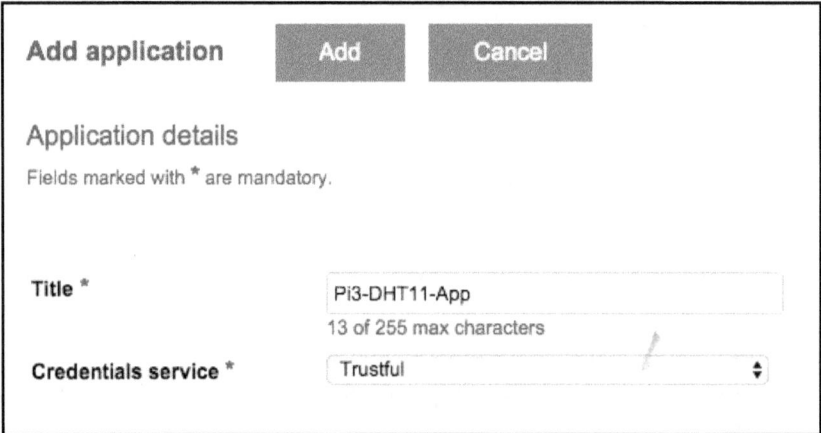

5. Once the application has been created, sign out of the administration UI and log back in with tenant developer credentials: `devuser` and `devuser123`.

6. From the **Applications** list on the left-hand side, expand **Pi3-DHT11-App** and click on **Application CTL**.

7. Now, we are going to add two common type libraries (CTLs):
     - The schema for the data collector
     - The schema for the sampler

We are going to create them as application-level scoped types.

1. First, anywhere on your machine, create a file named `config-schema.json` and update it as shown here:

```
{
  "type": "record",
  "name": "Configuration",
  "namespace": "org.myapp.schema",
  "fields": [{
    "name": "samplePeriod",
    "type": "int",
    "by_default": 15
  }]
}
```

2. The preceding configuration specifies that we are going to send the sampled data every 15 seconds.

3. Next, create another file named `data-schema.json` and update it as shown:

```
{
  "type": "record",
  "name": "DataCollection",
  "namespace": "org.myapp.schema",
  "fields": [{
    "name": "temperature",
    "type": "float"
  },
  {
  "name": "humidity",
  "type": "float"
  }]
}
```

4. The preceding schema defines the two data properties that we are going to send to the Kaa middleware and the data type.

5. Save both files and head back to **Administration UI** | **Pi3-DHT11-App** | **Application CTL** and then click on the **Add** button. Scroll to the bottom of this screen, and you should see the **Upload from file** option.

6. Now select `config-schema.json`, which we created earlier, and perform the upload:

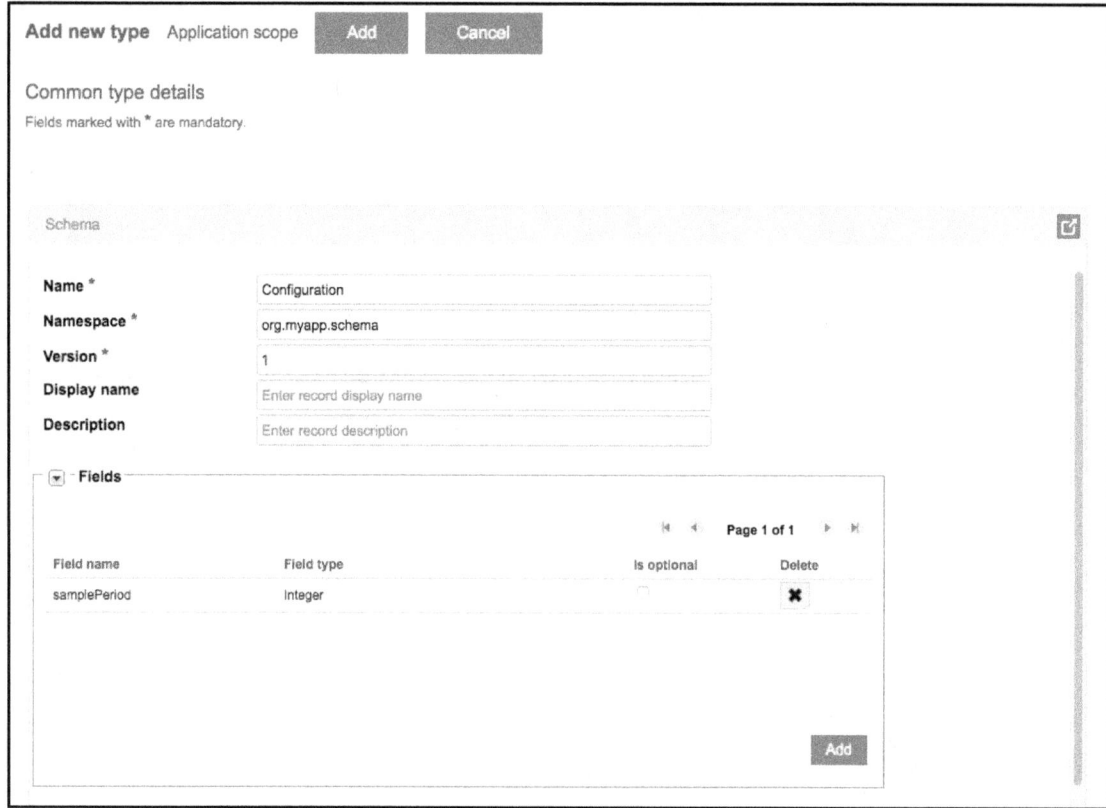

7. Once the schema has been successfully uploaded, we should see the schema we have defined appear in the form. Click on the **Add** button at the top of the screen to add this schema.

8. Now, we will follow the same process and upload `data-schema.json`:

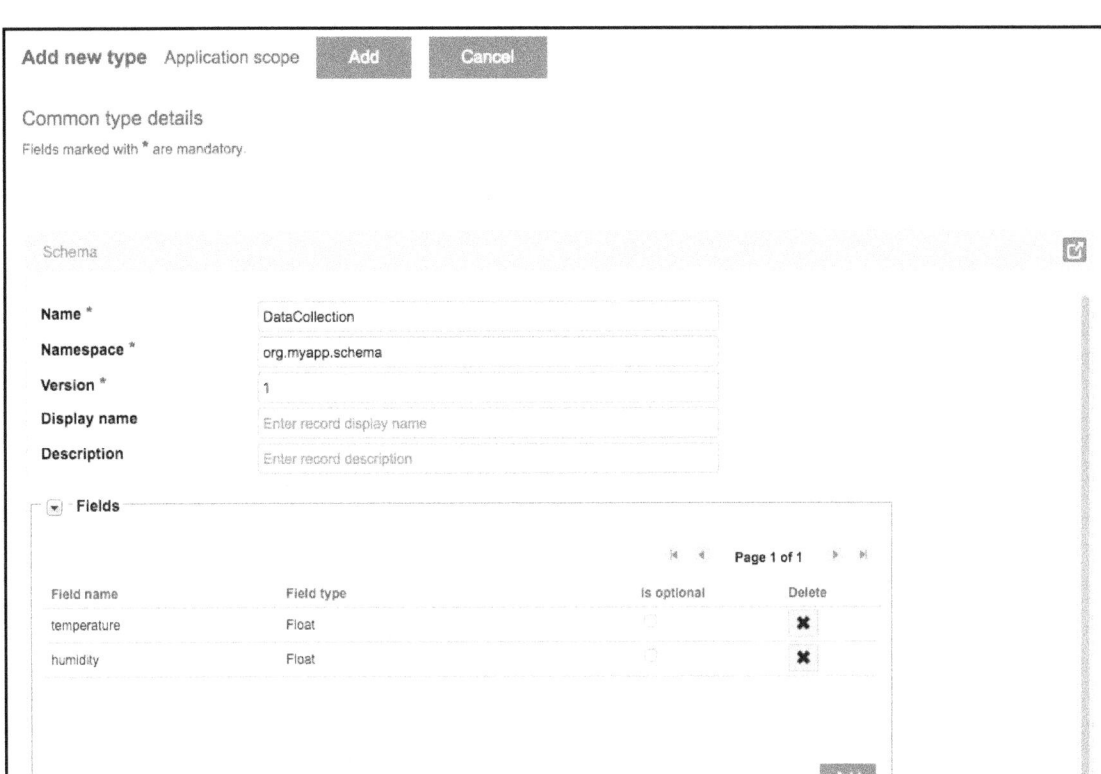

9. And add this CTL as well.

10. Now that we have created two, application-scoped CTLs, let's actually use them in this project.

11. From the left menu, select **Pi3-DHT11-App** | **Schemas** | **Configuration**. Next, click on the **Add** button.

12. Update the form as shown here:

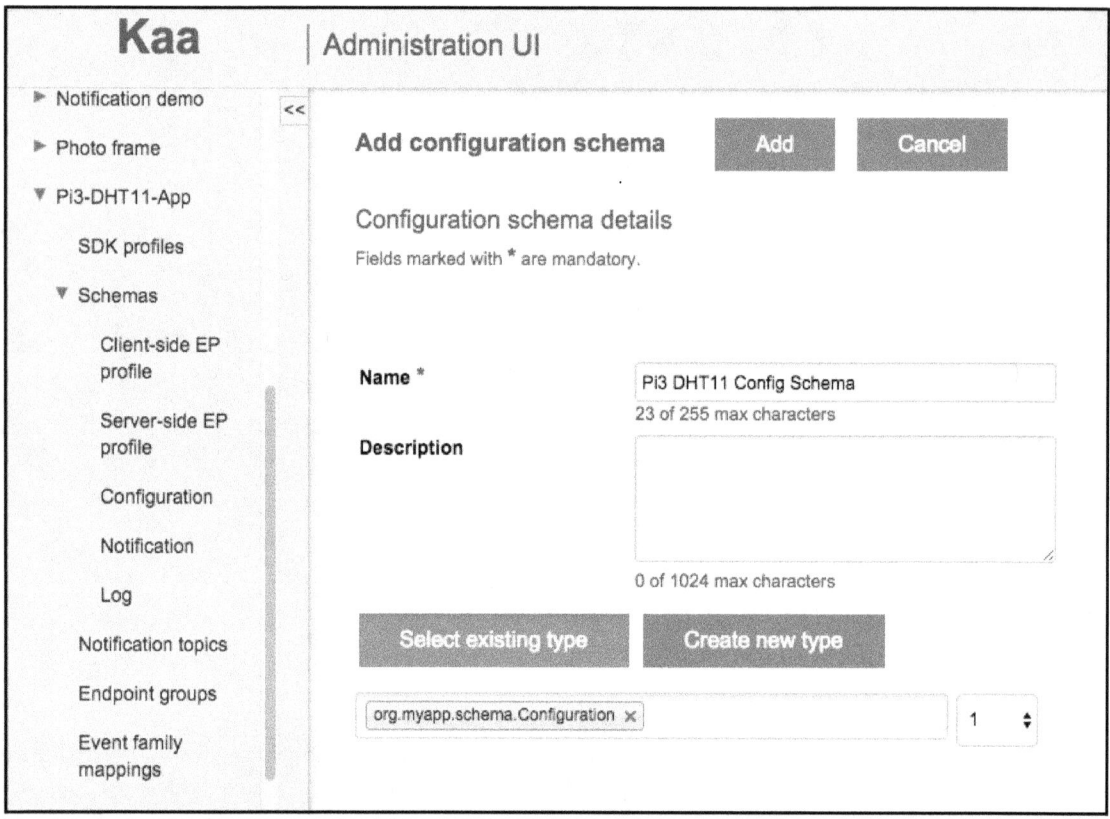

13. Click on **Add**. Once the schema has been successfully added, make a note of the **Version** field. This is very important while generating the SDK. If this is a new application and you have followed the previous steps as-is, the version number should be **2**.

14. Once the configuration schema has been added, next we will add the log schema.

15. From the left menu, select **Pi3-DHT11-App** | **Schemas** | **Log**. Next, click on the **Add** button.

16. Update the form as shown here:

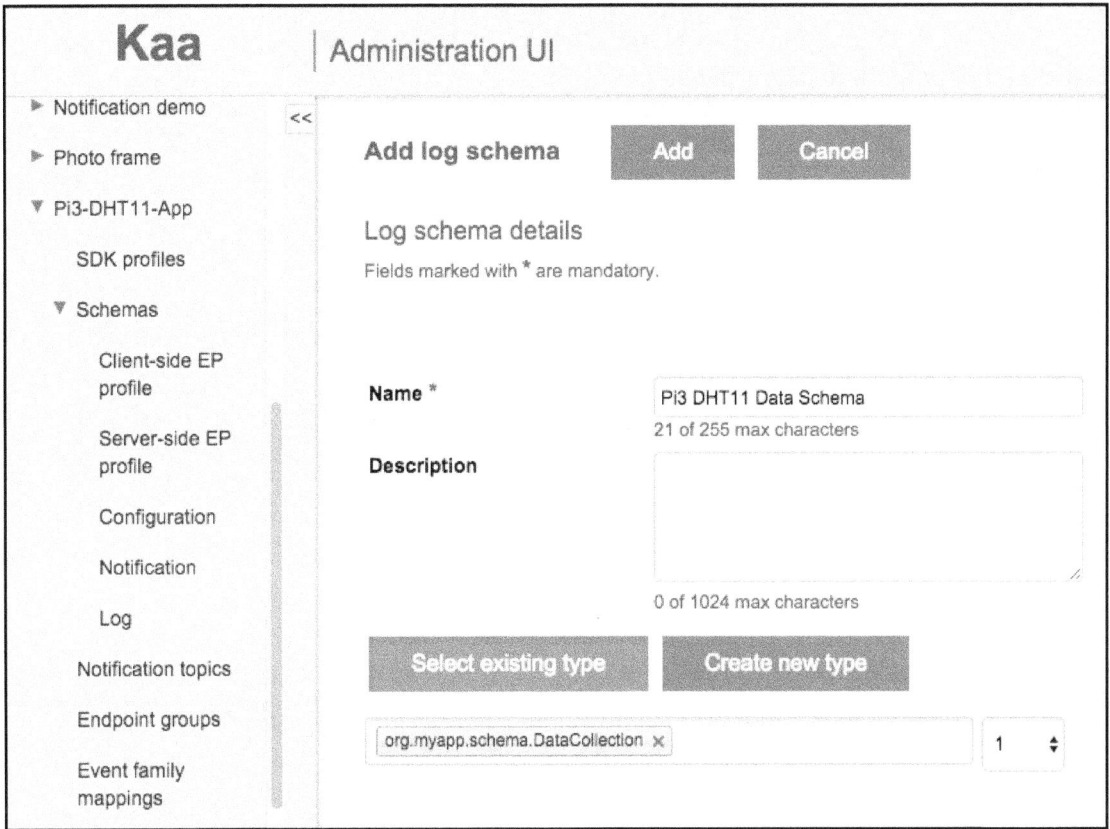

17. Click on **Add**. Once the schema has been successfully added, make a note of the **Version** field. This is very important while generating the SDK. If this is a new application and you have followed the previous steps as-is, the version number should be **2**.

18. In this section, we are going to set up two log appenders:
    - To send the data to a MongoDB database
    - To send data to a REST API endpoint to access the same data in real time

Setting up a MongoDB log appender

We are going to log one copy of the data into the MongoDB present inside the Kaa Sandbox. For that, from the left menu, select **Pi3-DHT11-App** | **Log appenders**. Next, click on **Add log appender** and fill in the form as shown:

Field	Value
Name	Pi3-DHT11-MongoDB-Logger
Min schema version	**1**
Max schema version	**Infinite**
Confirm delivery	False
Log metadata	Select the following: • **Endpoint key hash** • **Timestamp** • **Application token** • **Log schema version** • **Header version**
Type	**MongoDB**
MongoDB nodes | **Host**	localhost
MongoDB nodes | **Port**	27017
Authentication credentials	--
MongoDB database name	kaa-pi3-dht11-data
Include client profile data	True
Include server profile data	True

We will leave the remaining as defaults and click on **Add**. Or alternatively, you can save the following schema and upload it the **Add Log appender** page as well:

```
{
  "mongoServers": [
  {
    "host": "localhost",
    "port": 27017
  }],
  "mongoCredentials": [],
  "dbName": "kaa-pi3-dht11-data",
```

```
"connectionsPerHost":
{
  "int": 30
},
"maxWaitTime":
{
  "int": 120000
},
"connectionTimeout":
{
  "int": 5000
},
"socketTimeout":
{
  "int": 0
},
"socketKeepalive":
{
  "boolean": false
},
"includeClientProfile":
{
  "boolean": true
},
"includeServerProfile":
{
  "boolean": true
},
"minLogSchemaVersion": 1,
"maxLogSchemaVersion": 2147483647,
"pluginTypeName": "MongoDB",
"pluginClassName":
"org.kaaproject.kaa.server.appenders.mongo.appender.MongoDbLogAppender",
  "headerStructure": ["Endpointkeyhash", "Headerversion", "Timestamp",
"Applicationtoken", "Logschemaversion"]
}
```

 Instead of logging into the MongoDB on the Kaa Sandbox, you can log data to any remote node or nodes. You can use a service, such as `https://mlab.com/` to save your data externally as well.

Setting up a REST log appender

Next, we are going to create a REST log appender, which is going to publish the data that the Kaa middleware receives in real time to an HTTP(s) endpoint. This way, a client interested in real-time data can fetch it.

This REST log appender is going to transmit the data to a Node.js server and display it in the console. This can be any server and any application that can process incoming data in real time. For that, from the left menu, select **Pi3-DHT11-App** | **Log appenders**. Next, click on **Add log appender** and fill in the form as given in the following table:

Field	Value
Name	`Pi3-DHT11-REST-Logger`
Min schema version	**1**
Max schema version	**Infinite**
Confirm delivery	False
Log metadata	Select the following: • **Endpoint key hash** • **Timestamp** • **Application token** • **Log schema version** • **Header version**
Type	**REST**
Configuration | Host	`10.2.192.250` (This is the IP of the server where the Node.js application is running)
Configuration | Port	`3000` (This is the port of the server where the Node.js application is running)
Configuration | Use SSL	False
Configuration | Include Kaa header	True
Configuration | Relative URI path	`/`
Configuration | Method	**POST**
Request MIME type	**JSON**

We will leave the remaining as defaults and click on **Add**. Or alternatively, you can save the following schema and upload it the **Add Log appender** page as well:

```
{
  "host": "10.2.192.250",
  "port": 3000,
  "ssl": false,
  "verifySslCert": false,
  "username": null,
  "password": null,
  "connectionPoolSize": 1,
  "header": true,
  "path": "/",
  "method": "POST",
  "mimeType": "JSON",
  "minLogSchemaVersion": 1,
  "maxLogSchemaVersion": 2147483647,
  "pluginTypeName": "REST",
  "pluginClassName":
"org.kaaproject.kaa.server.appenders.rest.appender.RestLogAppender",
  "headerStructure": ["Endpointkeyhash", "Headerversion", "Timestamp",
"Applicationtoken", "Logschemaversion"]
}
```

With this, we are done with the setup of our application. Next, we will build a simple Node.js server that is going to receive data from the Kaa middleware.

Node.js server - REST Logger

Anywhere on your machine, create a folder named REST-Logger. In this folder, we are going to build the Node.js server application.

For this server, we need to have Node.js installed. You can visit https://nodejs.org/en/download/ to download the version of Node.js that is applicable for your machine.

Once Node.js is installed, we will go ahead. Open a new Command Prompt or terminal here and run:

```
npm init -y
```

Next, create a new file named `server.js` at the root of the `REST-Logger` folder and update it as shown:

```
var http = require('http');
var server = http.createServer(function(req, res) {
  var jsonString = '';
  req.on('data', function(data) {
    jsonString += data;
  });
  req.on('end', function() {
    var data = JSON.parse(jsonString); // to Object!
    console.log('>>>>>>>>> BEGIN >>>>>>>>>>>>n');
    console.log('Method:', req.method);
    console.log('URL:', req.url);
    console.log('Headers:', JSON.stringify(req.headers, null, 4));
    console.log('Data:', JSON.stringify(data, null, 4));
    console.log('>>>>>>>>> END >>>>>>>>>>>>>>n');
    res.writeHead(200);
    res.end();
  });
})
server.listen(3000);
console.log('Server listening on port 3000');
```

In the preceding code, we are starting an HTTP server on port 3000 and are listening for incoming requests. Once a new request is received, we will process the data and print it in the console.

We will start the server once we are ready to accept data. In the next step, we will download the SDK and run our application.

Downloading the SDK and running the app

Now that the application is set up on the Kaa IoT middleware and we have a Node.js REST logger application running, we are all set to send data from our device.

We are going to perform the following steps:

1. Set up a folder structure for our project
2. Download the SDK
3. Set up dependencies
4. Set up hardware
5. Run the application

Setting up a client app

On the Raspberry Pi, where we want to run this client, create a folder named `Kaa-IoT-Device` on the desktop. Inside the `Kaa-IoT-Device` folder, create three folders named, `kaa-sdk`, `src`, and `build`. Next, we are going to download the SDK and add it to our setup.

Downloading the Kaa SDK

Let's see how to download the SDK:

1. From within the Raspberry Pi, navigate to `http://10.2.192.250:8080/kaaAdmin` and login with the `devuser` and `devuser123` credentials.

2. Once logged in, navigate to **Pi3-DHT11-App** | **SDK profiles** and click on the **Add** button. Fill in the following screen as shown:

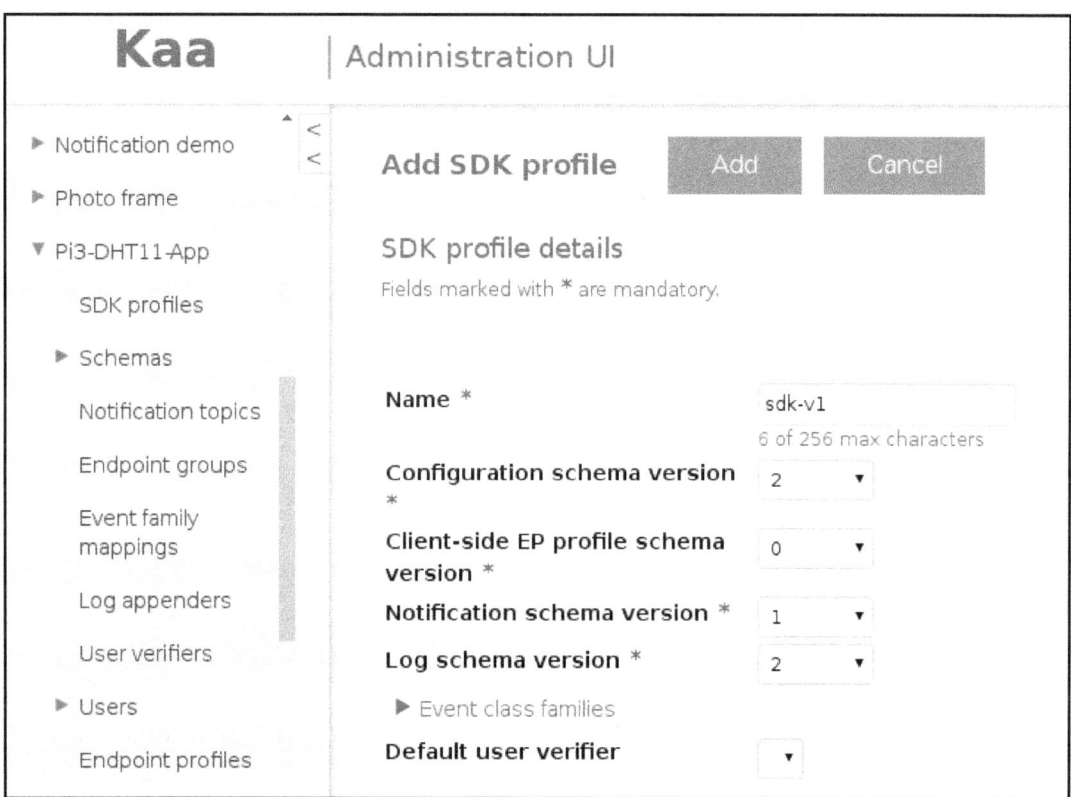

 Do note that the configuration schema version and log schema version should match with the version numbers of the schema we have set up.

3. Click **Add** and a new SDK profile will be created with the specified configuration.
4. Now, from the **SDK profiles details** page, click on the download icon under the **Generate SDK** column for the profile we just created.
5. Select **C** from the drop-down and click on **Generate SDK**, as shown:

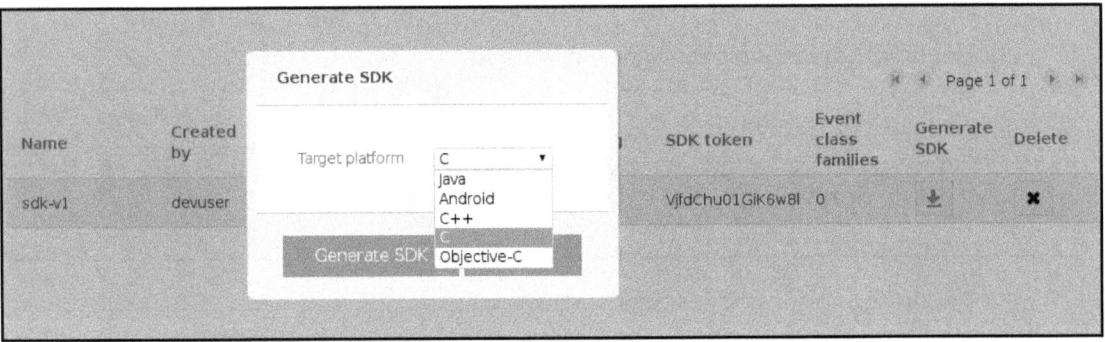

6. Now the SDK will be downloaded to the Raspberry Pi. From the downloaded folder, move the ZIP file to the `Desktop/Kaa-IoT-Device/kaa-sdk` folder and unzip its contents into the folder.
7. Next, we are going to set up a `CMakeLists.txt` file. At the root of the `Kaa-IoT-Device` folder, create a file named `CMakeLists.txt` and update it as shown:

```
cmake_minimum_required(VERSION 2.8.12)
project(kaa-application C)
set(CMAKE_C_FLAGS "${CMAKE_C_FLAGS} -std=gnu99 -g -Wall -Wextra")
add_subdirectory(kaa-sdk)
add_executable(kaa-app src/main.c)
target_link_libraries(kaa-app kaac wiringPi
${CMAKE_THREAD_LIBS_INIT})
install(TARGETS kaa-app DESTINATION bin)
```

In the preceding file, we have defined our project and added the required files and folders that need to be compiled and the final executable to be generated. We will install the required dependencies in the next step.

Setting up dependencies

Now that we have set up the project as well as the SDK, we are going to install the required dependencies. We need to install the following:

- CMake to build our Kaa C app
- WiringPi to interface with the GPIO pins on the Raspberry Pi

In the Raspberry Pi, open a Terminal and run the following:

```
$ sudo apt-get install cmake
```

Once this is done, install WiringPi by following the instructions on this page: http://wiringpi.com/download-and-install/. Once the required dependencies are set up, we will set up the hardware and start reading the data.

Setting up the hardware

Now that we have our set up, we are going to complete the remaining operation on the Raspberry Pi to send data.

Things needed

The prerequisites for setting up the hardware are:

- **One Raspberry Pi 3**: https://www.amazon.com/Raspberry-Pi-Desktop-Starter-White/dp/B01CI58722
- **One breadboard**: https://www.amazon.com/Solderless-Breadboard-Circuit-Circboard-Prototyping/dp/B01DDI54II/
- **DHT11 sensor**: https://www.amazon.com/HiLetgo-Temperature-Humidity-Arduino-Raspberry/dp/B01DKC2GQ0
- **Three male-to-female jumper cables**: https://www.amazon.com/RGBZONE-120pcs-Multicolored-Dupont-Breadboard/dp/B01M1IEUAF/

If you are new to the world of Raspberry Pi GPIO's interfacing, take a look at *Raspberry Pi GPIO Tutorial: The Basics Explained* at: https://www.youtube.com/watch?v=6PuK9fh3aL8.

Connect the DHT11 sensor to the Raspberry Pi as shown in the following schematic:

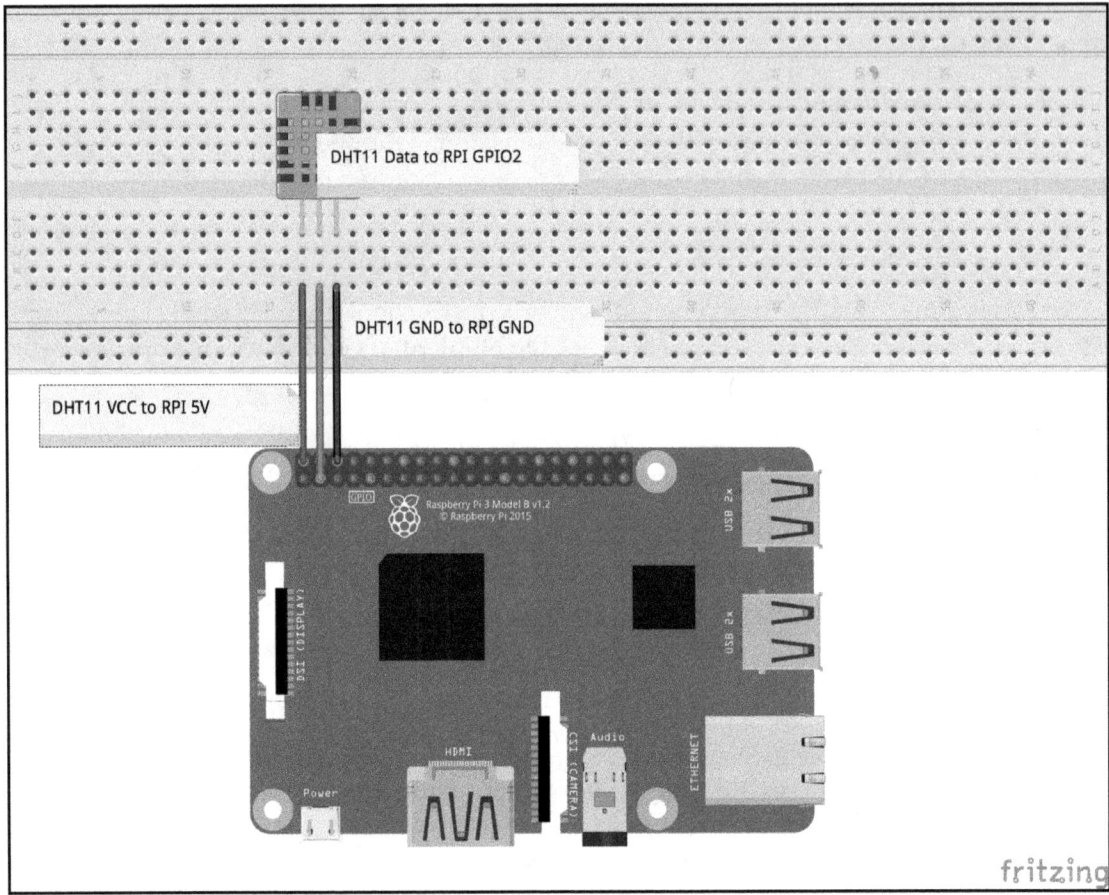

Now that we have our hardware as well as software set up, we will be building the client logic and running the application to send data to the cloud.

Running the application

From inside the `Kaa-IoT-Device/src` folder, create a new file named `main.c` and update it as shown:

```
// Modified version of:
https://kaaproject.github.io/kaa/docs/v0.10.0/Programming-guide/Your-first-
Kaa-application/
```

```c
#include <stdio.h>
#include <stdlib.h>
#include <stdint.h>
#include <time.h>
#include <kaa.h>
#include <platform/kaa_client.h>
#include <kaa_error.h>
#include <kaa_configuration_manager.h>
#include <kaa_logging.h>
#include <gen/kaa_logging_gen.h>
#include <platform/kaa_client.h>
#include <utilities/kaa_log.h>
#include <platform-impl/common/ext_log_upload_strategies.h>
#include <wiringPi.h>
#define MAXTIMINGS 85
#define DHTPIN 8 /* https://pinout.xyz/pinout/wiringpi */
int dht11_dat[5] = {
    0,
    0,
    0,
    0,
    0
};

static int32_t sample_period;
statictime_tlast_sample_time;
externkaa_error_text_unlimited_log_storage_create(void **
log_storage_context_p, kaa_logger_t * logger);

int dht11_read_val(int * humidity, int * temperature) {
    uint8_t laststate = HIGH;
    uint8_t counter = 0;
    uint8_t j = 0, i;

    dht11_dat[0] = dht11_dat[1] = dht11_dat[2] = dht11_dat[3] =
dht11_dat[4] = 0;

    /* pull pin down for 18 milliseconds */
    pinMode(DHTPIN, OUTPUT);
    digitalWrite(DHTPIN, LOW);
    delay(18);
    /* then pull it up for 40 microseconds */
    digitalWrite(DHTPIN, HIGH);
    delayMicroseconds(40);
    /* prepare to read the pin */
    pinMode(DHTPIN, INPUT);

    /* detect change and read data */
```

```
    for (i = 0; i < MAXTIMINGS; i++) {
        counter = 0;
        while (digitalRead(DHTPIN) == laststate) {
            counter++;
            delayMicroseconds(1);
            if (counter == 255) {
                break;
            }
        }
        laststate = digitalRead(DHTPIN);

        if (counter == 255)
            break;

        /* ignore first 3 transitions */
        if ((i >= 4) && (i % 2 == 0)) {
            /* shove each bit into the storage bytes */
            dht11_dat[j / 8] <<= 1;
            /* if ( counter > 50 ) */
            if (counter > 50) /* <- !! here !! */
                dht11_dat[j / 8] |= 1;
            j++;
        }
    }

    // verify checksum and print the verified data
    if ((j >= 40) && (dht11_dat[4] == ((dht11_dat[0] + dht11_dat[1] +
dht11_dat[2] + dht11_dat[3]) & 0xFF))) {
        * humidity = dht11_dat[0] + dht11_dat[1] / 100;
        * temperature = dht11_dat[2] + dht11_dat[3] / 100;
        return 0;
    }

    return -1;
}

/* Periodically called by Kaa SDK. */
static void data_sampling_callback(void * context) {
    time_tcurrent_time = time(NULL);
    /* Respect sample period */
    if (difftime(current_time, last_sample_time) >= sample_period) {
        int temperature = 0;
        int humidity = 0;

        if (dht11_read_val( & temperature, & humidity)) {

            printf("Temperature: %d\n", temperature);
            printf("Humidity: %d\n", humidity);
```

```
            last_sample_time = current_time;
            kaa_user_log_record_t * log_record =
kaa_logging_data_collection_create();

            log_record - > temperature = temperature;
            log_record - > humidity = humidity;

            kaa_logging_add_record(kaa_client_get_context(context) - >
log_collector, log_record, NULL);
        } else {
            printf("Invalid Data, Skipping...\n");
        }
    }
}


/* Receives new configuration data. */
statickaa_error_ton_configuration_updated(void * context,
constkaa_root_configuration_t * conf) {
    (void) context;
    printf("Received configuration data. New sample period: %i seconds\n",
conf - > sample_period);
    sample_period = conf - > sample_period;
    return KAA_ERR_NONE;
}


int main(void) {
    /* Init random generator used to generate temperature */
    srand(time(NULL));
    /* Prepare Kaa client. */
    kaa_client_t * kaa_client = NULL;
    kaa_error_t error = kaa_client_create( & kaa_client, NULL);
    if (error) {
        return EXIT_FAILURE;
    }
    /* Configure notification manager. */
    kaa_configuration_root_receiver_t receiver = {
        .context = NULL,
        .on_configuration_updated = on_configuration_updated
    };
    error = kaa_configuration_manager_set_root_receiver(
        kaa_client_get_context(kaa_client) - > configuration_manager, &
        receiver);
    if (orror) {
        return EXIT_FAILURE;
    }
    /* Obtain default configuration shipped within SDK. */
```

```
    constkaa_root_configuration_t * dflt =
kaa_configuration_manager_get_configuration(
        kaa_client_get_context(kaa_client) - > configuration_manager);
    printf("Default sample period: %i seconds\n", dflt - > sample_period);
    sample_period = dflt - > sample_period;

    /* Configure data collection. */
    void * log_storage_context = NULL;
    void * log_upload_strategy_context = NULL;
    /* The internal memory log storage distributed with Kaa SDK. */
    error = ext_unlimited_log_storage_create( & log_storage_context,
        kaa_client_get_context(kaa_client) - > logger);
    if (error) {
        return EXIT_FAILURE;
    }
    /* Create a strategy based on timeout. */
    error = ext_log_upload_strategy_create(
        kaa_client_get_context(kaa_client), & log_upload_strategy_context,
        KAA_LOG_UPLOAD_BY_TIMEOUT_STRATEGY);
    if (error) {
        return EXIT_FAILURE;
    }
    /* Strategy will upload logs every 5 seconds. */
    error =
ext_log_upload_strategy_set_upload_timeout(log_upload_strategy_context, 5);
    if (error) {
        return EXIT_FAILURE;
    }
    /* Specify log bucket size constraints. */
    kaa_log_bucket_constraints_tbucket_sizes = {
        .max_bucket_size = 32,
        /* Bucket size in bytes. */
        .max_bucket_log_count = 2,
        /* Maximum log count in one bucket. */
    };
    /* Initialize the log storage and strategy (by default, they are not
set). */
    error = kaa_logging_init(kaa_client_get_context(kaa_client) - >
log_collector,
        log_storage_context, log_upload_strategy_context, & bucket_sizes);
    if (error) {
        return EXIT_FAILURE;
    }

    /* Start Kaa SDK's main loop.data_sampling_callback is called once per
15 seconds. */
    error = kaa_client_start(kaa_client, data_sampling_callback,
kaa_client, 1);
```

```
/* Should get here only after Kaa stops. */
kaa_client_destroy(kaa_client);

if (error) {
    return EXIT_FAILURE;
}
return EXIT_SUCCESS;
}
```

The preceding code has the following methods:

- `main()`: This method will be invoked on application launch. In this method, we create a new Kaa client and configure it. Using `kaa_client_start()`, we register a callback to `data_sampling_callback()`, to be periodically called.
- `on_configuration_updated()`: This method will be invoked when there is a configuration update that happens on the Kaa IoT middleware, and the device is running.
- `data_sampling_callback()`: This will be invoked periodically by the Kaa SDK. On each invocation, we check if we have passed the `sample_period` (15 seconds) and if we did, we use `dht11_read_val()` to get the current temperature and humidity. Once we get the values, we update the `log_record` and, using `kaa_logging_add_record()`, we publish the record to the IoT middleware.
- `dht11_read_val()`: Implements the DHT11 protocol to extract the data from the sensor and send it back to the calling function. You can read more about the custom DHT11 protocol in the datasheet here: `https://akizukidenshi.com/download/ds/aosong/DHT11.pdf`.

Save this file. The final folder structure should be as shown:

Now we will build and run the app. Execute the following commands from inside the `Kaa-IoT-Device` folder:

```
$ cd build
$ cmake ..
$ make
$ ./kaa-app
```

If everything goes well, you should see the logs and then the data being published every 15 seconds as shown:

Now, the data is successfully being sent to the Kaa IoT middleware. First, let us check our MongoDB to see if the data is being persisted.

Validating MongoDB data

From any machine, SSH into Kaa Sandbox via following command:

```
$ ssh kaa@127.0.0.1 -p 2222
```

When prompted for the password, enter `kaa`. You can also use PuTTY (`https://www.putty.org/`) for this as well. Once logged in, let's access the MongoDB instance. Run the following command:

```
$ mongo
```

We should be logged in to the MongoDB shell as shown:

```
 →   ~  ssh kaa@127.0.0.1 -p 2222
kaa@127.0.0.1's password:
Welcome to Ubuntu 14.04 LTS (GNU/Linux 3.13.0-29-generic x86_64)

 * Documentation:  https://help.ubuntu.com/

  System information as of Tue Feb 20 00:10:10 PST 2018

  System load:   0.12           Processes:            88
  Usage of /:    14.3% of 35.31GB  Users logged in:   1
  Memory usage: 62%             IP address for eth0: 10.0.2.15
  Swap usage:    0%

  Graph this data and manage this system at:
    https://landscape.canonical.com/

New release '16.04.3 LTS' available.
Run 'do-release-upgrade' to upgrade to it.

Last login: Tue Feb 20 00:10:11 2018 from 10.0.2.2
kaa@kaa-sandbox.kaaproject.org:~$ mongo
MongoDB shell version: 2.6.1
connecting to: test
> show dbs;
admin                (empty)
kaa                  0.031GB
kaa-pi3-dht11-data   0.031GB
local                0.031GB
> ▊
```

As we can see from the preceding screenshot, there is a database named `kaa-pi3-dht11-data`, which we have set up while creating the MongoDB log appender.

Use this database, and list the collections to see what data has been populated, using the following two commands:

```
> use kaa-pi3-dht11-data;
> show collections;
```

We should get a collection named `logs_<<APP_TOKEN>>`. Now query the collection as follows:

> **db.logs_<<APP_TOKEN>>.find().pretty();**

We should see the data that has been logged, as shown:

```
> use kaa-pi3-dht11-data;
switched to db kaa-pi3-dht11-data
> show collections;
logs_77554414525095759343
system.indexes
> db.logs_77554414525095759343.find().pretty();
{
        "_id" : ObjectId("5a8bd8deef540e070bc62bf4"),
        "header" : {
                "endpointKeyHash" : {
                        "string" : "Z6fVxlDQsv76s0/+6FmKRiUP5ZI="
                },
                "applicationToken" : {
                        "string" : "77554414525095759343"
                },
                "headerVersion" : {
                        "int" : 1
                },
                "timestamp" : {
                        "long" : NumberLong("1519114462547")
                },
                "logSchemaVersion" : {
                        "int" : 2
                }
        },
        "event" : {
                "temperature" : 31,
                "humidity" : 33
        }
}
>
```

With this, we are able to persist the data into MongoDB and fetch it when we need it.

Validating the REST log appender

Next, we will validate the REST log appender. Head back to the REST-Logger folder, where we have created our Node.js application to receive the data from the Kaa REST log appenders:

1. Start the Node.js server by running the following command:

   node server.js

2. We should see a message from the server on port 3000. Now, we wait for the data from the device to go to the Kaa IoT middleware and then to this server.

3. Once the data starts coming in, we can see the logs as shown here:

```
→ REST-Logger node server.js
Server listening on port 3000
>>>>>>>>> BEGIN >>>>>>>>>>>

Method: POST
URL: /
Headers: {
    "content-length": "260",
    "content-type": "application/json; charset=UTF-8",
    "host": "10.2.192.250:3000",
    "connection": "Keep-Alive",
    "user-agent": "Apache-HttpClient/4.3.2 (java 1.5)",
    "accept-encoding": "gzip,deflate"
}
Data: {
    "header": {
        "endpointKeyHash": {
            "string": "Z6fVxlDQsv76s0/+6FmKRiUP5ZI="
        },
        "applicationToken": {
            "string": "775544145250957593343"
        },
        "headerVersion": {
            "int": 1
        },
        "timestamp": {
            "long": 1519114729806
        },
        "logSchemaVersion": {
            "int": 2
        }
    },
    "event": {
        "temperature": 32,
        "humidity": 25
    }
}
>>>>>>>>> END >>>>>>>>>>>>>>
```

We can build any application based on this data, as required, or simply attach a web socket using socket.io (`https://socket.io/`). You can also take a look at this Stack Overflow post named, *What is an example of the simplest possible socket.io example?*: `https://stackoverflow.com/a/9916153/1015046` to get idea of the implementation.

With this we are done with implementing the end-to-end flow for our sample application. In the next section, we are going to work on building a dashboard for this application.

Building a dashboard

Now that we have seen how a client can read data from our device on demand, we will move to building a dashboard, where we show data in real time.

For this we are going to use the ThingsBoard platform.

ThingsBoard.io

ThingsBoard is an open-source IoT platform for data collection, processing, visualization, and device management.

It enables device connectivity via industry-standard IoT protocols—MQTT, CoAP, and HTTP—and supports both cloud and on-premises deployments. ThingsBoard combines scalability, fault-tolerance, and performance so you will never lose your data.

You can read more about ThingsBoard here: `https://thingsboard.io/`.

In the solution we are building using the Kaa IoT middleware, we are going to use the ThingsBoard platform for visualization, since Kaa IoT itself does not provide any visualization tools.

Setting up ThingsBoard

For this chapter, we are not going to set up an instance on our local machine; instead we are going to use the live demo instance:

1. Head over to `https://demo.thingsboard.io/signup` and sign up for a new account, if you don't already have one.

2. Now that we are logged in, click on **DEVICES** from the side menu. Once we are on the **Devices** page, we should see a bunch of pre-configured devices for us. We are not going to use any of them; instead we are going to create one of our own.

3. Using the + sign in the bottom right-hand corner, we will create a new device.

4. Fill in the new device form as shown:

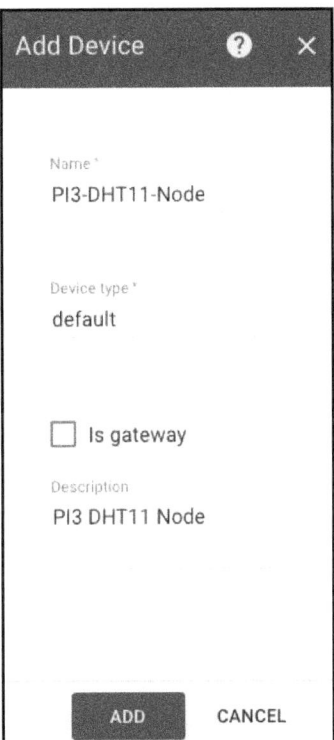

5. Click on **ADD** and then click on the newly created device to see the device information:

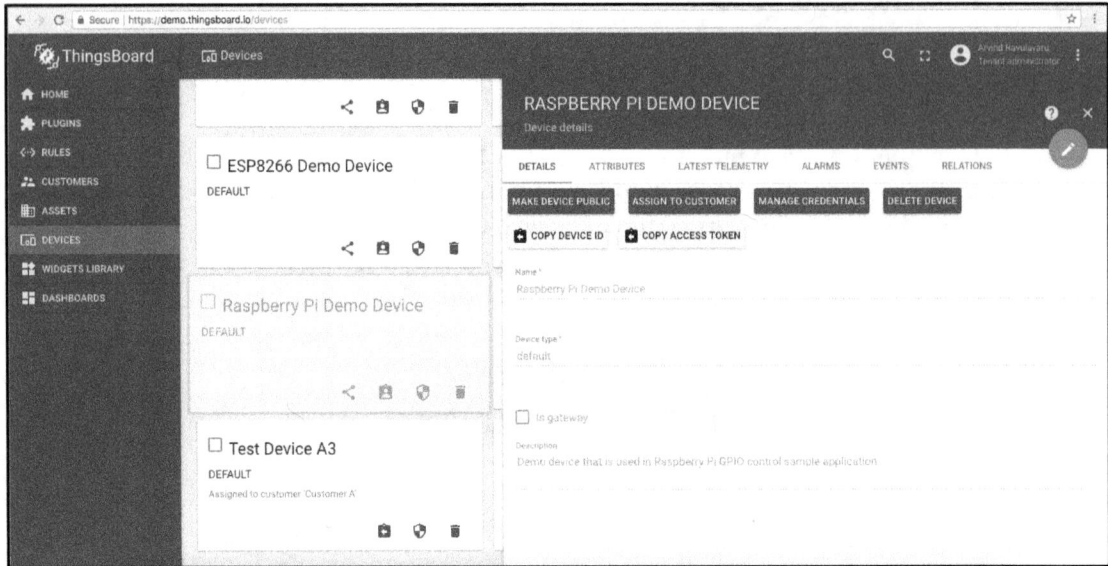

6. Using the access token of this device, we are going to make an HTTP request from Kaa IoT middleware using the REST log appender to a ThingsBoard REST endpoint.

 You can read more about *HTTP Device API Reference* here: `https://thingsboard.io/docs/reference/http-api/`.

Adding a REST log appender

Now, we are going to create another REST log appender to send the data from our device to ThingBoard.io:

1. Head back to the Kaa administration UI and log in as a tenant developer using the `devuser` and `devuser123` credentials. Navigate to **Pi3-DHT11-App** and then **Log appenders**, create a new log appender, and fill it in as shown:

Field	Value
Name	Pi3-DHT11-ThingsBoard-Logger
Min schema version	1
Max schema version	**Infinite**
Confirm delivery	**False**
Log metadata	Do not select any metadata
Type	**REST**
Configuration | Host	demo.thingsboard.io
Configuration | Port	80
Configuration | Use SSL	**False**
Configuration | Include Kaa header	**False**
Configuration | Relative URI Path	/api/v1/ACCESS_TOKEN/telemetry
Configuration | Method	POST
Request MIME type	**JSON**

2. In the form, under **Configuration | Relative URI Path**, we need to provide the device's *access token*. For this, head back to the device page in ThingsBoard.io, select the device, and under the **Details** tab, we should see a button named **COPY ACCESS TOKEN**. Copy the token from here and update the relative path.

3. We will leave the remaining defaults in place and click on **Add**.

Or alternatively, you can save the following schema and upload it the **Add Log appender** page as well:

```
{
    "host": "demo.thingsboard.io",
    "port": 80,
    "ssl": false,
    "verifySslCert": false,
    "username": null,
    "password": null,
    "connectionPoolSize": 1,
    "header": false,
    "path": "/api/v1/ACCESS_TOKEN/telemetry",
    "method": "POST",
    "mimeType": "JSON",
    "minLogSchemaVersion": 1,
    "maxLogSchemaVersion": 2147483647,
    "pluginTypeName": "REST",
    "pluginClassName":
"org.kaaproject.kaa.server.appenders.rest.appender.RestLogAppender",
    "headerStructure": []
}
```

With this, we are done with the setup of the REST log appender. In the next section, we will publish the data to the ThingsBoard platform.

Building the dashboard

Start the Kaa client app on the Raspberry Pi, if it is not already running. This will start sending data to MongoDB, the Node.js server, and the ThingsBoard server:

1. Head over to the **Devices** page on **ThingsBoard** and click on the **LATEST TELEMETRY** tab and we should see the data coming in as shown:

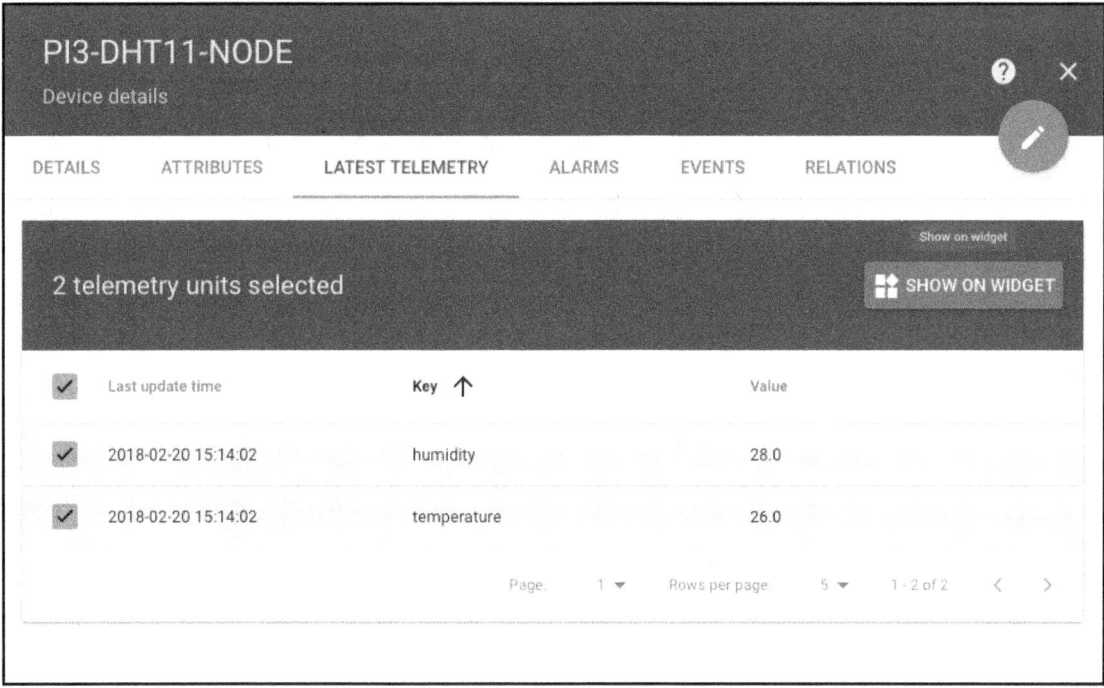

2. Select the two rows and we should see a button named **SHOW ON WIDGET**. Click on **SHOW ON WIDGET**, select **Charts** from the drop-down, and then click on the *third chart* type to view time series data as shown:

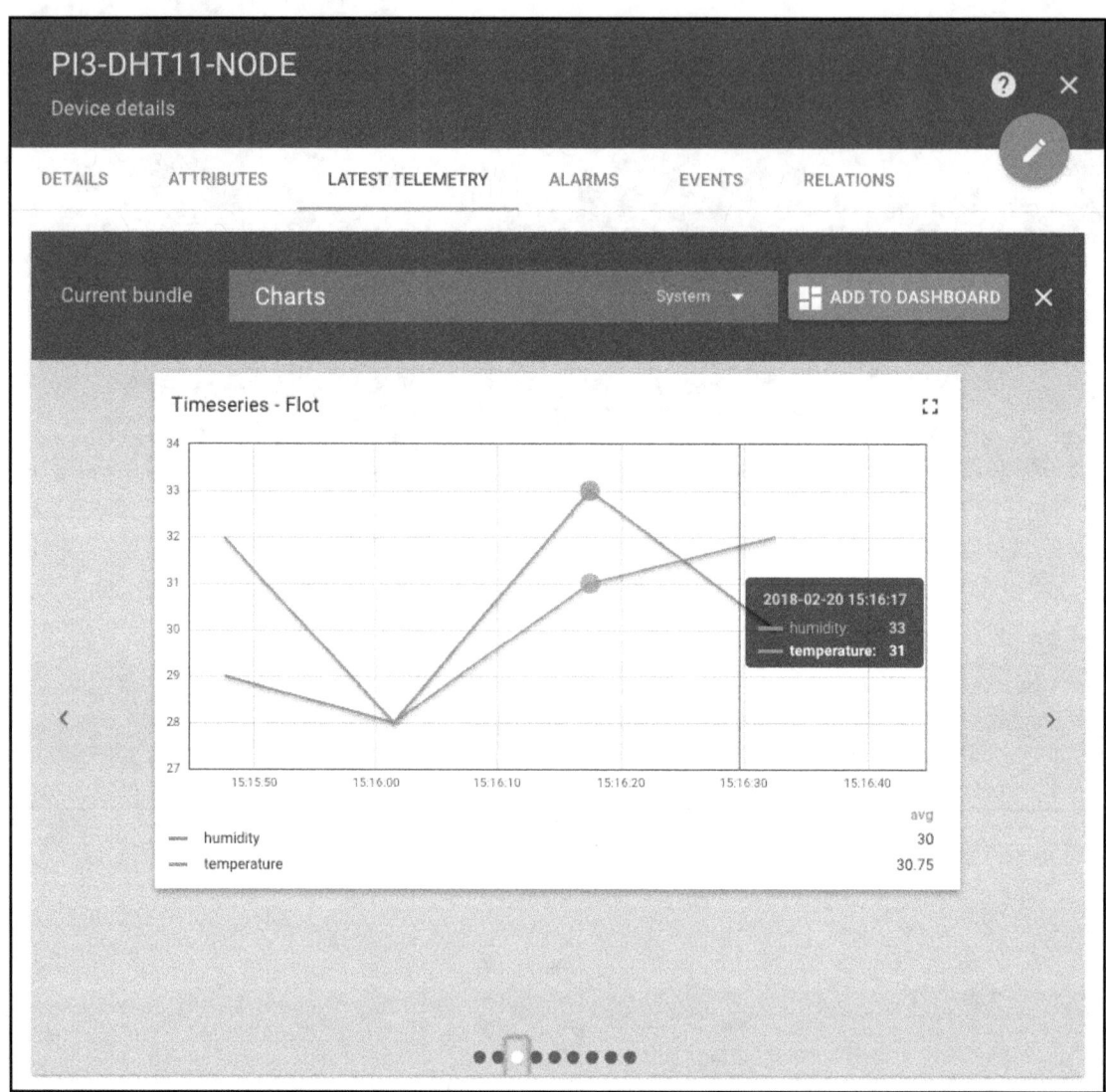

3. Next, click on the **ADD TO DASHBOARD** button and then create a new dashboard named PI3-DHT11 Dashboard. Using the left-hand side menu, navigate to **Dashboards** and open the newly created dashboard and we should see the following:

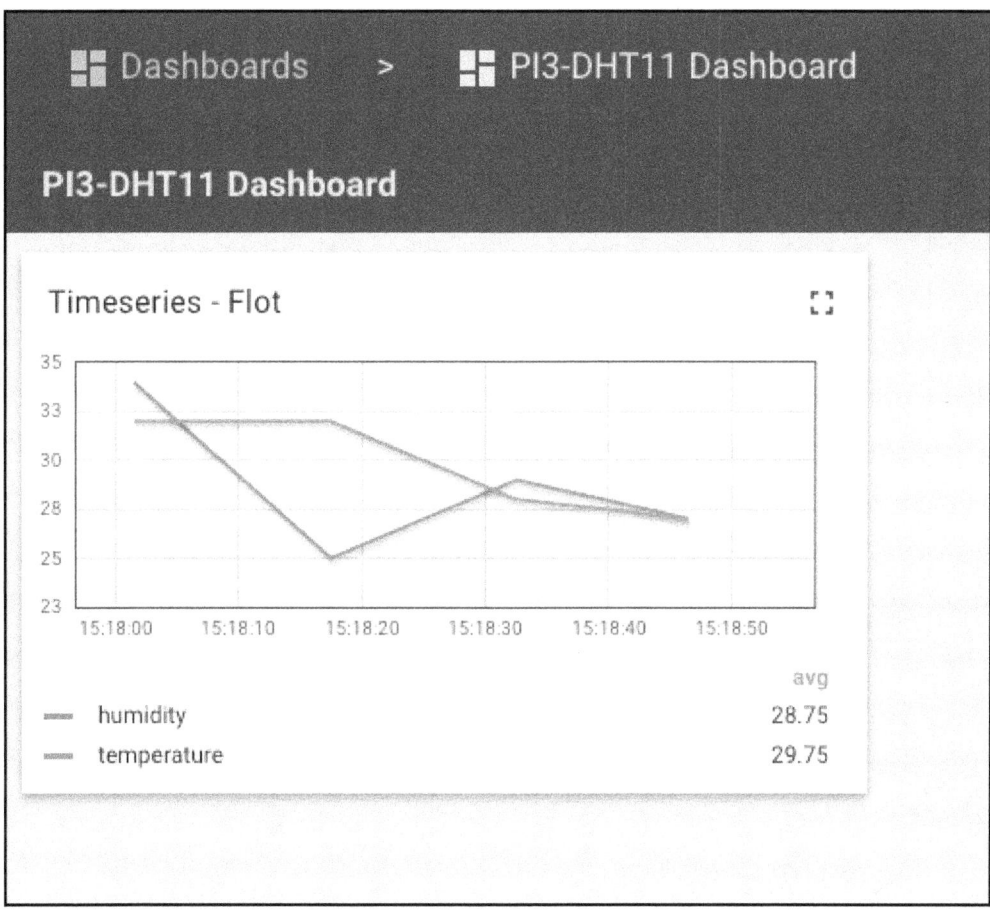

4. We will make a couple of changes to this dashboard to make it more presentable. Click on the **Edit** button on the bottom right of the page.

5. Now, resize the chart to occupy the full screen, or according to your own taste.

6. From the top menu, update the **REALTIME** settings as shown:

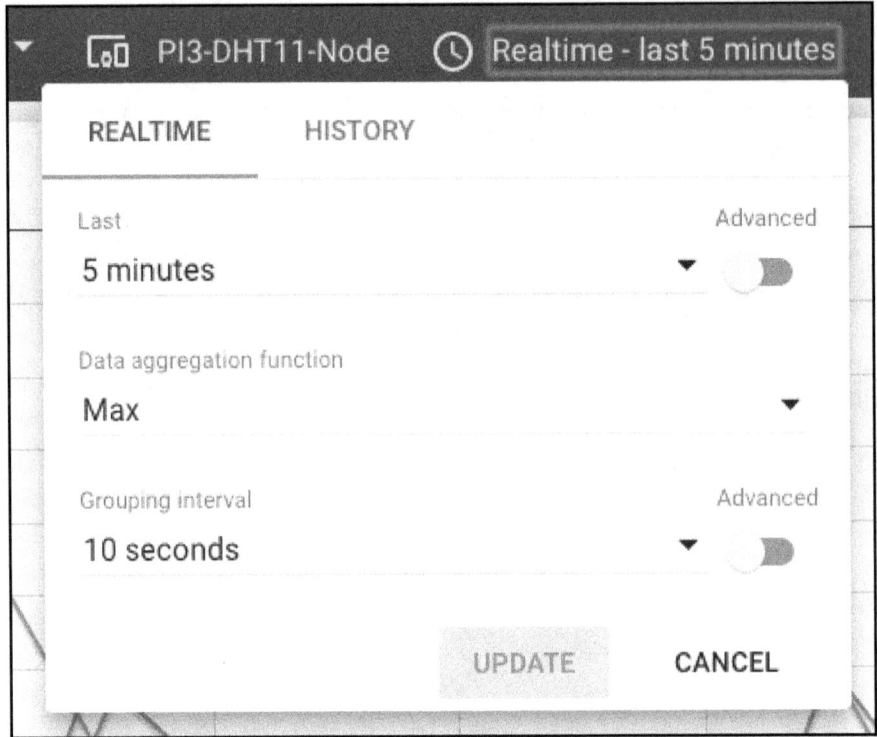

And our final dashboard will be as shown in the preceding screenshot.

 I was playing with the sensor to generate data as previously, so we can see an interesting chart instead of two straight lines.

With this, we have seen the basic features and implementation process for working with the Kaa IoT middleware as well as the ThingsBoard platform.

Summary

In this chapter, we have seen how to work with the Kaa IoT middleware. We started off by downloading and setting up the Kaa Sandbox image on our local machine. Then we created a new application and configured the required schema.

Then, we created two log appenders to send data to MongoDB as well as to a REST endpoint, that we built using Node.js.

For the visualizations, we used the demo setup provided by ThingsBoard and we have configured another REST log appender to send data to the ThingsBoard platform. Finally, we built the dashboard using the telemetry data that we received on ThingsBoard.

This chapter wraps up our walkthrough of five IoT platforms at a basic level.

In the next chapter, we are going to work on data analytics using Azure IoT Cloud and Azure Machine Learning Studio.

IoT and Machine Learning 9

In the last five chapters, we have learned how to work with five different IoT platforms, performing the simple operation of sending data from our smart device to the platform, as well as the means to build visualization.

In this chapter, we are going to take this process one level forward by adding intelligence to the solution that we are building.

We are going to use **Azure Machine Learning** (**AML**) Studio to build a **machine learning** (**ML**) model from existing weather data, and from this data model, we are going to make a prediction as to whether it will rain using temperature and humidity as an input.

The topics covered in this chapter are as follows:

- What is machine learning?
- What is AML and how do we use it?
- Building and validating the AML model using web services.

What is machine learning?

Machine learning is the process by which a system learns by itself without programming. The main goal of machine learning is to answer a question based on the data model that was created during the process of machine learning.

Let's say that we have a climate and weather dataset that has a correlation between temperature, humidity, and rainfall. The machine would observe this dataset using various algorithms and would generate a data model. A data model is the gist of the dataset, which can then be used to answer questions such as, *"If the temperature is x and the humidity is y, will it rain?"*.

I may have over-simplified ML, but this is what lies at its core.

Tom M. Mitchell (http://www.cs.cmu.edu/~tom/) defined ML as the following:

> *"A computer program is said to learn from experience E with respect to some class of tasks T and performance measure P if its performance at tasks in T, as measured by P, improves with experience E."*

You can read more about this at http://www.cs.ubbcluj.ro/~gabis/ml/ml-books/ McGrawHill%20-%20Machine%20Learning%20-Tom%20Mitchell.pdf.

To get started with learning ML, you can watch the following five-part video by Brandon Rohrer on the basics of machine learning to get an idea of the subject: https://docs. microsoft.com/en-gb/azure/machine-learning/studio/data-science-for-beginners-the-5-questions-data-science-answers.

A person who works on ML in terms of understanding data, building data models, and validating them is called a **data scientist**. The field is called **data science**.

Machine learning workflow

The following diagram shows a typical workflow of an ML project:

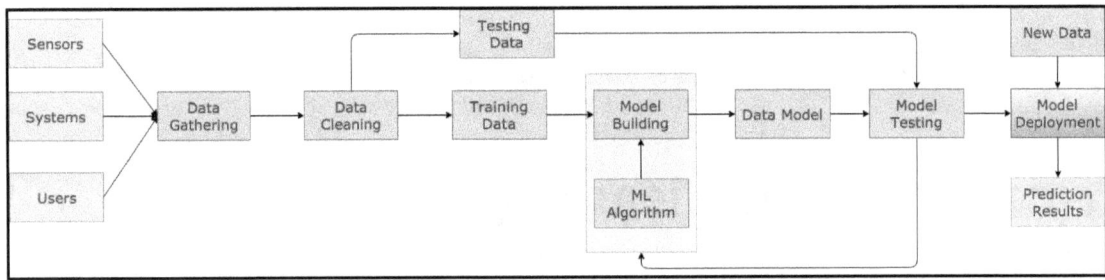

Everything starts with the gathering of data. The data can come from various sources in various forms. Once the data is stored, we clean and preprocess it. Then we split our data into two parts. The first set is for training and the second set is for testing.

The training data, along with an ML algorithm, is used to build a data model. This data model is evaluated against the testing dataset that we have kept to one side. This results in a more accurate prediction. If the accuracy is acceptable, then we deploy this data model.

If new data comes in, we pass it to the model to get a prediction.

Now, let's look at different types of machine learning algorithms.

Types of machine learning algorithms

The following diagram illustrates different types of machine learning algorithms:

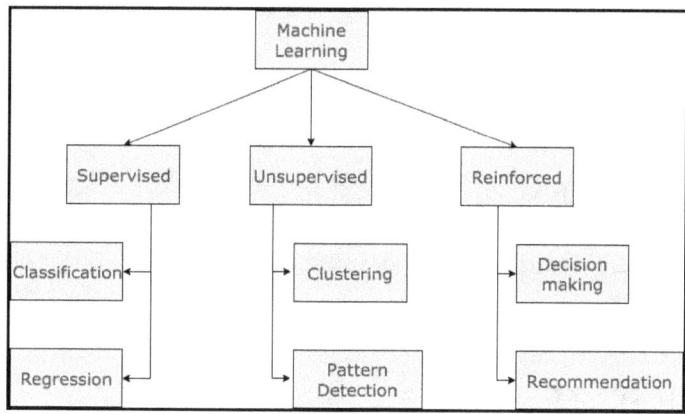

There are three types of machine learning algorithms: **Supervised**, **Unsupervised**, and **Reinforced**. Each of these is used depending on what kind of activity we want to perform.

Supervised ML algorithms

A supervised ML algorithm would be used if we have historic data that shows a correlation between inputs (**features**) and outputs (**labels**). For instance, in our earlier example, we were predicting rainfall based on the data we had for the temperature and humidity. Using a supervised machine learning algorithm, we would build a data model that can predict the chance of rainfall based on a new data record.

Unsupervised learning algorithms

An unsupervised ML algorithm is where we let the system figure out how the data has been structured or grouped, and based on this model, new incoming data can be placed in one of the clusters that define the data. For instance, say that a bank has a user's credit card usage pattern, and they build a cluster model of this pattern. When a new transaction takes place on that user's card, then based on the data model, the system can tell if this was a genuine purchase made by the intended user or if it is fraud.

Reinforced learning algorithms

The final type of ML is reinforced learning. This is a process where the machine learns by itself based on a reward system. In reinforced learning, there is generally an environment and an agent, and the agent is typically the machine. Let's say that the environment is in **state A** and an agent performs **action A** on this environment and observes how the state changes. Based on the action, the new state, and the reward returned by the environment, the machine learns.

Think of reinforced learning as a machine learning how to ride a bike. If the machine is able to move forward, it receives a reward, and if the machine falls down because it lost its balance, it is not rewarded.

Reinforced learning forms the basis of a lot of AI systems.

If you wish to learn more about machine learning, please refer to the following resources:

- **Python Machine Learning - Second Edition**: https://www.packtpub.com/big-data-and-business-intelligence/python-machine-learning-second-edition
- **Python Deep Learning**: https://www.packtpub.com/big-data-and-business-intelligence/python-deep-learning
- **Practical Machine Learning**: https://www.packtpub.com/big-data-and-business-intelligence/practical-machine-learning

Machine learning platforms

There was a time when people used to lease machines and set up data centers to run extensive machine learning algorithms and research. Thanks to the cloud, now all the cloud-based services are available on demand.

A data scientist can load a petabyte of data into a cloud server by running a bunch of algorithms on top of it, saving the data models, extracting the results, and deprovisioning the cloud resources, and will not be billed more than $50.

Isn't this a great time we live in?

Having said that, there are multiple platforms available on the market, some offered as cloud services, some proprietary, and some open source. In the following sections, I have listed a few of them in no particular order of preference.

Amazon machine learning

Amazon machine learning is a managed service for building machine learning models and generating predictions, enabling the development of robust and scalable smart applications. It enables you to use powerful machine learning technology without requiring an extensive background in machine learning algorithms and techniques.

Amazon machine learning comes with the following properties:

- Data visualization and exploration
- Model evaluation and interpretation tools
- Modeling APIs
- Machine learning algorithms
- Data transformations
- APIs for batch and real-time predictions

 You can read more about Amazon machine learning at `https://aws.amazon.com/machine-learning/`.

You can also explore other machine learning services offered by AWS, such as the following:

- Amazon SageMaker
- Amazon Rekognition
- AWS DeepLens
- Amazon Comprehend

 You can read more about these services at `https://aws.amazon.com/machine-learning/`.

To give an idea of how to use Amazon Rekognition, we can upload a picture to the **AWS Rekognition** demo service and the API will return some information concerning it.

Take a look at the following example, where I have uploaded the picture of the most handsome creature I know—Dexter. The following screenshot shows the rendered result of the picture:

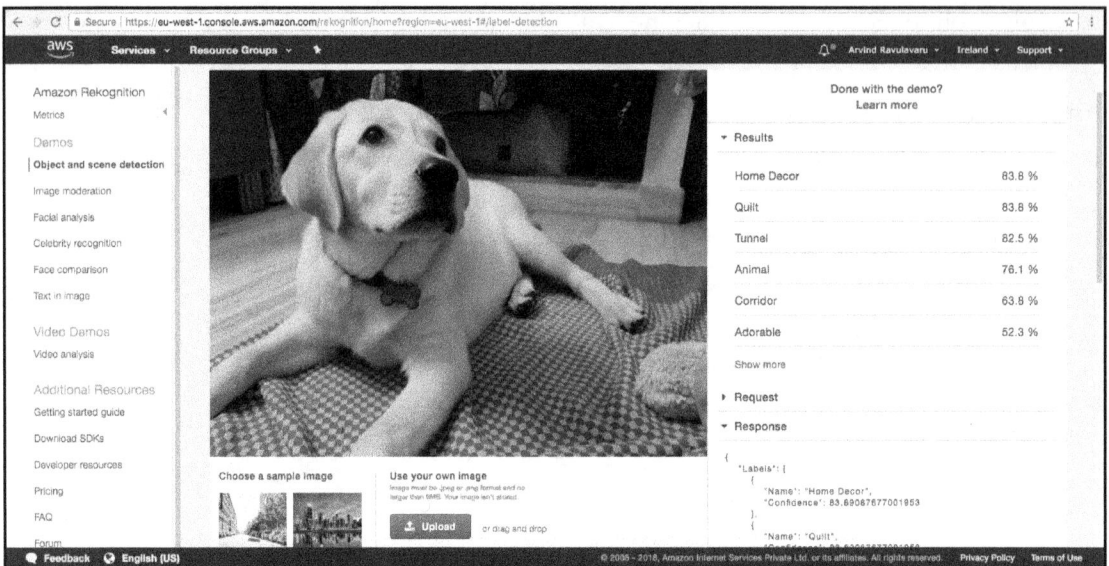

You can find AML pricing details at https://aws.amazon.com/aml/pricing/.

Azure Machine Learning Studio

Microsoft Azure Machine Learning Studio is a collaborative, drag-and-drop tool you can use to build, test, and deploy predictive analytic solutions on your data. Azure Machine Learning Studio publishes models as web services that can easily be consumed by custom apps or **business intelligence** (**BI**) tools, such as Microsoft Excel.

You can read more about Azure Machine Learning at
`https://azure.microsoft.com/en-us/overview/machine-learning/`.

You can read more about Azure Machine Learning Studio at
`https://azure.microsoft.com/en-us/services/machine-learning-stud`
`io/`.

You can read more about Azure Machine Learning services at
`https://azure.microsoft.com/en-us/services/machine-learning-serv`
`ices/`.

You can read more about Azure Data Science Virtual Machine at
`https://azure.microsoft.com/en-us/services/virtual-machines/data`
`-science-virtual-machines/`.

Along with machine learning, Azure also provides common AI services
similar to AWS. You can read more at `https://azure.microsoft.com/en-`
`in/services/cognitive-services/`.

I have uploaded the same sample image to the Google Cloud Vision API, with the following
results:

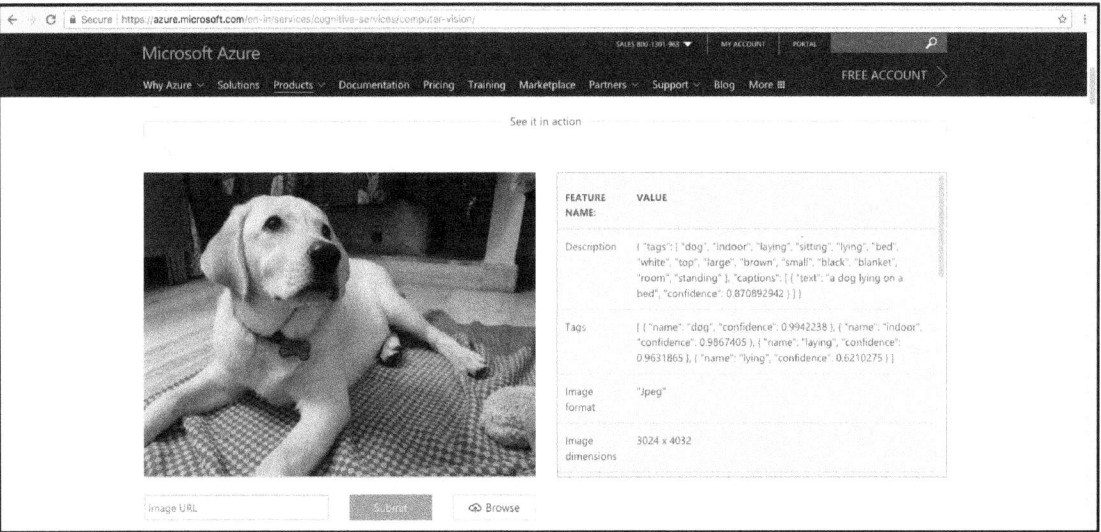

You can find in-depth pricing details at
`https://azure.microsoft.com/en-in/pricing/details/machine-learning-studio/`.

Google Cloud Machine Learning

The Google Cloud Machine Learning engine brings the power and flexibility of TensorFlow (`https://www.tensorflow.org/`) to the cloud. We can use its components to select and extract features from our data, train our ML models, and get predictions using the managed resources of Google Cloud Platform.

You can read more about Google Cloud Machine Learning at
`https://cloud.google.com/ml-engine/`.

Apart from machine learning, Google also offers their popular AI services over APIs. This service is called **Google Cloud AI**.

Google Cloud's AI provides modern ML services, with pre-trained models and a service to generate our own tailored models. Google Cloud's neural-net-based ML service has better training performance and increased accuracy compared to other large-scale, deep learning systems. Major Google applications use Google Cloud Machine Learning algorithms, including Google Photos (image search), the Google app (voice search), Google Translate, and Inbox by Gmail (smart reply).

Here is an output from the Google Vision API:

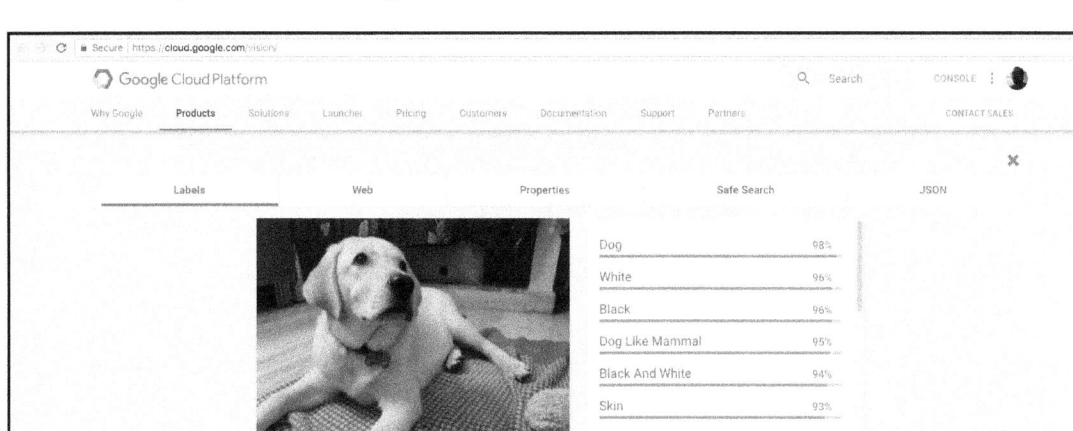

You can explore other Google Cloud AI services at `https://cloud.google.com/products/machine-learning`.

For pricing details, visit `https://cloud.google.com/pricing/list`.

IBM Watson Machine Learning

IBM **Watson Machine Learning** (**WML**) also provides a similar platform to its counterparts for work with machine learning. It helps us build sophisticated analytical models by using our own data, and deploys the models it generates for use in applications.

You can read more about IBM Watson Machine Learning at `https://developer.ibm.com/clouddataservices/docs/ibm-watson-machine-learning/`.

IBM Watson, along with its machine learning platform, provides other cognitive services that you can explore at `https://www.ibm.com/watson/products-services/`.

Here are the results from IBM Watson's visual recognition service for the same picture that we used previously:

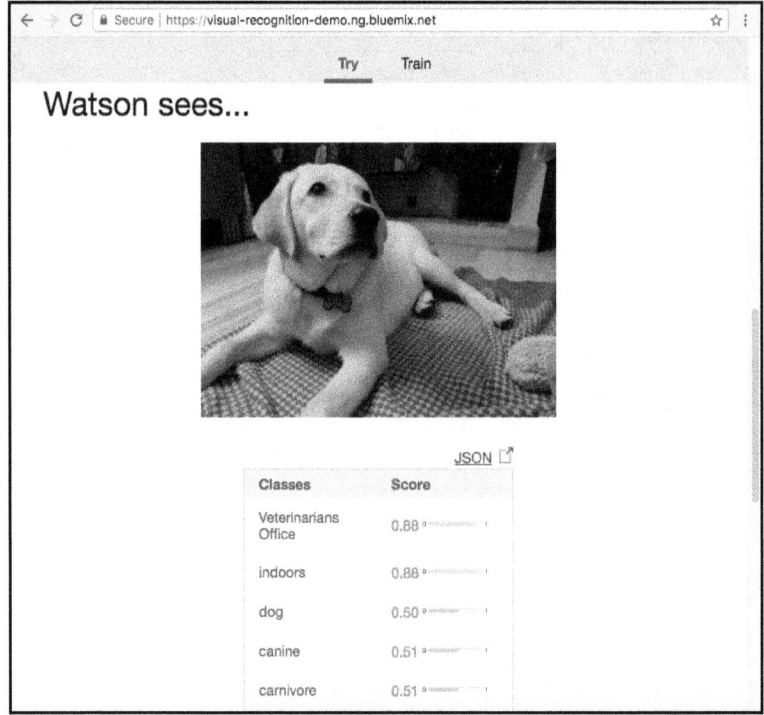

As you can see, so far, the results and recognition patterns are different for different providers.

Open source tools

The platforms we have discussed are the four major cloud platforms for performing ML operations on our data.

There are other open source tools available that you can run on your machine to generate results.

You can explore these other open source tools at
`http://opensourceforu.com/2017/01/best-open-source-machine-learn`
`ing-frameworks/` and
`https://dzone.com/articles/5-open-source-machine-learning-framew`
`orks-and-tool`.

Rain prediction

Now that we understand machine learning, and we have already worked on IoT, let's work on a simple experiment that shows the value of using ML in IoT.

In this chapter, we are going to perform the following operations:

1. Use historical data to build a data model
2. Get real-time data from a sensor and feed it to the model
3. Based on the inputs to the model, predict the output

Here, we are going to use historical weather data and then build a data model that accepts temperature and humidity values and returns the probability of rain.

We are going to use Azure Machine Learning Studio for this, and we are going to work along the lines of an article named *Weather forecast using the sensor data from your IoT hub in Azure Machine Learning* at `https://docs.microsoft.com/en-us/azure/iot-hub/iot-hub-weather-forecast-machine-learning`.

We are not going to implement all the use cases—only enough to get the hang of it. So let's get started.

Setting up Azure Machine Learning Studio

Navigate to `https://studio.azureml.net/` and sign up for a new studio account, if you do not already have one. Once signed up, log in to the Azure Machine Learning Studio. You should land on the projects page.

If you are new to Azure Machine Learning Studio, I recommend watching the five getting started videos on the `https://studio.azureml.net/` homepage.

Importing experiment

The following are the steps to import the experiment into ML Studio:

1. Navigate to
   `https://gallery.cortanaintelligence.com/Experiment/Weather-prediction-model-1` and click on the **Open in Studio** button, and this experiment will be imported into our list of experiments.

2. Select the following setting for the appropriate section, as illustrated in the following screenshot:

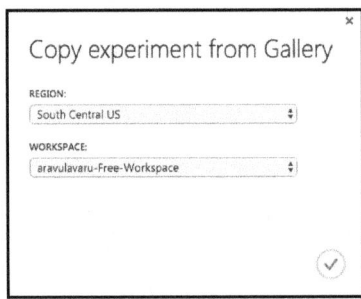

3. Now, the experiment will be opened by default, and we should see a pictorial representation similar to the following screenshot:

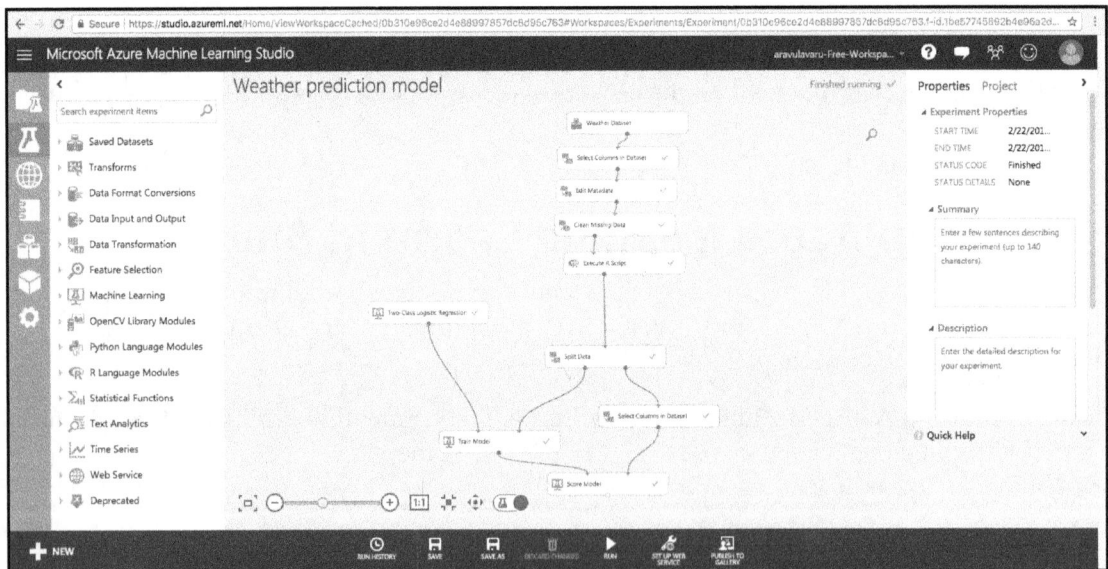

4. The left pane consists of the experiment's items, the right pane displays the **Properties** of the experiment item that is selected, and the center canvas is where we build our experiment.

 The previously illustrated flow chart or experiment loosely follows the steps we have defined in the flow diagram of typical machine learning projects.

5. Before we start exploring every item in this experiment, let's run the experiment to see if everything is okay. In the footer of the page, click **RUN** button. This may take a minute or so to complete.

6. Once completed successfully, you should see a green tick mark next to each of these items, similar to the one shown in the following screenshot:

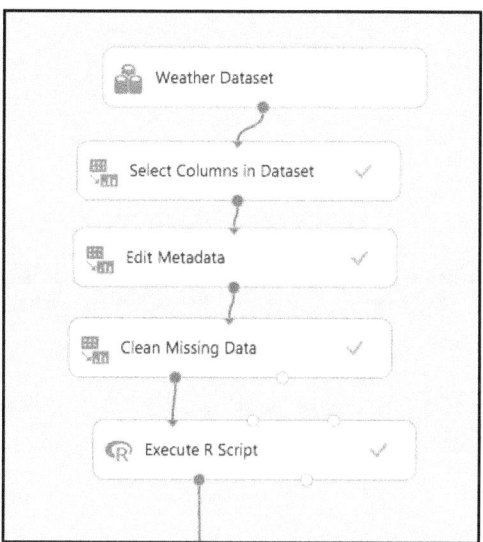

Now, let's explore each of these items in the experiment.

Weather dataset

The weather dataset is the dataset that we are going to use to generate our data model. Click on the **Weather Dataset**, and on the output connector, right-click and select **Visualize**. This process will open a popup, which will display the first few rows of the dataset and its metadata, as shown in the following screenshot:

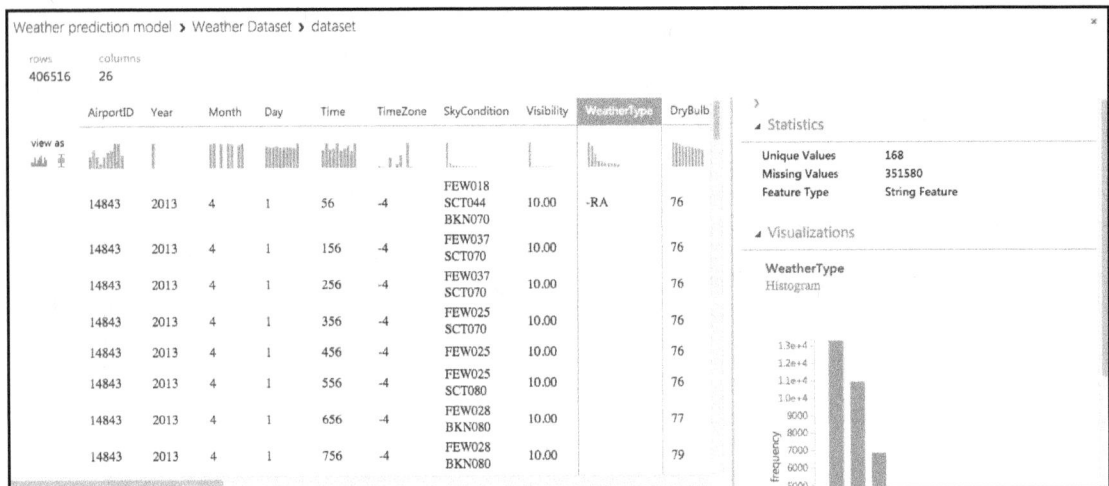

When we click on any column, a new panel will show more details about it, as shown in the previous screenshot. In this dataset, there are 351580 values for the **WeatherType** data column.

In our rainfall prediction experiment, we are going to use the **DryBulbCelsius** and **RealtiveHumidity** columns as features and the **WeatherType** as the label or outcome.

Selecting columns in the dataset

In the next step, we are going to select the pertinent fields in the dataset, which are **DryBulbCelsius**, **RealtiveHumidity**, and **WeatherType**. Click on the **Select Columns in Dataset** item, and in the output connector, right-click and select **Visualize**, and we should see the data from the selected columns only:

Editing the metadata

Using the **Edit Metadata** item, we shall rename the columns. If we click on **Edit Metadata** on the right-hand pane, we should see its values, as illustrated in the following screenshot:

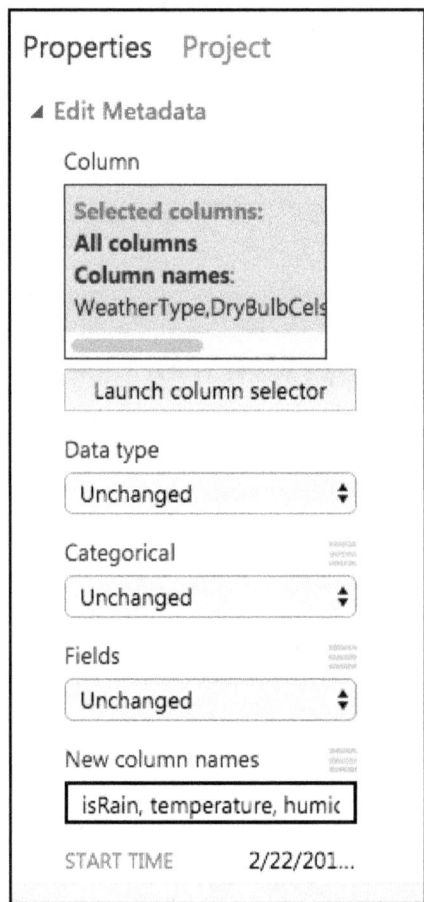

We have mapped **WeatherType** to **isRain**, **DryBulbCelsius** to temperature, and **RelativeHumidity** to humidity.

If we visualize this, we should see the updated dataset.

Cleaning the missing data

As part of our data cleaning process, we want to clean up the missing data. As we have already seen, there are `351580` values for the **WeatherType**. So, using the **Clean Missing Data** option, we are going to remove the missing data.

There are a number of techniques that can be used to clean data, and this is where a data scientist comes into the picture. Based on the type of data and the weightage of data in deriving the model, a technique is selected.

Remember that the way we clean our data also adds to the quality of the data model and thus the accuracy of the prediction. Take a look at the video titled *Is your data ready for data science?* (https://docs.microsoft.com/en-in/azure/machine-learning/studio/data-science-for-beginners-is-your-data-ready-for-data-science), if you have not already done so.

If we click on the **Clean Missing Data** item on the right pane, we should see that the **Cleaning mode** selected is **Remove entire row**.

Now, if we visualize the output from this item, we should see that the number of our rows has reduced to `54936`, with `0` missing data for the **isRain** column:

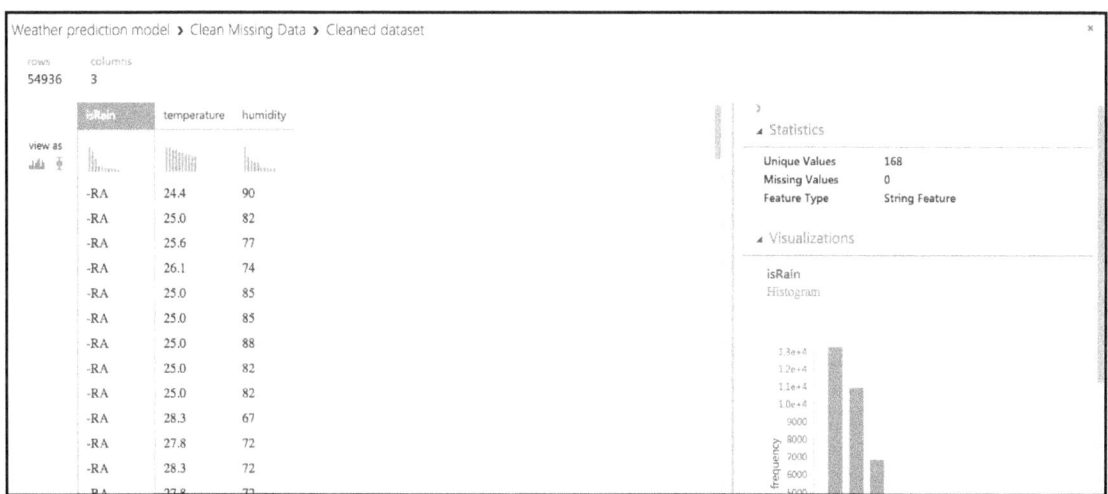

Of course, we lost a big chunk of data, but this dataset is way cleaner and the quality of the model from this dataset is higher than it would be otherwise .

Executing the R script

In this step, we are going to do data munging. We are going to rewrite the values of the **isRain** column in such a way that we get a Yes or NO answer instead of the **WeatherType**:

1. In the experiment, click on the **Execute R Script** item. On the right pane, we should see the following R script:

    ```
    # Map 1-based optional input ports to variables
    data <- maml.mapInputPort(1) # class: data.frame

    data$isRain[grepl(""RA"", data$isRain)] <- ""Yes""
    data$isRain[grepl(""SN"", data$isRain)] <- ""Yes""
    data$isRain[grepl(""DZ"", data$isRain)] <- ""Yes""
    data$isRain[grepl(""PL"", data$isRain)] <- ""Yes""
    data$isRain[data$isRain != ""Yes""] <- ""NO""

    # Select data.frame to be sent to the output Dataset port
    maml.mapOutputPort(''data'');
    ```

     R is a programming language centered around statistical computation and graphics. For data scripting in ML, we use either R or Python. You can read more about R at https://www.r-project.org/about.html.

2. In the previous script, we are reading the dataset from **Port 1**. The **Execute R Script** item has three ports. The first two are to load the datasets and the third one is to load additional R modules.

3. Once we read the dataset, we mung the **isRain** column using the grepl (https://stat.ethz.ch/R-manual/R-devel/library/base/html/grep.html) function to match a given pattern and replace it with a Yes or NO.

     We need to understand what the data means before we start working on it. Since this is a predefined dataset, you can learn more about it at https://www.ncdc.noaa.gov/orders/qclcd/. You can find more information on how this dataset is saved in the Azure sample datasets at https://docs.microsoft.com/en-us/azure/machine-learning/studio/use-sample-datasets.

4. Now, when we visualize the output of this item, we should see a similar result to that shown in the following screenshot:

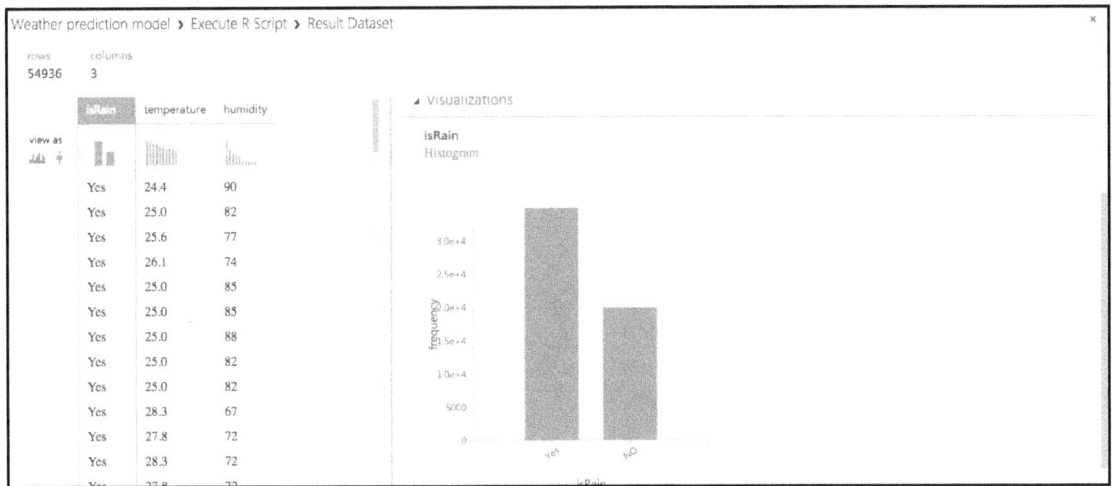

Now our dataset can answer a `Yes` or `NO` question.

Splitting data

Now that we have our data ready to be processed, we will split it into two sets, one for training and another one for testing. Again, there are multiple techniques on how to split the data. In this experiment, we are using 90% for training data and the remaining 10% for testing.

You can click on **Split Data** and view the properties in the right-hand pane.

Train model

Now that we have split the data, we will train the model. This experiment uses a *two-class logistic regression* algorithm
(`https://docs.microsoft.com/en-us/azure/machine-learning/studio-module-referenc e/two-class-logistic-regression`) to build the data model.

We feed the training data and the algorithm to the **Train Model** item.

If we click on the **Two-Class Logistic Regression** item, we should see the parameters that can be configured in the right-hand pane:

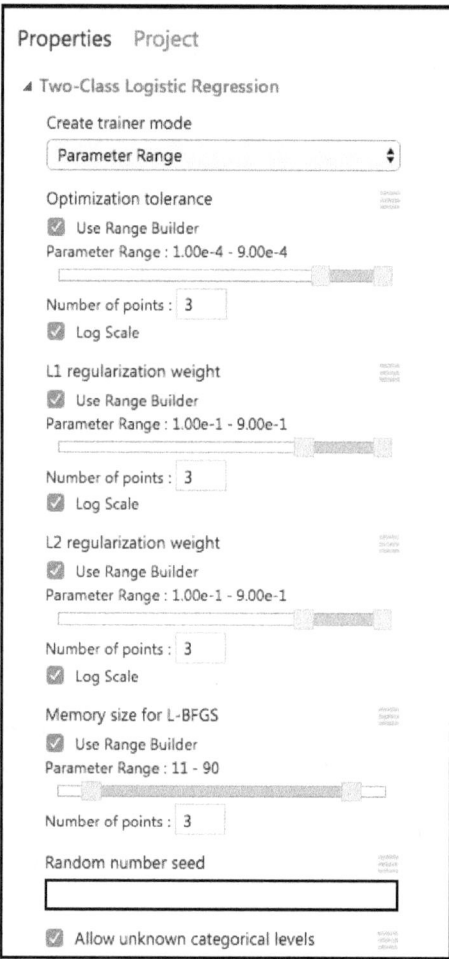

As data scientists, our role is to understand the dataset and prediction model, and then based on that, we define the settings, as illustrated in the previous screenshot.

 Have a look at the video *Azure Machine Learning Studio: Two-Class Logistic Regression* at `https://www.youtube.com/watch?v=ZmVrw1oIkdg` by *Mark Keith* about working with two-class logistic regression in Azure Machine Learning Studio. You can check out this playlist at `https://www.youtube.com/playlist?list=PLe9UEU4oeAuXMUWqhhJQrGVWz UWY6pS9j`.

If we right-click on the output node of the **Train Model**, we should find more information on the model that was trained from the dataset and the algorithm we have selected.

Algorithm selection

Algorithm selection is a very important task when working in the field of data science. The wrong algorithm can lead to invalid or misguided predictions.

There are a few rules that we generally follow when selecting an algorithm.

You can check out *Machine learning algorithm cheat sheet for Microsoft Azure Machine Learning Studio* at
`https://docs.microsoft.com/en-gb/azure/machine-learning/studio/a lgorithm-cheat-sheet` for more information.

A gist of the cheat sheet is shown in the following screenshot:

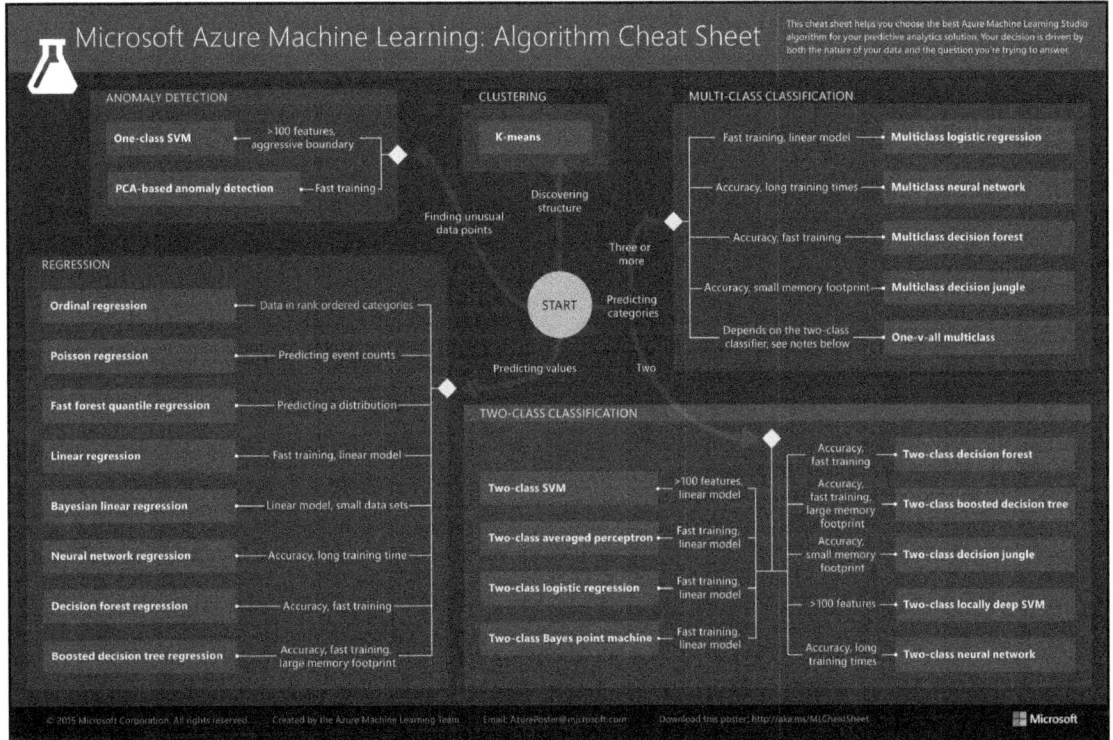

Score model

Now that we have trained the model, we will see how well this model works on the testing dataset. As we saw in the experiment, the test data output from the **Split Data** item is fed into **Select Columns in Dataset**.

In the **Select Columns in Dataset** section, we select the columns that need to go in as inputs to the model so we can predict the output. Here, we have selected the **temperature** and **humidity** columns, and we are going to predict the isRain property.

The output of **Select Columns in Dataset** is fed into **Score Model**, along with the output of the **Train Model**.

If we right-click on the output of **Score Model**, we should see a new column named **Scored Probabilities**, which shows the results of our prediction against the original **isRain** column or **Scored Labels**.

Any value greater than 0.5 is consider as a Yes, indicating that it would rain, and any value less than 0.5 is a NO, indicating that it is not likely to rain, given the temperature and humidity:

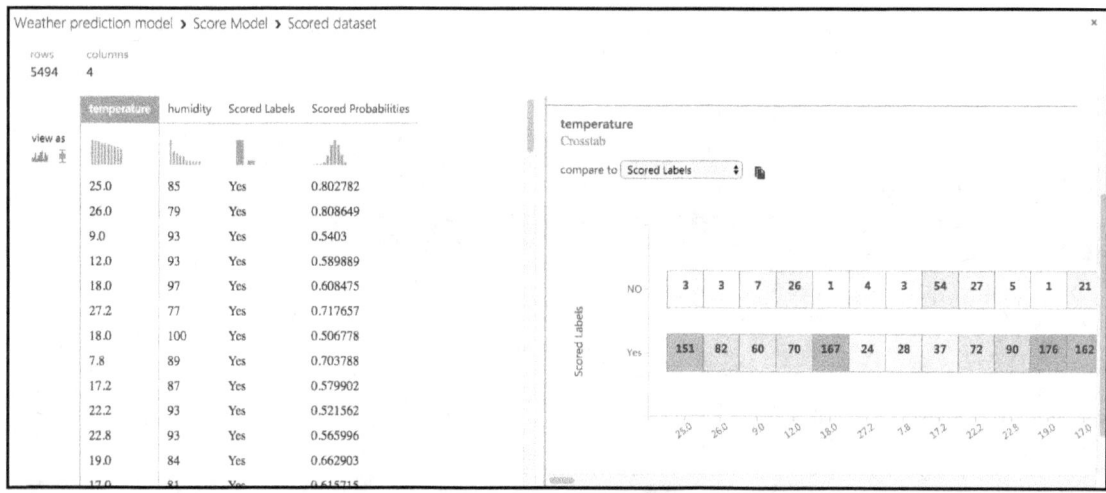

As shown in the previous screenshot, if I select the **temperature** column and compare it with **Scored Labels**, I can see a crosstab (https://www.researchoptimus.com/article/cross-tab.php) chart of the chances of rain versus the temperature and the weight of the chance of rain.

You can play around with this experiment and see how changes to the algorithm or columns will change the scoring pattern.

Deploying web service

Now that we have seen how the model is able to predict the outcome of rain, based on temperature and humidity values, let's convert this data model into a web service so that we can use a REST API to pass values to this model and get the results in real time:

1. From the footer of the experiment, select **Set up Web Service** | **Predictive Web Service**.

   If this option is disabled, delete any existing web service items in the experiment, save, and then run the experiment, and you should be good to go.

2. This will take a couple of minutes and generate a new tab in our experiment named **Predictive experiment**:

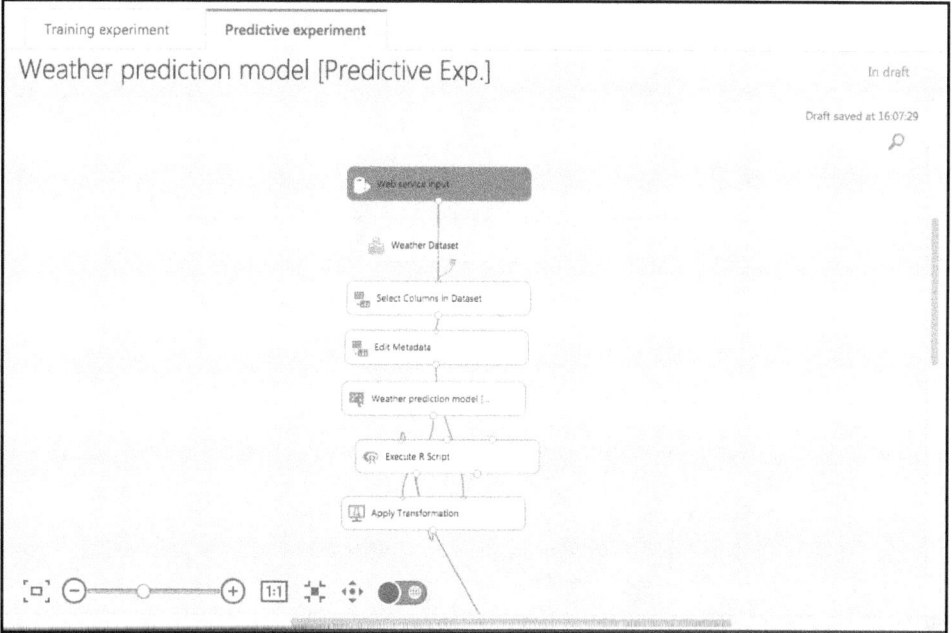

3. By default, the **Web service input** item will be connected to the **Select Columns in Dataset** item. Delete this link and drag the **Web service input** item next to **Score Model**, and then connect the output of **Web service input** to the **Score Model** dataset input, as shown in the following screenshot:

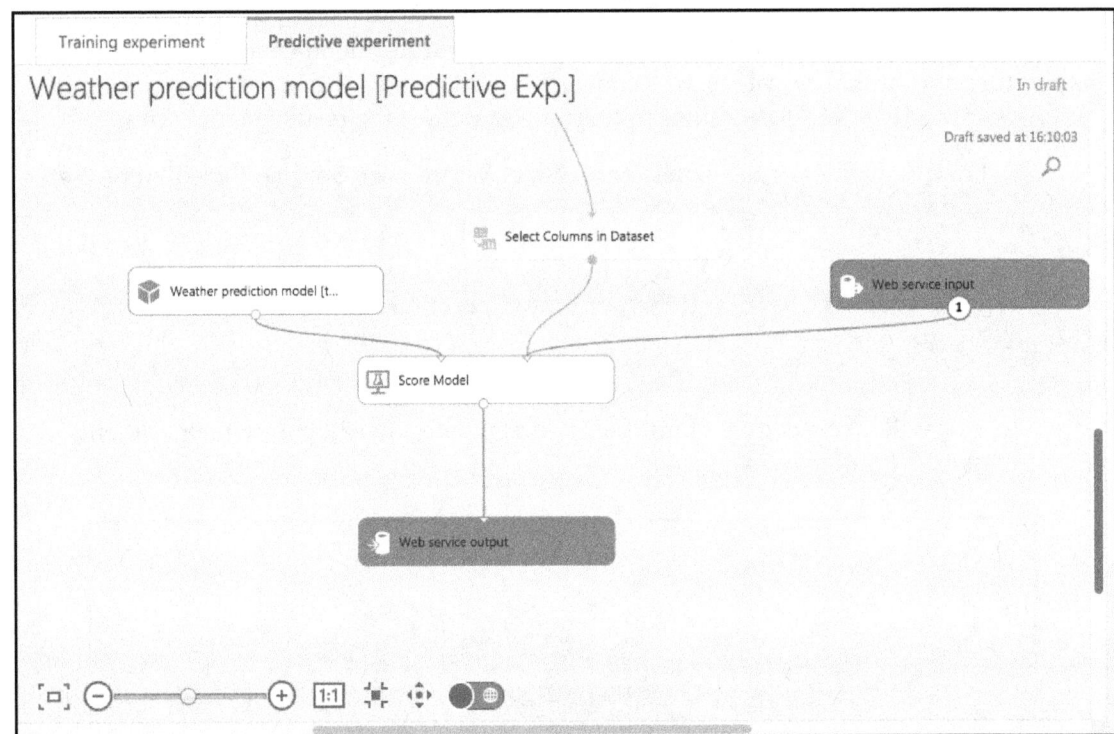

4. Now, we are going to run this experiment, and once it is successfully executed, we will deploy the web service. If everything goes well, we should be automatically taken to the web services page. Here, we should see two endpoints, as shown in the following screenshot:

You can look at an article titled *How to call a Azure Machine Learning Web Service from NodeJS* at `https://blogs.msdn.microsoft.com/bigdatasupport/2016/02/18/how-to-call-a-azure-machine-learning-web-service-from-nodejs/` to see how to work with this web service using a programming language such as Node.js.

For now, we are going to use the **Test** button, as illustrated in the previous screenshot, to test this service.

Testing web the service

Let's now test the web service:

1. Click on the **Test** button on the **REQUEST/RESPONSE** endpoint row. We should see a similar form to the one shown in the following screenshot. Fill in the details as applicable:

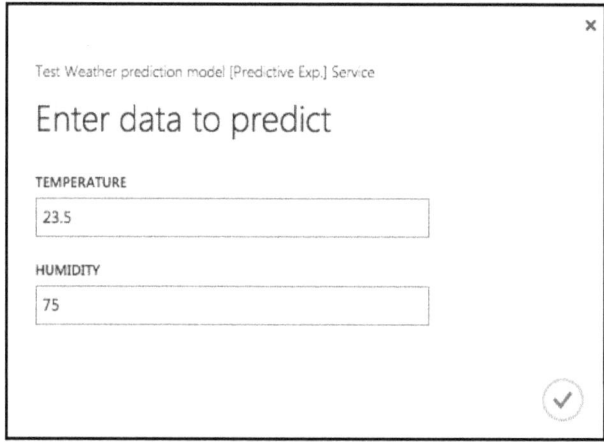

2. After providing the correct values, submit the form. After a moment, we should see the results:

This concludes our walkthrough of the basics of machine learning using Azure ML Studio.

As practice, you can read the remaining part of the article *Weather forecast using the sensor data from your IoT hub in Azure Machine Learning* at
https://docs.microsoft.com/en-us/azure/iot-hub/iot-hub-weather-forecast-machine
-learning to learn how to link your Raspberry Pi 3 to the DHT11 sensor output and the machine learning web service we have just created, and then save the results from the web service's interaction onto Azure storage and then visualize the results. This should give you a better idea of how the entire flow is completed.

I hope this chapter has shown you how to use machine learning with IoT to perform real-time predictions. What is shown in this chapter does not even scratch the surface of what is possible with the powerful duo of machine learning and Internet of Things.

Summary

In this chapter, we have learned what machine learning is and some of its basic concepts. Then we looked at the various ML options on offer from platform providers, as well as possible open source solutions.

We then tried to implement a machine learning model using Azure Machine Learning Studio, and saw how we can predict the probability of rain if we pass in the temperature and humidity. We concluded the chapter by building a web service and exposing the model so anyone can get predictions based on the model we just created.

In the next chapter, we are going to look at the various IoT use cases that can leverage what we have learned so far and add value to their systems.

10

Platform Comparisons

In the last nine chapters, we have gone through the world of IoT. We started off with the building blocks, and we moved on to the real-world applications of IoT. Then we experienced it's implementation on five different IoT platforms and looked at how to work with an end-to-end IoT solution and off-the-shelf platforms. We have also taken a quick plunge into IoT and machine learning using the Microsoft Azure platform.

In this last chapter of our enterprise IoT journey, we will compare and contrast the IoT platforms we have looked at and define the situations in which they would be suitable.

Topics covered in this chapter are:

- What is an IoT platform?
- Features of an IoT platform.
- Comparison between AWS IoT, Azure IoT, Google Cloud IoT, IBM IoT platform, and Kaa IoT.

What is an IoT platform?

We have already seen in `Chapter 3`, *Getting Started with IoT Platforms*, what an IoT platform is. In this section, let's dig a bit deeper into the same architecture.

I had the privilege to architect and design an IoT platform named The IoT Suitcase. I started working on it in mid-2015 and finished the basic stack by the end of 2015. My goals in designing the platform involved these factors:

- Data processing
- Security
- Seamless hardware and cloud software integration
- Device management for individual devices and groups of devices
- User interfaces and dashboards
- High scalability
- Enterprise readiness
- Most important of all, the ability to add intelligence

Do check out this other book, titled *Practical Internet of Things with JavaScript* (https://www.packtpub.com/hardware-and-creative/advanced-iot-javascript), where you are shown how to design an IoT platform using only JavaScript and how to build various solutions.

Everybody defines platforms differently. For some, a platform is the software running on the cloud. For others, a platform is only a form of data collection software from the devices. For some a platform is end-to-end, which includes data originating from a device to data being notified on to the end user's devices with intelligence.

As we have seen in Chapter 3, *Getting Started with IoT Platforms*, the following are the various layers that constitute an IoT platform:

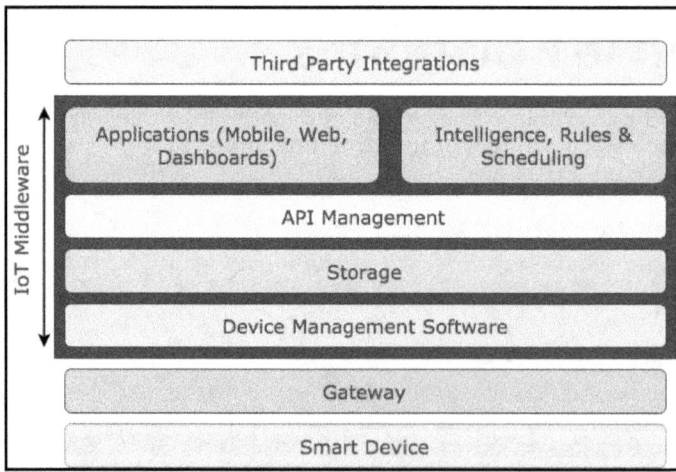

We have the **Smart Device**, the **Gateway**, and the **Device Management Software**. These are the core parts of the IoT. These pieces form what I call the *last mile connectivity between the real world and the virtual world.*

For any basic IoT solution, all we need is these three blocks. How we want to utilize that data and take it forward defines the other blocks in the previous diagram.

Now, depending on the use case, a lot of blocks can come and go. If we were building a simple application, where the data from sensors was just stored and queried manually, our stack would look like the following diagram:

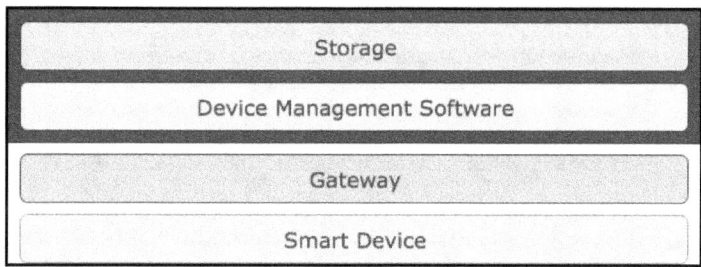

There is the **Smart Device** that talks to the **Device Management Software** over a **Gateway**, and the gateway persists the data into **Storage**. Then a developer/user would query the storage directly.

The previous architecture is more suitable for the management of administration-level applications, where the user accessing the data is not worried about the visual interface and is more interested in data itself.

Another possible setup of an IoT solution is where the data from the smart device is live streamed without any persistence. The proposed stack would look like this:

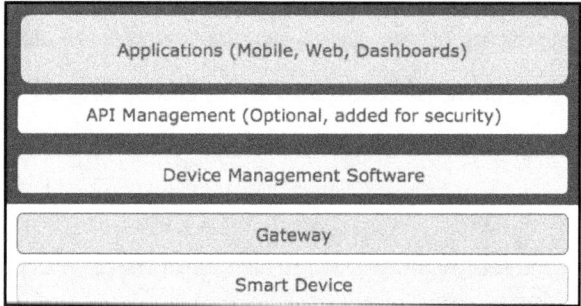

The **Device Management Software** illustrated in the previous diagram feeds the data into an **API Management** layer, which then connects the end devices to the **Device Management Software** to steam data from one end to another in real time.

The previously depicted architecture is suitable for real-time monitoring without the worry of storage and intelligence.

The following diagram is another solution stack, where the platform is responsible for the last mile connectivity and nothing else. Here is what it would look like:

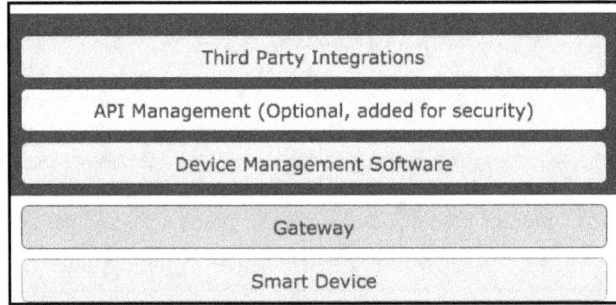

The data is fed directly from the **Device Management Software** to the third-party integration point. This can be a web socket connection, a MQTTS/COAP, any message queue-based connection, or a simple database endpoint that accepts data from the management software.

Now, if we were only collecting data from the smart devices to run analytics on top of it, this is what our stack would look like:

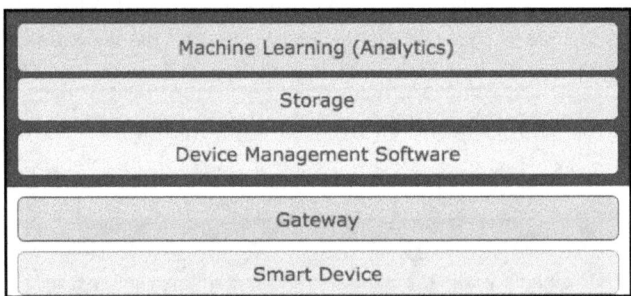

The data from the sensor is fed into the storage and from there our ML setup would start the learning and analytics process.

These are some of the few ways one can design an IoT platform/solution, depending on the use case and requirements.

And we have always had the mothership of all IoT solutions, where we have had all the components, using which data collection and data analysis can be achieved.

Given that there are many possible combinations for building an IoT solution, what are the key features that we need to look for in an IoT platform?

Features of an IoT platform

A very important note before we get started with the features is that in IoT there is no *cookie cutter* solution for building an IoT solution, be it a start-up or be it an enterprise, the application, the use case, the boundaries of the problem we are solving determines the ideal platform and it will vary from problem statement to problem statement.

Also note that various layers in the IoT can be plugged and played, as I have shown in the previous section.

So, what features are bare essentials?

Essential features

Let's look at some of the essential feature of an IoT platform.

Security

Authentication and authorization of users is a challenge that we have already conquered. Now, we are adding new types of users called smart devices. And they also need to be authenticated and authorized in a similar fashion, and every packet that comes and goes between the cloud and the device needs to be monitored closely for data integrity as well as secured communication.

Not only does the communication between the device and the device management software need to be secure, but also the other entities that are interested in exchanging data with the IoT middleware need to be authorized. Another layer of protection can be added by encrypting data while persisting in the database. This would be an additional layer of security on the data even though the database servers get hacked.

Remember, in today's era, *data is money!*

Secure device communication

The next feature is to secure the communication between the hardware and the device management software running on the cloud. This is a bare essential for any communication. Sensor data from the device always needs to transmit over a secure line. Otherwise, things like man-in-the-middle attacks or replay attacks can be simulated and the integrity of data will be lost.

In today's world, we have TLS/SSL-based solutions that provide end-to-end encryption between the device and cloud management software. Things like packet scrambling and simple encryptions are also an option.

Device management

This is one of the most important management features that needs to be part of any IoT platform. Given the various reports that we have seen in this book, we are talking about billions of devices.

Managing 5, 10, 100, or 1,00,000 devices is very simple. Imagine the interconnection between multiple devices across multiple users; performing different activities is not that easy to manage.

A good device registry or a catalog that can define each device and query it individually or as a part of a group of devices is highly important.

Imagine one device of your 8,000-device group goes rogue and stars performing a DDoS attack on your own servers. This is when the value of a good device management stack is realized.

The ability to disable the device remotely or block a certain device on the fly is very essential as one rogue device can bring the entire solution to its knees.

Device and cloud integration

Device and cloud integration is a key feature for developers. How easy it is for a device to connect to cloud software securely and start transmitting data makes a lot of difference to the developer's time.

In the platforms we have explored so far, we are have seen how each of them provides a way for the device software to communicate with their cloud counterpart.

AWS, Azure, Watson, and Google IoT Core rely on libraries that they have developed or third-party MQTT libraries that can be used to work with the platform. On the other hand, we have looked at Kaa, which generates the device SDK depending on the device/platform on which the software is going to run.

Each platform would have a different approach and ease of use is very important so that the developer doesn't spend too much time integrating but rather can focus on the application use case.

Communication protocols

Another very important feature that can make or break a platform is its ability to communicate using multiple protocols. Today, there are plenty of low power, reliable, and small footprint protocols available that are ideal for IoT solutions.

A platform's ability to support these protocols at the device management layer and expose a protocol-agnostic API to the higher layers is essential.

I have worked with hardware that transmits scrambled plain text TCP/IP packets and I have also used MQTTS and similar for the communication. A good platform supports both and the communication layer is decoupled from the data processing layer, keeping the entire platform flexible and scalable.

Storage

Persistence is another important aspect of IoT. Data in IoT is like a constantly flowing river. Knowing when to store what is half of the job. Depending on what our application is, we can persist information.

A good storage solution should be able to do millions (not exaggerating) of reads and writes per seconds. It should have a flexible query interface and adapters to plug in to various big data and data streaming tools.

Beneficial features

The following features do not get to the core of the IoT solution itself but will definitely add more value to the overall solution. Again, these features are more effective in certain use cases than in others:

- Visualization
- Third-party integration
- Analytics and intelligence

Visualization

The ability to build dashboards that can extend the power of data visualization within the platform is always a good feature to have. These dashboards should be extendable as well as flexible as we don't know what kind of data would come in.

In this book, we have seen various ways to create dynamic and static dashboards. Some dashboards as an output of data processing and others as static dashboards which only display raw data.

Visualization also needs to have its own level of data abstraction. A dashboard that gets created should be centered around an administrator, a data scientist, or an end user, who would view the final data after processing.

Third-party integration

This is another key feature that adds scalability to the platform. The ability for the application to send and receive data between various other services as well as IoT platforms will by definition increase the value of the end solution.

Imagine an IoT platform that can talk to various weather providers and integrate that data with incoming sensor data and produce better information to a user-this adds huge value. A platform that has configurable integration endpoints and which lets other platforms push or pull the data would be another great feature. An open integration between popular voice assistance services like Amazon Alexa or Google Assistant, which can be directly configured to a type of device, is always helpful for rapid solution development.

Analytics and intelligence

Software that can run in parallel with other IoT platform pieces, which keeps monitoring the data and generates analytics on the fly, is a good feature to have. One of the end goals of IoT, as we have seen in `Chapter 9`, *IoT and Machine Learning*, is the ability to generate reports and analyze data to get the desired outcome from the entire system.

We have looked at the major platform providers like Amazon, Microsoft Azure, Google, and IBM Watson Cloud, which provide easy integration with IoT middleware and their big data services. This will definitely help any enterprise get insights into the data as the data is being gathered.

These were some of the key features that are good to have in an IoT platform.

Again, a lot of solutions do not have a generic solution and various pieces need to be mixed and matched to achieve the primary goal.

Comparison between platforms

Now that we have gone through the various features that an IoT platform should have, we are going to compare the five platforms and provide a matrix that can help define a use case:

Feature	AWS	Azure	Google IoT	IBM Watson	Kaa
Device Inventory Management	Yes	Yes	Yes	Yes	No (management is more on an application level)
Device SDK	Yes-provided	Yes-provided	Yes-can use any MQTT client software	Yes-provided	Yes-provided
Security	Yes	Yes	Yes	Yes	Yes
Data protocols	MQTT(s), HTTP(s)	MQTT(s)	MQTT(s)	MQTT(s), HTTP(s)	HTTP(s)
Storage support	Yes	Yes	Yes	Yes	Yes
Dashboard	Not built in	Not built in	Not built in	Not built in	Not built in

Has dashboard tools as part of the platform	Yes	Yes	Yes	Yes	No
Big data support	Yes	Yes	Yes	Yes	Depends on the infrastructure
Integration with machine learning tools on the platform	Yes	Yes	Yes	Yes	No
Scaling on demand	Yes	Yes	Yes	Yes	Platform supports this but it depends on the end infrastructure
Pricing (IoT core service) #	Per million minutes of connection: $0.080. Per million messages (up to 1 billion messages): $1.00.	S1 edition- $50 per unit with 4,00,000 messages with a maximum size of 4 KB.	Monthly data volume of 250 MB to 250 GB billed at $0.0045 per MB. Number of devices-unlimited, within **queries per second (QPS)** maximums.	Up to 450 GB per month, charged at $0.001 per MB of data exchanged. Unlimited devices.	Depends on the infrastructure on which this stack is running.
Ease of (first time) use (in terms of interfaces, integration, and configuration)*	Good	Good	Good	Good	Poor
Third-party integration support or interoperable standards	Yes (REST API and MQTT)	Yes (MQTT)	Yes (REST API and MQTT/Pub/Sub)	Yes (MQTT)	Yes (REST API and database dumping)

Supports fog computing (edge devices)	Yes	Yes	No	Yes	Yes
Managed cloud	Yes	Yes	Yes	Yes	No
Open source	No	No	No	No	Yes
Code complexity while implementing*	Low	Low	Low	Low	Low
Configuration centric or code centric*	Equally balanced	Equally balanced	Code centric	Equally balanced	Configuration centric
Device SDK supported languages	Embedded C, JavaScript, Arduino Yun, Java, Python, iOS, Android, and C++ SDK	C, Python, Node.js, Java, and .NET	Can use any MQTT client in any language	Python, Node.js, Java, Android, Node Red, Embedded C, iOS, C#, and Arduino	Java, Android, C++, C, and Objective C

* My opinion on this feature.
\# Dependent on various factors

This summarizes the comparison between the five platforms that we have worked with. Do note that these are not the only platforms on the market; there are others, which you can explore. The previous comparison factors can be used as a rule of thumb when exploring other IoT platforms.

Summary

In this chapter, we have looked at what defines an IoT platform as well as some essential and beneficial features of an IoT platform. Then we compared the five platforms we have worked with against the various features of an IoT platform.

With this, we conclude the book titled *Enterprise Internet of Things Handbook*. I hope I have helped you in gaining some perspective for picking an IoT platform for your enterprise needs.

Other Books You May Enjoy

If you enjoyed this book, you may be interested in these other books by Packt:

Internet of Things for Architects
Perry Lea

ISBN: 978-1-78847-059-9

- Understand the role and scope of architecting a successful IoT deployment, from sensors to the cloud
- Scan the landscape of IoT technologies that span everything from sensors to the cloud and everything in between
- See the trade-offs in choices of protocols and communications in IoT deployments
- Build a repertoire of skills and the vernacular necessary to work in the IoT space
- Broaden your skills in multiple engineering domains necessary for the IoT architect

Learning AWS IoT

Agus Kurniawan

ISBN: 978-1-78839-611-0

- Implement AWS IoT on IoT projects
- Learn the technical capabilities of AWS IoT and IoT devices
- Create IoT-based AWS IoT projects
- Choose IoT devices and AWS IoT platforms to use based on the kind of project you need to build
- Deploy AWS Greengrass and AWS Lambda
- Develop program for AWS IoT Button
- Visualize IoT AWS data
- Build predictive analytics using AWS IoT and AWS Machine Learning

Leave a review - let other readers know what you think

Please share your thoughts on this book with others by leaving a review on the site that you bought it from. If you purchased the book from Amazon, please leave us an honest review on this book's Amazon page. This is vital so that other potential readers can see and use your unbiased opinion to make purchasing decisions, we can understand what our customers think about our products, and our authors can see your feedback on the title that they have worked with Packt to create. It will only take a few minutes of your time, but is valuable to other potential customers, our authors, and Packt. Thank you!

Index